Ray Hill bega e
extreme right -
ment in the N b
South Africa, he underwent a dramatic change of heart
and, returning to the UK, he worked as a 'mole' inside
the far right for almost five years. His activities took him
to the heart of far-right terrorism in Europe, and formed
the basis of a 75-minute documentary on Channel 4 in
1984.

Andrew Bell is news editor of *Time Out* in London.

RAY HILL with ANDREW BELL

The Other Face
of Terror

Inside Europe's Neo-Nazi Network

GRAFTON BOOKS

A Division of the Collins Publishing Group

LONDON GLASGOW
TORONTO SYDNEY AUCKLAND

Grafton Books
A Division of the Collins Publishing Group
8 Grafton Street, London W1X 3LA

A Grafton Paperback Original 1988

Copyright © Ray Hill and Andrew Bell 1988

ISBN 0-586-06935-6

Printed and bound in Great Britain by
Collins, Glasgow

Set in Times

Contents

Acknowledgments

Both Andy Bell and myself would like to extend our deep gratitude to Gerry Gable and his *Searchlight* colleagues for the painstaking and unflinching help they have given us from their unique archives while we have been writing this book. It would have been impossible without them. We would also like to thank Sarah Whyatt and Minnah who between them typed the manuscript.

Preface

This book is the complete and unabridged record of my involvement with some of Europe's most notorious and psychotic nazi thugs and terrorists. It does not, in all its parts, reflect well upon myself – it is the story of my political life, warts and all.

I believe that to some extent I have made amends for some of my misguided actions in pursuit of political ideology, but the reader must be the final judge of that. The reader can also judge just how easy it is for a reasonably intelligent but uneducated young man, of whom there are even more around today, to fall prey to this seductive ideology, whatever name or title it may be temporarily masquerading under. To a large extent it is my experience that the young skinhead with NF tattoos is as much a victim of nazi poison as is the young Asian whom he attacks. I say this not in an effort to excuse him but in an effort to understand him, and in an effort to urge the reader to win the hearts and minds of such working-class young men before their infection becomes terminal.

It is always difficult to admit that one has been totally wrong. In my case it was made easier by my stable family life, for which credit is entirely due to my completely apolitical, long-suffering and hard-working wife, Glennis. We have been married now for 22 years and her down-to-earth common sense, fortitude, good humour and self-discipline have been the qualities that have sustained me through periods of self-doubt and depression such as cannot be imagined by those who have been fortunate enough to go through life without a major crisis of conscience. She has been a gem of a woman and, knowing her as I do, I have no doubt that she will continue to be such.

Good friends are nearly, although not quite, as important as a good family. Gerry Gable, as any anti-fascist would know, is the most dedicated and consistent of all that distinguished group of people. For those who have not met the man I must record that he is also, when the mood takes him, an extremely funny comic. When, during my period 'underground', things started to get on top of me, I could always rely on Gerry to put me back on top of the world. Always fair, even to his enemies, Gerry Gable is as good a friend as any man could wish to have, and I am proud to have worked with him and even more proud to regard him as 'my mate, Gerry'.

There are many more really great people I have met during the course of activities, including film producer Geoff Seed, and even more whom I cannot name for a variety of reasons. One man, known as 'Pink Spot', is still on the 'inside' and doing just as valuable a job as I ever did.

I cannot, of course, claim that I would not change a great deal of the course of my past life if I could do so. Even so, it has had its compensations. Without my initial involvement, which I do regret, there would have been no film on Channel 4 entitled 'The Other Face of Terror'; dozens of violent nazis would have remained unexposed; film producer Ludi Boeken and I would have been unable to shatter the confidence of the international fascist establishment, as I'm sure we did; and this book, with the good that I hope it will do, would have remained unwritten.

The Other Face of Terror takes you from a working-class terraced house in Leicester to fascism in South Africa, terrorism in France, nazi fugitives in Ireland, nazi festivals in Belgium and back again to England, with my account of plots to cause explosions in London and to set up a pirate nazi broadcasting station in the Midlands. It is my story. And every word of it is true!

Ray Hill
August 1987

Prologue

'How would you like to go out with a bit of a bang?'

A grin flickered on his lips as he lazily stirred his coffee in a crowded North London burger bar.

Oh hell, I thought, what's he got lined up for me now?

'Go on. Tell me more.'

My companion was Gerry Gable, a journalist who had been investigating and exposing the activities of racists and fascists for almost twenty years. For the previous five years we had been working together: I was his 'deep throat' deep inside the nazi movement in Britain, providing him with information which went on to appear regularly in his anti-fascist magazine *Searchlight*. A little less regularly it featured in television programmes and Fleet Street articles about the activities of nazi groups at home and abroad.

The burger bar in King's Cross was our regular meeting place. From Leicester, where I lived, I travelled to London every couple of weeks or so to report on what was happening in far-right circles. Just opposite St Pancras Station, where my train pulled in, it was simply a convenient – and suitably anonymous – place where we could get our heads together, discussing what was going on and what my course of action for the next few weeks should be.

Gerry was an old hand at this business and had achieved almost legendary status in the far right itself. It wasn't simply that he managed to reveal with awesome regularity the most secret deliberations and acts of the right-wing groups; it was more the way he did it. For almost two decades he had been running his own network of informants inside the extreme right, often to devastating effect. On more than one occasion, so the stories went, the collapse of right-wing parties had been caused directly by the disruptive activities of his agents, who often held quite senior positions in the party hierarchies. One of the ironic side effects of this was a debilitating paranoia which certainly afflicted most of the fascist groups I had been involved in. They were always hunting 'moles', and anyone who stepped out of line in any way at all quickly faced the accusing finger of his racist comrades: 'You're working for *Searchlight*.' It had reached the point where it almost did not matter whether they were or not. The suspicions and lack of trust were themselves disruptive enough.

Those accusing fingers had been pointed in my direction more than once during my political career, but my reputation as a hard-line nazi leader had been more than enough, on each occasion, to bring many other 'comrades' rallying indignantly to my defence.

In all of this, ever since I had made contact with *Searchlight* back in 1979, I had been guided by Gerry, and together we had succeeded in avoiding the many pitfalls into which any 'agent' can tumble. We had to be careful, for instance, never to make public information which was known only to a very small number of people. Usually I would safeguard us against this by passing on such titbits to a few more of my far-right friends before they were revealed openly. In this way the trail back to me was obscured. On occasion, however, we judged it so vital that information was made known without delay that we had been forced to go public before it was, strictly speaking, completely secure to do so. Happily, suspicion usually (and luckily) came to rest on people other than myself, and when such suspicions were raised I was more than happy to add my observations about the unreliability of certain characters. In general, though, such risks were to be avoided like the plague, and on the whole they were.

In the weeks leading up to that fateful King's Cross meeting, I had been working with former National Front chieftain John Tyndall, setting up a new political party of the far right. Tyndall had quit the NF in 1980 after its disastrous showing in the general election and, railing against the 'homosexuals and pederasts' whom he alleged were now in control of the Front, he had embarked on a new path with a group which he named, with a staggering lack of originality, the New National Front. Now he felt the time was right to launch a new outfit with a distinctive name which could garner the remnants of one or two other right-wing groups which were floundering. At the time I had a considerable following among younger members of the hard-line British Movement, from which I had been 'expelled' two years earlier, to the fury of my supporters. I had also established a close relationship with the Leicester-based British Democratic Party, then on the verge of collapse following a television programme detailing its involvement in a gun-running racket. No wonder that Tyndall targeted me as the man who could help him sweep up these leavings from someone else's table. What he didn't know was that my dispute with the British Movement leader, Michael McLaughlin, had been carefully engineered precisely with the aim of splitting the organization. Nor could he have imagined, even in his wildest flights of fancy, that I had worked closely with the television programme-makers who had so decisively pulled the rug from under the BDP. As far as he was concerned, I was a prize catch.

What he certainly didn't know, and what I had only recently confided to Gerry, was that I was beginning to consider just how long I could carry on leading a double life. For four years now I had been publicly known not only as a leader of the far right, but as one of its hard men; ruthless and uncompromising; a nazi demagogue who could whip up the faithful with vitriolic, venomous speeches at rallies and demonstrations. More than once my over-the-top rhetoric upstaged more senior nazis on public platforms, and there were gangs of young fascist thugs who regarded me, and not any of the established party leaders like Tyndall or McLaughlin, as their true leader.

But it does all take its toll. Genuinely occupying such a role is exhausting enough: the constant travelling to meetings and marches; the effort that goes into writing articles or leaflets and organizing meetings; the constant encroachments on family life as domestic obligations take second place to political duties or even just attending to a constantly ringing telephone. When all your effort is no more than a pretence kept up twenty-four hours a day to deceive those around you, it can be a peculiarly draining business. And the stress is only ever partly compensated by the knowledge of what you are personally contributing to the struggle against a political creed incomparably and intrinsically evil. Although, of course, this does help. In short, my life as a 'mole' was beginning to place an increasingly intolerable strain upon me personally, and upon my family. I had come to feel that very soon I would want to be able to devote to them the time and attention that they had been denied, more recently by my under-cover life, and before that by my years as a genuinely committed nazi activist.

As it happened, my reservations about carrying on

coincided with an approach that had been made to *Searchlight*, which Gerry now proceeded to outline over several cups of coffee in King's Cross.

A Dutch television company, with whom *Searchlight* had co-operated before, making programmes about European nazi groups, was proposing what they called 'the definitive investigation' of the neo-nazi movement. There had already been a couple of meetings between the company's principal producer, Ludi Boeken, and *Searchlight* journalists to discuss the areas that could profitably be explored, and some development money had been made available by Channel 4 in Britain. It was planned to show the programme on television networks all over Europe. However, after I had told Gerry of my reluctance to carry on much longer, one of his *Searchlight* colleagues had suggested that, if I agreed, the programme could be dramatically enhanced by building it around my own personal experiences. What better way of exposing what is going on in those fanatical circles than by hearing it from someone who has been there? I was extremely well qualified to speak: not only had I held leading positions in British nazi groups, but I had travelled to Europe, moving among the very men who had planned and carried out terrorist bomb outrages in Italy, France and Germany. I was also intimately acquainted with secret high-level nazi operations, like the publishing networks which flooded Europe and the United States with racist and anti-semitic literature. If I were happy to do it, Gerry concluded, it could be sensational. But, given the sensitivity of much of what I could say, there was really nothing to be gained by my appearing anonymously or in silhouette to protect my identity. My former nazi colleagues would know immediately who was spilling the beans. It was all or nothing.

'You'll want to think about it,' he said. 'No one's trying to twist your arm. If you feel it's too risky and you'd rather just retire quietly, that's fine by everyone concerned. No one will think any the worse of you for it. You've done more than most already; you've taken risks that most people wouldn't even think about. Take a few days and let me know what you think. If you decide not to, we'll talk about arranging your retirement.'

As it happened, I didn't need a few days. Not even a few hours. I had already considered what would happen if the worst were ever to come to the worst and I were to be uncovered by the nazis as a *Searchlight* informer. Long before, I had bought myself a small property in another part of the country to which my family and I could decamp at short notice and begin new lives if the need arose. I could not be cavalier with my family's welfare and on their account proper arrangements had to be made to minimize the danger when the truth about the life I had chosen to lead was finally revealed.

On the whole, the nazi 'comrades' who might be upset to find out about my true role were not the sort to inspire fear or awe. True, they could be vicious and dangerous, but only ever in the manner of the coward or the bully. Their 'operations' were only ever carried out in gangs, or at night, or both. I had seen at first hand how their acts of revenge were planned, and while it meant there would be certain dangers, I refused to let myself be reduced to terror by the cowardly antics of the night-time hit squads. As soon as you allow yourself to be intimidated by such things, the tactics of the thug and the bully boy have won the day.

So I only needed a few moments' thought. In fact, nothing could have excited me more than the opportunity of dealing such a devastating blow to the thugs and bigots with whom I had been associating. Ever since my retreat from national socialism during a spell of emigration to South Africa, I had become more and more convinced that these men and their ideas represented something fundamentally evil. The only thought that kept me going in those subsequent years was the certain knowledge that I was doing something to scotch their efforts; to guarantee that their policies of hatred and violence – and, ultimately, murder on a massive scale – never became a reality. And, if truth be told, to make some amends for the years when I had genuinely been one of them. Now I was presented with the opportunity of delivering a blow from which it might take them years to recover; a massive propaganda bombshell that would expose them before an audience of millions. Far from frightening me, the prospect actually filled me with glee. How on earth could I say no?

I had just one reservation. At this stage, I would have to put the idea to my wife. A major change in our lives would be inevitable after the programme had been shown, and I felt obliged to get her consent. Taking risks was one thing, but this time the consequences were more certain. We would have to face the fact, for instance, that Leicester could no longer be our home. But if she agreed, I would make the programme.

Back in Leicester, she and I sat up until the early hours going over what it would mean for us. As can be imagined, she did not exactly leap at the prospect of having to pack up and leave the town where she had lived most of her life, but in the end, she agreed with me that the thing had to be done. I telephoned Gerry at his home late the following night and told him to arrange a meeting with his Dutch film-maker friend. I was raring to go.

A week later, I was again standing on the platform at Leicester railway station, waiting for a train to take me to London. This time, however, it was not for one of our regular King's Cross assignations. On this occasion a meeting had been arranged for later in the evening at the Soho offices of Ludi Boeken's production company, Belbo Films.

On Gerry's advice, we had stepped up security precautions. If any of my nazi friends had bumped into me that afternoon at the railway station, I am convinced that they would never have recognized me. A black wig covered my rather thinning locks, and I had dressed in a smart blue suit and tie and a navy overcoat. To complete the deception I wore a pair of dark glasses. It was a truly startling transformation. Even the closest of acquaintances would have had great difficulty in identifying me.

Gerry and I were to meet in the street near a particular Soho pub. He was already waiting as I arrived, and I could see him eyeing somewhat tentatively this dark, imposing figure looming towards him. He didn't realize it was me until I stopped next to him and asked, 'How are you, Gerry?'

Inside the pub we had a drink while we waited for one of his *Searchlight* colleagues to arrive. I had met this chap a few times while working on other stories, so I recognized him as he came through the door. But he certainly did not recognize me, and I saw him look quizzically at Gerry as he approached our table. Gerry by this time could barely contain himself, and was giggling uncontrollably as he realized he was actually going to have to introduce us.

But these two were, to some extent, hardened to this sort of theatre, by virtue of their work for years with informers of one sort or another, and their reaction was nothing compared to that of poor Ludi Boeken, the unsuspecting film producer. As his secretary ushered us into his small office, his jaw visibly dropped and he very nervously extended his hand. I think he expected me to break it off. Clearly, he had been expecting either a young thug or a middle-aged, seedy misfit, and if anything, I resembled more some lumbering mafia godfather. If he needed to be impressed, my little performance that evening certainly did the trick.

For the next hour or so, we discussed how my story could fit together with the lines of investigation which Channel 4 had agreed for the programme.

Two years earlier, nazi groups in France, Italy and Germany had initiated a wave of terror bombings aimed at innocent civilians. The three most notorious outrages, at Bologna railway station, the Rue Copernic synagogue and the Munich Oktoberfest, had claimed more than a hundred lives. Only a timely intervention by myself and *Searchlight* colleagues had prevented a similar act of carnage being visited upon the streets of London in 1981. Ludi wanted to get to the heart of the conspiracy which lay behind these events.

Secondly, he wanted to investigate the apparent flood of racist and anti-semitic literature which had been pouring out in Europe and the United States over the previous five years. Enormous quantities of books, pamphlets and periodicals were being printed, many of them expensively produced and dwelling upon the holocaust carried out against the Jews by the Hitler regime. Typical of this 'historical revisionism' was *Did Six Million Really Die?*, a booklet which originated in Britain, written by a National Front leader, and which disputed whether the Holocaust had actually taken place. It was printed in runs of hundreds of thousands and in several European languages. None of the European nazi groups had the funding or resources to finance such a prolonged and expensive propaganda campaign on their own, but the question 'Where does the money come from?' had remained largely unanswered. Ludi wanted to get to the bottom of it.

Some parts of these stories had already been patched together and published – not least in *Searchlight*. But there was still much to be uncovered and much which, while known, had hitherto had to be kept secret because to do otherwise would have jeopardized my cover as a nazi. I was one of only a very few who was privy to such sensitive information.

We covered all of this ground in much detail, but even as we spoke it became clear that it would not, even now, be enough for me to appear on the screen telling all that I knew. There were gaps to be filled; things still to be proven. I knew what was coming, but it was Gerry's *Searchlight* colleague who finally, and rather tentatively, asked the question.

'How would you feel, Ray, about travelling round to meet some of these characters for one last time? Only this time you'd be wired up to record everything that was said. Hopefully, you could draw out of them what we still need to know, and it would all be on the record. I don't think there's any other way.'

A pause.

'Oh, what the hell,' I sighed.

Gerry grinned at me. 'I knew you would.'

'Why?'

'Because you're a wicked bastard.'

When we adjourned it was to Leoni's, an Italian restaurant in a neighbouring Soho street. It was something of a celebration lubricated by several bottles of fine wine, and spiced with a mood of excited anticipation. We all knew that, if things worked out, we were going to make a film that would be rather unique. With *Searchlight*, who had helped him draft the original programme proposal for Channel 4, Ludi already had a fairly comprehensive list of individuals who would feature in the investigation and on whom further evidence would have to be collected. They were to be the principal 'targets' in one of the most penetrating exposés of the extreme right's dirty secrets ever to be shown on television.

1
The Making of a Nazi

Ever since I revealed publicly, back in early 1984, that for several years I had been working as an infiltrator in the ranks of British and European nazi movements, I have constantly been asked the same question: 'What made you change sides?' Many people obviously found it hard to come to terms with the idea of a hardened nazi, someone who had harboured such a fierce hatred of people of other races, being transformed, and spending years of his life working secretly for the destruction of the same political movements in which he had been a driving force for more than a decade.

I can understand their curiosity. It was not as if I were an infiltrator from the beginning; someone who loathed racism and fascism and decided from the outset to work within these movements in order to subvert them. For years I was as dedicated and convinced a nazi as any of those who called me their comrade. Nor was I just some character on the fringes without a particularly strong attachment, who could, under the pressure of relatively insignificant events, be swayed in one direction or the other. No, from my earliest days in the far-right movement almost twenty years ago, I threw myself totally and enthusiastically into the heart of things. I was an organizer, a leader, an orator, totally committed to the national socialist ideology I had embraced. So my conversion, while not exactly on a par with that of St Paul on the road to Damascus, was nevertheless of sufficiently dramatic proportions to arouse intense curiosity – not so much among those I had deserted, but certainly among those anti-fascists and democrats who, although they were not to know it, I had secretly joined.

But, looking over my career on the extreme right in the relative tranquillity that has followed my public disclosures, I cannot help feeling that this is not the most interesting question. My answer, which a part of this book tries to provide, may satisfy a certain curiosity, but it does little to help us comprehend what we are up against. More important, to my mind, is the question: 'How did you become a fanatical racist in the first place?' How did a relatively ordinary, recently married, working-class chap become transformed into what the popular press likes to call 'a strutting stormtrooper' for the nazi movement? Seen in these terms, my story is far from unique, and in comprehending what happened to me, we might come to grasp a little more clearly what happened to so many others who came to embrace the same ideology of uncompromising racial hatred.

My story, from apolitical working man in Leicester to nationally known racist activist, is a textbook example of how simple prejudices, born out of an over-simplistic understanding of one's own personal difficulties, can be exploited by quite sinister forces behind the scenes; how racial ill-feeling, rooted in ignorance, can be led gently by the hand until it explodes into fully-fledged nazism, of which, it must be said, genocide is the logical conclusion.

In this sense, it ceases to be my story. It is the story of thousands of right-wing extremists in Britain and many other countries. For over five years, I worked underground in the nazi world on the precept 'Know Thine Enemy'. Perhaps we can learn equally important things from the years when I was genuinely part of the enemy as from those later, possibly more exciting years, which I spent fighting it.

I was born in 1939 in what was then the Lancashire mill town of Mossley. Mossley has since been 'moved' by politicians into the ridiculous conurbation of 'Greater Manchester', but this has not, thankfully, made the locals regard themselves as anything other than Lancastrians. It is a highly individual little community with its own non-League football team, which once got to Wembley, its own particular version of a Lancashire accent, and its own highly doubtful claim to have 'the world's oldest fish and chip shop'.

Situated some eight or ten miles to the north-east of Manchester proper, Mossley is within walking distance of Saddleworth Moor and the Peak District. Through the town runs the river Thame. There is something incongruous about it all – row upon row of dismal *Coronation Street*-type houses running in all directions, some from top to bottom of incredibly steep hills; others running across what must once have been bare hillsides, all part of the Pennine chain. Yet this dismal setting is surrounded by some of the most glorious countryside in the British Isles. Within a dozen miles or so of Mossley is the village of Holmfirth (better known for the magnificent scenery which provides the backdrop to the television series *Last of the Summer Wine*), the rugged 'Snake Pass' and the Ladybower Reservoir, the scenic Chew Valley, and the dark and brooding Saddleworth Moor where the infamous 'Moors murderers' buried their young victims.

In the early years of the war Mossley was a poor town. Very few houses had indoor toilets; ours was situated about fifty yards from the back door and shared with three other families. I remember my father spending many hours in the winter of 1947 digging through the snow so that we were able to get to the lavatory. The modern technology of the water closet had still not reached Mossley when we left in 1955. The lavatory still consisted of a large bucket or bin which was carted away on a horse and cart once a week.

Despite these conditions, cleanliness was still considered to be in close proximity to godliness. The stone floor of this abominable outside toilet was scrubbed daily, in turn, by the three women of the families which shared it. The front doors of the houses opened directly on to the street and every week the pavement outside the front doors would be scrubbed, soft sandstone rubbed over it, and then mopped, making it, for an hour or two anyway, a bright and shining yellow patch among the drab grey-stone houses.

I started school at the age of four years in 1944. My first school was the local Church of England school, St John's. I remember my first teacher as if it were yesterday: Mrs Rawse was one of the most hateful women I ever met. She arrived at school each day in a car, itself a source of wonder to kids who were used to seeing the family waste carted away weekly by the local council's horse and cart. Even the headmaster, a great old chap called Jack Andrews, who had been invalided out of the army before qualifying as a teacher, arrived on a bike. But Mrs Rawse alighted each day from the car driven by her shopkeeper husband like some Lancashire Lady Docker, and spent the entire day trying to correct our accents.

Corporal punishment, or 'the strap', was the order of the day. Seldom a day passed without my being punished in this way by Mrs Rawse. I expect it was largely my own fault, as I was by nature a bit of a rebel, and would argue the toss with anyone over anything.

My father was called up into the Army when I was only a few months old, and I didn't see him again until I was five. I clearly remember his return at the end of the war and how proud I was of his photograph in the local paper. While he was waiting for demobilization after his return to England, my mother and I went to stay in lodgings near his camp in Wiltshire. Those were happy days. I was almost six years old and it was a great adventure.

All too soon this delightful interlude was over and it was back to Mossley, St John's School and Mrs Rawse.

At the age of eleven I left St John's to go to Stamford Secondary School in nearby Ashton-under-Lyne. I had never been happy at St John's, but this new school was a nightmare by comparison. The cane – not the strap – was used unmercifully. If Mossley was a tough area, Ashton was a battlefield. Punch-ups in the playground were a daily way of life. The response of the staff was to wield the cane with ever-increasing vigour.

I endured four miserable years at Stamford, although I am quite prepared to admit that much of the unhappiness was probably my own fault. I hated teachers and authority in general and had done ever since I had come under the jurisdiction of the awful Mrs Rawse.

After leaving school I worked in a variety of jobs until I reached the age of eighteen, when I joined the Army on a three-year engagement. Why, with my dislike of authority, I chose to join the Army, I really do not know. Looking back, I suppose it was just a case of not really knowing what I wanted to do and finding somewhere to fill in my time until I made up my mind.

The Army didn't prove to be too bad; I did have a stripe on my sleeve for at least part of my service although, to be honest, it didn't stay there very long. I suppose my outstanding achievement was to be the welterweight representative in the team which won the Western Command Boxing Championship. I had always been keen on boxing and the Army gave me the opportunity to find out if I was any good.

But I had reached adulthood without having acquired any commercial or industrial skills, and when I left the Army I was again at something of a loose end. My education in the service had been furthered in the formal scholastic manner, taking various Army Education Certificates. This, however, had only taken me up to around the standard of GCE 'O' levels; a standard which I really ought to have achieved by the age of sixteen, had I made any effort at all at school. At the age of twenty-one they weren't a great deal of use to me.

The next five years were spent doing nothing much other than scraping a living as best I could in a variety of jobs, often taking up challenges in fairground boxing booths and spending every moment of my spare time reading. It was this instinct for self-education which kept me alive intellectually, and which has stayed with me all my life. I read avidly anything I could lay my hands on, from James Hadley Chase to James Joyce.

But even so, it was a miserable period of my life, as I wandered around the Midlands taking whatever work I could find wherever I could find it. On one occasion, employed in a scrap metal yard in West Bromwich, I was sacked for belting a foreman who tried to bully us into working in pouring rain by telling us that he could 'always get a gang of niggers to do the job'. It was one of the many experiences which convinced me at the time that people like myself were suffering as a direct result of immigration into this country.

It was in Leicester, again employed in casual labouring work, that I met Glennis, who was to become my wife.

We married in June 1966, and after a long and depressing search for somewhere to live, settled down in a rather humble bedsit in Kimberley Road, Leicester. It was small and cramped but, for a recently married and far from affluent young couple, it was at least a start.

Within three months, however, my wife became pregnant with Susan, our first child. Children were barred from most bedsit accommodation in those days, and ours was no exception: we immediately had to start looking for somewhere else to live.

Finding somewhere larger proved even more difficult, given what we could afford out of my meagre wages as a warehouseman. Eventually we moved into a small terraced house which, although giving us more room, was the sort of place that these days would bring the health authorities crashing down upon a landlord's head. Our lives were a daily struggle.

Leicester during those years was undergoing something of a transformation. It had become one of the main centres of immigration from the Indian sub-continent and the ethnic communities were growing rapidly. It all seemed a bit much to many people like myself. We found their habits and culture strange and threatening, but, worse, we believed that our own difficulties in finding work and housing were being aggravated by the arrival in increasing numbers of unwelcome foreigners. In Leicester's traditional industries, like textiles, we were convinced that wages and conditions were being undermined by the willingness of these new arrivals to work long hours for low rates of pay. It did not occur to us that what was happening was that they were actually being exploited far more ruthlessly than ever we had been. At the time it seemed simply that we were being deprived of what was rightfully ours.

Like many other people who suffered the same problems, I saw the situation in stark and simple terms; in black and white, so to speak. Without immigrants there would be enough jobs and houses for native-born, white British people like myself. Why should we go short for them? At the same time, looking back, I believe there was a certain psychological defence at work here, as well. I was not unusual in being brought up to believe that as a man it was my duty to provide for my family. That I hadn't been able to led naturally enough to a feeling that I had failed; that as a breadwinner I was inadequate. That feeling of shame evaporates quickly if you can identify someone else who is to blame for your misfortunes. So, in my own mind, racial prejudice restored my standing as head of my family. The difficulties we had no longer reflected badly upon me as provider. The blame lay with the immigrants, and it followed that to fight immigration was to fight for my family.

One evening there appeared in our local paper, the *Leicester Mercury*, a full-page advertisement for a group called the Anti-Immigration Society – AIMS. It argued bluntly against any further immigration to Leicester, and echoed everything of which I had already convinced myself. At the bottom of the page was a tear-off slip, which readers were invited to sign and return if they agreed with the sentiments of the advertisement. Almost without thinking, I posted it off.

By return I received an invitation to a public meeting organized by AIMS to be held the following week in a school hall in Aylestone, a suburb of Leicester. I decided to go, and with about a hundred other people, squeezed into the hall to hear various speakers discuss immigration and the work of AIMS.

AIMS seemed to be a perfectly respectable organization, headed by a local teacher, Denis Taylor. He spoke in suitably moderate terms about the impact that immigrants were having on our city. At his right hand, as AIMS secretary, was one Mary Dwyer, whom I came across several years later as a National Front activist in Manchester. I didn't disagree with a word that was said. Without exception, the people there were concerned with what they saw as a swelling flood of immigrants. I shared their fears without reservation.

But on each chair in the hall we found leaflets from another organization, called the Racial Preservation Society. And from the platform, Denis Taylor told us that while AIMS was not in any way linked to RPS, nevertheless the two groups shared similar views on the issue of immigration, and members of AIMS were perfectly free to contact RPS individually if they so wished. I took the leaflet home and, the following day, wrote to RPS at one of the two addresses provided, expressing my interest in their activities.

A week or so later I received a reply: more leaflets about immigration, and a coupon to return if I wanted to be added to the RPS mailing list. I returned it with a £1 subscription.

At the time I didn't realize what was happening; only later did I see how I was being very gently enticed into a completely new political world. Through my vague interest in anti-immigration activity I had been drawn into the Racial Preservation Society. I had no way of knowing that it was being run by hardened fascists, some of them former Mosley blackshirts, like Alan Hancock, Jimmy Doyle and Ted Budden. There were no names on any of the literature I received, but even if there had been, they would have meant nothing to me. My full conversion to extremist politics was to come later; at this stage, I would still probably have given such people short shrift if I had any inkling at all about their backgrounds. But they made quite sure that I had none.

Over the following months I received copies of the RPS newsletter, a duplicated leaflet-sized effort, and of its newspaper *Southern News*. They also sent long lists of books and pamphlets which were available from RPS, and which I ordered several at a time. I think I must have read almost everything they had to offer.

This was the turning point in my 'nazi education'. These publications did not confine themselves, as the earlier leaflets had done, simply to matters of immigration. Over a period of time, under their influence, my views came to change quite dramatically.

My original standpoint had been simply this: a misguided or incompetent government was storing up problems for future generations through a policy of virtually uncontrolled immigration. From the RPS and its literature I learned of a gigantic, secret conspiracy, designed to destroy the British nation genetically, economically, and socially. Behind it were forces determined to replace nation states with a system of world government, and a policy of immigration and 'race-mixing' was designed to pave the way by destroying national, racial and cultural differences. Of course, in those years there was a tremendous debate going on about whether Britain should join the Common Market, so to me it appeared that the pressures from the main political parties towards EEC membership fitted exactly with what RPS described as this conspiratorial drive towards world government.

It really was not difficult for me to add two and two

together in such a way. As I have said, I wasn't particularly well educated, and had had to leave school at fifteen. But with all modesty, I do like to think that I am fairly bright. Employed in mundane manual work, I was simply bored. Some sort of intellectual pursuit – and that was how the RPS reading material appeared to me – was meat and drink. At the same time, I harboured a strong streak of anti-establishment rebelliousness, and for a whole bundle of reasons connected with the circumstances in which my family lived, I had quite a chip on my shoulder.

I was still only in my mid-twenties and, although it's not a very flattering admission to have to make, I was probably not very mature even for that age. The RPS, if nothing else, appeared radical, and addressed itself directly to what I felt was the big issue. Compared with Westminster politicians of all parties who expressed vague reservations about the level of immigration, or who made (so it seemed) milk and water statements that things would all turn out for the best, the RPS came across as an organization of people with conviction – clear-sighted, committed and courageous. They made a dynamic stand, saying, 'No, we think it's wrong,' and at the time I admired them for it. Once attracted to them, I was easy meat and swallowed all the pseudo-academic claptrap that they used to drive home their message.

By the time, years later, that I came to know that those who had been running RPS were nazis, it simply didn't matter. By then I was one of them.

But before that there was still one more turning point. By now I accepted all they had to say about the world conspiracy, but they were not open, in their newsletter at least, about who they believed was behind it. They talked of 'international finance' or used similar phrases, and it never really occurred to me to wonder whether it meant anything more significant than banks, building societies and finance companies. But once again, the final piece of the ideological jigsaw was put into place for me by the RPS, or, more precisely, by their literature, from which I learned – and came to believe – that the problem was the Jews.

The particular work which had this effect on me was *Fraudulent Conspiracy* by Colin Jordan, a man whose name I was familiar with, and whom, I admit, I was just a little surprised to find on the RPS booklist. At that stage I still regarded RPS as a perfectly respectable, well-intentioned anti-immigration pressure group. Colin Jordan, however, was known to everyone as Britain's most notorious Hitler-worshipper. When he married the perfume heiress Françoise Dior, pictures of them cutting their fingers to mingle blood over an open 'virgin' copy of *Mein Kampf* were splashed all over the papers. Members of his National Socialist Movement had worn SA-style uniforms and swastikas and made no bones about their devotion to the Third Reich. They plastered bus stops, walls and public lavatories with stickers saying 'Hitler was right', a sentiment which provoked a riot when Jordan proclaimed it from the plinth in Trafalgar Square during an NSM rally in 1962.

There was no way, at that point, that I felt any attraction to his nazi theology. My knowledge of the Second World War was pretty thin, but my father had done his bit in the army, and I knew and believed that we were the goodies and the nazis were the baddies. But, at the same time, I did sympathize with some of his more amusing – if juvenile – antics, like his attempt to have Harold Wilson arrested for treason. He had a natural nose for publicity, and I just thought of him as 'a bit of a nutter' – albeit an amusing and probably harmless one. I wasn't aware then of the right-wing gangs, under his nominal leadership at least, roaming Notting Hill carrying out attacks on black people and trying to stir up race riots. His members had also been organizing a campaign of arson attacks against Jewish synagogues. Dozens, mainly in London, were destroyed in an orgy of fire-raising, and NSM members later received hefty gaol sentences for their part in it. When I did find out it didn't matter because by then I was wholly devoted to the cause.

When I read Jordan's *Fraudulent Conspiracy*, I was taken quite by surprise. Here was a man described as a Cambridge graduate, using words quite beyond my comprehension, who gave the impression of having devoted considerable thought to the subject of 'the conspiracy', but whom I had only ever seen presented in the popular press as some sort of buffoon. I had already learned from the RPS that the media were themselves part of the great conspiracy, so it was a logical step from that to my new conviction that the ridiculing of Colin Jordan, and the fact that no one gave serious attention to his economic message, was merely further evidence of 'the conspiracy'. In my mind, Jordan was no longer a clown; he was the main victim of the conspirators.

Fraudulent Conspiracy seemed to make complete sense, in a very simple way. Britain's problems, it said, are the fault of the financial system. The financial system is run by Jews. Therefore, the problem is the Jews.

It may seem quite incredible that someone like myself, who takes pride in being reasonably bright and independent of thought, could have rushed to embrace transparent nonsense like this. But it did happen, and it happened to many others like me. After the softening-up process I went through with AIMS and RPS, it all appeared perfectly logical.

Almost immediately I wrote to Jordan congratulating him on the booklet, saying that while I was not myself any authority on the subject, I had been very impressed with what he had to say. By return I received an extremely courteous reply and an invitation to meet him. We met, and I was even more impressed.

Despite being an obsessive Hitlerite, he was very different from other right-wing leaders I met during my years as an activist. He could inspire tremendous affection and respect, and possessed the sharpest sense of humour I ever witnessed. Over the years, and particularly in those early days, there is no doubt that these talents inspired others to enormous destruction and damage; especially when the NSM arson gangs were going wild in London. As a leader he was in a league of his own, unchallenged by any of his rivals. Many on the extreme right feel that he still is, and even these days he is constantly fending off pleas from the despairing faithful to return to active politics and lead this or that group. For whatever reason he has decided to live as a sort of political hermit in Yorkshire.

But despite the high regard I once had for him, I now feel extremely bitter towards Colin Jordan, not least because I consider he owes me about ten years of my life. If any one man was responsible for enticing me into the nazi underworld it was he. I may have been baptized by RPS, but Colin Jordan was my political godfather.

Looking back now, trying to view things in a fairly detached, objective fashion, I always end up asking myself, 'How on earth could I believe such ludicrous, unbelievable nonsense?' Part of the answer (but only part) is that Colin Jordan was such a remarkable political educator. A schoolteacher by training, he brought his professionally-acquired skills to bear when it came to recruiting new members to his cause, coaxing them to embrace an ideology which was, in my case and many others, so fundamentally alien to everything we had grown up believing to be right. He had little trouble persuading me of the all-pervading existence of this 'Jewish conspiracy for world domination'.

None of what I have described in my 'education' as a dedicated nazi is intended in any way as an excuse for my later actions, but rather as an explanation. At the end of the day I remained a free agent, and had not been coerced into anything by anybody. In that respect, I have to accept full responsibility for my activities in the following years, and, given my record, it is not a light responsibility to have to bear. It was largely an acknowledgement of this that led me later to my decision to try to make some sort of amends for what went before by staying inside the nazi movement as a 'mole'. I wanted to undo some of the damage I had done. But even so, I believe people can learn from my experience how easily perfectly ordinary people can be sucked into such a world, and how simple common prejudices can easily and quickly be cultivated into the most evil political ideology the world has known, where the horrors and the tragedies of the past are forgotten, or endorsed, or, more frequently, denied as part of a gigantic propaganda hoax that Jews have perpetrated upon the world. Racism always has within it the potential to develop into something profoundly evil and murderous. And there are always the hard-line nazi and fascist agitators plugging away, openly or in secret, trying to guide it in exactly that direction.

It took less than a year before I was totally immersed in the idea of a Jewish conspiracy, and at this point I was thrown headlong into nazi activism: Colin Jordan asked me to become the Leicester leader of his recently formed British Movement.

I was to organize the Leicester branch, but with a brief which extended across the East Midlands and included Nottingham and Derby. We quickly built up quite a successful branch of two dozen or so activists.

Before long I had my first taste of political violence. The National Front, which in those early days had most of its support concentrated in London, had also managed to establish a reasonably active branch in Leicester, led by Brendan Wilmer, whom I was later to encounter again in South Africa. In the late summer of 1968, a South African trade delegation visited Leicester and set up shop at the Grand Hotel in Granby Street. Needless to say, supporters of the Anti-Apartheid Movement, mainly from the local University, turned up to demonstrate against the visit and, equally needless to say, we arrived in some numbers to demonstrate against them.

At a national level there was little contact between BM and the NF, but on this occasion, as on so many specifically local initiatives, grassroots members of the two groups joined forces to launch themselves at the students. A number were injured and there were several arrests. We were more than pleased with ourselves; we had given the reds a bloody nose and won some useful publicity in the local press, and we went on organizing similar stunts. On another occasion about fifteen of us disrupted a Secular Society meeting discussing immigration at the Secular Hall. We chanted, stamped our feet, handed out our leaflets – all the usual tactics we would use to make a democratic public meeting impossible. Whenever the question of immigration came up we were there, causing disruption, provoking angry responses until, if the opportunity arose, we would wade in with our fists and feet.

These activities went on for a couple of years. As Leicester organizer I was in almost daily contact with Colin Jordan, whom we all referred to as 'The Leader'. Under British Movement rules I had to attend monthly meetings of the party's directorate at which we would discuss the next piece of inflammatory literature to be produced or the next (usually 'soft') opposition meeting to be targeted for disruption. Of course, the last word always rested with 'The Leader', and I made frequent visits to Jordan's home in Tile Hill, Coventry, to discuss our work in Leicester. The more aggressive and provocative we were the better he was pleased. We spoke almost daily on the telephone and I became one of his most trusted lieutenants – so trusted that he 'honoured' me in June 1969 with the task of working as his election agent in the parliamentary by-election at Birmingham, Ladywood.

We ran a predictable campaign – election addresses and leaflets which blamed everything on blacks and Jews and unashamedly proclaimed our devotion to national socialism. Bill Clarkson, a dyed-in-the-wool nazi activist, brought a team of members down from Liverpool to add numbers and muscle to our efforts. Not surprisingly, our propaganda led to angry exchanges – and not a few violent incidents – in shopping centres or on housing estates. We did not mind in the slightest; this was exactly what they were intended to do. Even at the count on election night itself we managed to provoke a fight, and I made my first appearance on national television. I was rapidly making a name for myself as one of the most eager and uncompromising members of Jordan's nazi street gangs.

When the result was announced we were cock-a-hoop. Having made no efforts at all to disguise our nazi sympathies we persuaded 3½ per cent of the voters in the constituency to place their cross beside Colin Jordan's

name. To most people this might seem a pitiful performance. To us it meant that in just one West Midlands
constituency there were hundreds of potential nazi supporters. How many more would we attract as the lessons
of unfettered immigration sank home to more and more
people? After years of public hostility, we felt it was the
beginning of a rebirth. Like the Phoenix which featured
so often as an illustration of our propaganda, we felt we
were rising from the ashes of 1945.

Ladywood later came to achieve almost mythological
status amongst British nazis, and was invariably cited in
the arguments which raged over the years between the
'open' nazis and the 'closet' nazis. While we paraded
proudly with swastikas on our sleeves and published
photographs of Hitler on the covers of our journals, the
National Front was playing a very different game. There
was virtually no disagreement between us on policy or
ideological matters, but the leaders of the NF had decided
to abandon any public expression of nazi sympathies to
attract broader support from people who were worried
about immigration. Every nazi might be a racist, but not
every racist was a fully-fledged nazi. These were the
people they were after, hoping to succeed with them
exactly as the Racial Preservation Society had succeeded
with me: get them involved over immigration and then
slowly bring them round to accepting the more obnoxious
elements of national socialist ideology.

But, having worked at this strategy for almost ten
years, the Front themselves fought Ladywood in 1977. At
the time I was in South Africa, but it was the Front's
heyday. They were holding public marches of thousands
of members, and polling thousands of votes in some
areas.

Although their candidate in Ladywood was a superficially respectable solicitor, a perfect 'kid-glove' nazi, they managed only 5½ per cent – and treated it as a major victory. The 'open' nazis, however, never let them forget that 'old Jackboots' Jordan had polled only 2 per cent less only eight years before, in a campaign where swastikas, jackboots, and pictures of Hitler figured prominently. Why bother hiding what you really believed, they asked, when the results were only marginally better?

All of this hyper-activity carried on until late 1969, when various pressures led my wife and I to discuss emigrating. It was a subject we had considered many times, but I had been arrested in September of that year, and this event made us consider it rather more seriously. It all arose out of an incident in a Leicester café, where a group of BM members – myself included – had stopped for a sandwich and a cup of tea. When a scuffle developed between ourselves and some Leicester University students, the proprietor intervened and pushed me against a wall. Losing control a little, I punched him on the nose. Police arrived and I was charged with assault and actual bodily harm.

My wife had never been particularly happy about my political activity, but she was by and large prepared to put up with what she called 'all this stormtrooper stuff'. Quite understandably, however, she did draw the line at being telephoned in the middle of the night to be told that her husband was locked up in a local police cell and would be charged with causing bodily harm. She issued an ultimatum: if our marriage was going to last, there would be no more of this.

After some considerable deliberation – we had a young child to think of, after all – we decided to go ahead and emigrate. It goes without saying that, with my political views at the time, South Africa came a clear first for me on the list of countries where we might settle. The necessary arrangements took about three months and a couple of visits to the South African Embassy. Whether the South Africans knew of my political background or not I do not know. Anyway, they didn't appear to care.

My emigration date came up in December, conveniently before I was due to appear in court in Leicester. I simply dispensed with the formalities – I boarded a plane at Heathrow and left for South Africa, with my wife due to follow me later.

2

On Apartheid's Front Line

On New Year's Day 1970 my plane from Heathrow touched down at Jan Smuts Aairport near Johannesburg. Clearing immigration and customs with no hold-ups, I stepped out into what was to be a new life. Here in South Africa, my family was going to have all those things I believed we had been denied in England. I had been assured by the immigration officials at South Africa House in London that there would be no problem finding work and that the standard of living we could expect would far outstrip anything we could hope for back home. I wasn't so daft that I did not realize that much of this was due to South Africa's huge pool of cheap, if not slave, labour, but at that time such things did not trouble my conscience at all. If anything, they added to South Africa's attractions. In England, as I saw things then, an unremitting influx of blacks and Asians was souring life for me and millions of hardworking British people like me. We were being cheated of work, good housing and a decent education for our kids, things that we believed were our birthright, while thousands of interlopers seemed to have little trouble in grabbing work, houses and every state benefit on offer, and they got all this with help and encouragement from politicians of every political hue. Well, here in South Africa, the boot was well and truly on the other foot – and why not? I thought.

Johannesburg was seven miles by bus from the airport, and when I got off at the central railway station clutching my single suitcase, I confess I felt just a little lost and scared. It was a big place, especially to someone who had spent all his earlier life in small Yorkshire and East Midlands towns, and I knew nothing of the people or culture. I had no friends. The future, though big on promise, was at the moment completely unknown. I made for the nearest hotel, the Stern on the corner of Pritchard and Delvers. If that sounds a bit American, the similarity does not stop there. Like Manhattan, Johannesburg is built in strictly symmetrical blocks, so everything is located by reference to the nearest corner.

It was about 2 o'clock in the afternoon when I checked in, and I admit to a slight feeling of smug satisfaction when a black porter was summoned and curtly told to take my case to my room. I watched him do as he was told meekly and obediently, and I decided this was the way things should be. South Africa was truly the place for me.

Despite the hour, the hotel was buzzing with activity. The bar downstairs was crowded with drinkers. Very few of them, it seemed, were resident at the hotel, and without much hesitation this lost soul decided to join the party. It was more like England than England: revellers singing Ilkley Moor and other uniquely English tunes in that semi-drunken fashion so familiar in English pubs shortly before closing time on a Saturday night. I was quickly introduced to everybody there, and barely had to buy a drink all afternoon, until things began to tail off at about 5 o'clock when people began to drift home – considerably the worse for wear.

It had been a long day, so, after a shower, I slept for a couple of hours, assuming that life in the bar would begin again later in the evening. It wasn't to be – until the bar closed at midnight it was like a desert, and I spent the first Saturday night of my new life propping up an empty bar and trying to engage the barman in increasingly laboured conversation.

This, I discovered, was the pattern of Johannesburg weekend social life. There were no licensing laws, and everybody (at least among the expatriate English community) poured into the bars as soon as they opened at 11 o'clock on a Saturday morning with the single-minded object of getting utterly incapacitated as quickly as possible. This was usually accomplished by late afternoon when they staggered off home, not to resurface until the following day. As a result, Saturday night, in England the high point of weekend drinking, was like a grave.

My wife Glennis and our three-year-old daughter flew out a few weeks later, and we settled down into a comfortable enough existence. I found well-paid work quickly, and there was no difficulty finding agreeable accommodation among people we saw as our kind.

But while the British expatriate community into which we settled clung on to many of the facets of working-class life from the mother country, there were many respects in which life in the two countries could not have been more dissimilar. I had been brought up, for instance, to have regard to the future. The Midlands of Britain had always been the repository of those cautious, conservative values which characterized the 'aristocracy of labour' – the skilled well-paid workers who traditionally delivered so many votes for the Conservative Party, and whom the Tories had appealed to so successfully ever since Disraeli, over a hundred years ago, had shrewdly realized that universal male suffrage would not necessarily lead inexorably to socialism through the ballot box. Individual endeavour, hard work, saving for the future and general self-improvement were all highly prized. In other words, we learned to live, if anything, for tomorrow, even if this

meant sacrificing some of life's pleasure today. It was a
system of values that working people had copied from the
commercial middle classes, and it was based economically
on the relatively privileged position that skilled workers
in some areas of industry had enjoyed ever since the
Industrial Revolution.

In South Africa, people lived for today, taking whatever lucratively paid but temporary work was going, and
blowing the high rewards virtually overnight in a non-stop
cycle of drinking and party-going. While work was plenti-
ful during the country's frequent construction booms,
men like myself could take home two hundred pounds a
week – a fortune in those days. But then there would be
spells when no new building projects were starting up,
and things could be extremely tight for several months.

When jobs began again, there was never any problem
getting skilled work – even if you had no particular skills
to offer. When I was taken on at the huge Carlton Centre
project in Johannesburg, I worked first as a joiner and
then as an electrician – my only experience in either of
these trades was a bit of do-it-yourself odd-jobbery at
home. It really was little short of a miracle that the
building went up at all: there were people whose only
skills were in men's hairdressing and installing fire sys-
tems. One man I knew had only ever worked as a chef,
now he was pretending to be a civil engineer. All they
wanted, it seemed, was bodies. As long as they could
make up numbers on the work force and finish the job
eventually, the construction companies were prepared to
turn a blind eye to this bizarre state of affairs.

The sky-high wage rates and the general 'live for today'
attitudes which prevailed contributed to the orgiastic life-
style which swept the English community. Social drinking
on a prodigious scale was accompanied by a freebooting

sexual life-style which, I am sure, most of us had only read about in the Sunday papers back home. Wife-swapping parties were all the rage. One of the most popular forms was the 'car key party'. At the end of an evening's revelry, all the men present would put their car keys into a pot. Each woman would then pick out a key – and go home with its owner. Not surprisingly, the divorce rate was phenomenal – many people we knew were into their fourth or fifth marriages, and showed no signs of stopping there. Marriages which had survived happily for fifteen or twenty years were often lucky to last six months after emigration.

A wide and varied social life was one thing, but neither my wife nor I were keen to become embroiled in this semi-institutionalized 'musical beds' life-style. We were a close-knit and devoted family and we had no desire to put that at risk for the dubious delights of a few inter-marital romps.

We decided to move away from Johannesburg and went to live in a quiet suburb called Florida, just outside the city. After two years as a 'chancer' I felt it was time to try for more secure employment, so I enrolled at the government's Miners' Training College and from there I went to work in the nearby West Rand Consolidated Mines. Soon we had saved enough to buy a smallholding about five miles from Randfontein in the Transvaal, where we spent what were probably the happiest years of my time in South Africa – if not of my whole life. We lived in almost total isolation on our own idyllic little patch of God's earth. Each day I travelled the ten miles or so to and from the mine where I worked. My wife cultivated the small plot of land we owned, and in my spare time I indulged myself in a life-long ambition to breed dogs. Our quiet little farm (as we called it) echoed to the yaps and barks of the finest little pack of Airedale terriers you would see in a long time. In 1971, we had our second child, a son.

But just how quickly all of this could crumble in a society like South Africa was brought home to us brutally in 1975.

Very much a family man, I rarely went anywhere on my own. If we went out for an evening, or away for a weekend, it was always a family outing. The one exception was my occasional trip to Johannesburg for a boxing match. I had always been a keen fight fan and even to this day, one of my greatest pleasures in life is a night out at a good fight.

One Saturday night I travelled to the city to see Pat McCormack matched against a local boxer at Ellis Park. It promised to be a good, closely fought contest, and I had been looking forward to it for weeks. A few hundred yards from the stadium I was run down by a speeding car which shot through a red light and threw me over the bonnet, leaving me unconscious and badly hurt in the road. It disappeared without stopping.

My right arm was badly smashed although, as it turned out, I was lucky to be alive. All that had saved me from more serious injury was my army judo training. Purely by reflex, I went into a break fall as I hit the car's bonnet. The doctors told me this had saved my life – but it wasn't enough to save my right arm, which had taken the full force of the blow from the car and was shattered in several places.

At Johannesburg Hospital began one of the most dreadful experiences of my life. For four days I lay unattended in a ward, pieces of shattered bone protruding from the skin of my arm, while an argument raged over who was to pay for my treatment. Both the Miners' Medical Aid Society and the local municipal authority were insisting that the other should pay for my operation. While they bickered, I was left lying there, my arm simply tied up in a sling, suffering extraordinary pain.

After four days I couldn't stand it any longer. Struggling to the pay phone I called my doctor and told him that if something didn't happen damned quick I was going to walk to the British Consulate in Johannesburg and kick up a row, the like of which he would never have witnessed. It did the trick and I was operated on the next morning. To this day, however, I am still partially disabled, having lost what the doctors call the power of pronation and supranation – in other words, I cannot swivel my arm from the elbow.

The next several months were spent in a hospital bed, which meant that there was no income at all to provide for my wife and my two young children. My wife had to take an office job, starting at five in the morning to walk the kids, one still in a pram, to the child-minder who looked after them while she was at work. In the evenings she travelled in to Johannesburg to visit me at the hospital. Only her herculean efforts kept the family fed, clothed and together throughout this disastrous period. She never complained but it was obviously sheer hell for her.

Eventually, with my arm in as good repair as it was ever going to be, I was discharged, only to discover just how hard life could be in a get-rich-quick society where the survival of the fittest was still the governing principle. My job in the mines was gone, and now that my disability made similar work impossible, no one was the least bit interested in employing me. They were very tough times. I scratched a living selling insurance, breeding my Airedales and taking whatever odd jobs I could find, but we seemed to be permanently on the edge of financial ruin.

In many ways I was in the same position as I had been as a newly-married young man in Leicester and, perhaps not surprisingly, my thoughts began to wander in the same direction as they had then.

It was one of those spells when there was increasing pressure on the government to reform some of the harsher aspects of apartheid. The *Rand Daily Mail*, for example, was campaigning for electrification of black townships like Soweto. It was, looking back, a very modest proposal, but at the time it seemed to undermine everything I had come to South Africa to take advantage of. Here was the liberal press accusing the government of harshness and a lack of sympathy for black people, while my family often did not know where the next meal was coming from. Once again, I believed, ordinary white folk like us were being forgotten while demands were raised on behalf of blacks. All the old notions were welling up inside me again, obviously only having been temporarily laid to rest while we, like most of South Africa's whites, had enjoyed the fruits of 'separate development'.

By now, of course, I had been out of active politics for a few years. I had not really missed it, I must admit, and I suppose in some respects, by South African standards, I had mellowed just a little. Not exactly a liberal, I was nevertheless not the hard-line nazi who had packed his bags and quit Leicester four years earlier.

But I did resent bitterly the position in which I and my family now found ourselves. For all the calamities which had been visited upon us following my accident, we had received no help at all. Not a finger was raised on our behalf, but hearts seemed to be bleeding profusely for the 'poor, oppressed black' in the townships.

In late 1978, I dipped my toe, a little hesitantly at first, back into the waters of racist politics. It seemed natural at the time, given my feelings, to team up with people who were most active in campaigning against the 'reforms' which were being proposed. There were two obvious outlets for my newly awakened resentments – the recently formed South African branch of the British National Front, and the Herstigte National Party, a far right, basically Afrikaans party whose leader had been expelled from the ruling National Party after attacking it for its 'creeping liberalism'. In 1981, the HNP mopped up almost 200,000 votes (out of a white population of about 4 million) and in 1985 it had its first MP elected in a by-election. As the pressure for reform has grown in the Republic, so racist voters disaffected with the NP have slowly turned to the HNP as the vehicle to protect their position and their privileges. But in 1978, it was still very much on the margins, a small, noisy irritant, but one growing slowly and with considerable potential.

Founded by former National Party member and government minister Albert Herzog in 1969, the HNP quickly tried to combine monopolization of the 'no surrender' wing of white Afrikaans opinion with a firmly anti-Jewish explanation of South Africa's problems. Black encroachment into white privileges had to be resisted by whatever means were necessary, and it should not be overlooked, the HNP would stress, that behind black demands were communist agitators and Jewish interests. The 'Jewish conspiracy', for the HNP, was the key to understanding what made the world tick – and who the enemy really was.

At first, my involvement was confined to writing occasional articles for its paper *Die Afrikaaner*, whose editor, Mr Schoeman, I met on several occasions to discuss how best I could help the party's endeavours. We got on well, and he presented me, for my efforts, with an autographed copy of his book *Die Sluipmoord van Dr Verwoerd* (The Secret Murder of Dr Verwoerd), which alleged an international conspiracy in the murder of the architect of apartheid.

He was prompted to make this particular gift by my work for the HNP during a parliamentary by-election in Alberton, near Johannesburg. As I said, the HNP was at that time an exclusively Afrikaans party, but during the campaign I became the first person to address a party meeting in English – a rare privilege, I was assured at the time.

The 'Herstigtes', as they were known, were clearly impressed by the skills which I had acquired in England as a nazi activist, and were anxious to make use of them. One person who held my talents in particularly high regard was the party's founder and former leader, Dr Albert Herzog, who, when we met, voiced his true beliefs to me with a degree of frankness which, had it become known, would have severely damaged the party's chances of becoming a political force to be reckoned with. On one occasion he confided in me his belief that Premier John Vorster was 'in the pay of the Jews'.

Before launching the HNP, Herzog had been Minister of Post and Telegraphs in Vorster's cabinet. A few modest proposals from Vorster, made in the face of considerable international pressure, to liberalize some of those regulations which enforced apartheid in sport in South Africa, had convinced Herzog that his leader had been 'corrupted and bought by the Jews' during his internment as a nazi sympathizer in the Second World War. Vorster's apparent intention to introduce what were, after all, paltry reforms of the apartheid system, was more than enough to goad Herzog into bitterly attacking his party leader, who retaliated by expelling him. He immediately set up his own 'not an inch' alternative, the HNP.

In this enterprise he was joined by another cabinet minister, Jaap Marais, who later succeeded him as party leader, presiding over the disturbing gains which the 'Herstigtes' have made in South Africa over the last few years. Marais too was expelled from the NP in the 1969 row over the possibility of Vorster liberalizing sporting activities.

Unfortunately, the HNP's steady growth at the polls was not even set back by allegations in October 1979 that one of its leading members and election candidates, Neville Warrington, had fathered no less than three children by different black mothers. The HNP, staunch defenders of the notorious Mixed Marriages and Immorality Acts, which prohibited sexual relations between people of different races, was acutely embarrassed, and had to suspend Warrington from the party.

Two signals that the HNP had become a force to be reckoned with were seen in 1981. In April, in the general election, they picked up as much as 30 per cent of the white vote in some areas, and it was estimated that up to thirty-three Parliamentary seats might be within their grasp. Then, only a few months later, the Broederbond, the Afrikaaner secret society through which the establishment maintains its power and passes it on from generation to generation, lifted a ban on HNP members joining the society. The 'Broeders', who form the backbone of the ruling National Party, had declared HNP members beyond the pale in 1969. Faced with dozens of resignations from the brotherhood as members deserted the National Party, it had no choice but to open the doors to the HNP to stop the haemorrhage. Marais, needless to say, welcomed it as a victory for the Hestigtes – which, in a sense, it was. In his understanding of the world, Marais was no less uncompromising than Herzog, and told me himself that he believed the Second World War to have been 'a massive defeat for the white man'.

When I addressed a Herstigte election rally in 1979, shortly before returning to England, the *Johannesburg Star* estimated the audience at close to a thousand. My standing with the Herstigtes, and my welcome on their public platforms, was undoubtedly enhanced by the fact that in the meantime my star had also been rising rapidly in the predominantly English-speaking South African National Front, into whose activities I had also thrown myself.

SANF had been set up in March 1978 by Jack Noble, an English expatriate who, unlike me, had not been involved in racist politics in Britain before he emigrated to South Africa in 1971. Quite the opposite, in fact: under the *nom de plume* 'Albion' he had written many letters to the *Johannesburg Star* in which he argued a thoroughly liberal and enlightened point of view. At one stage, for instance, he organized a public petition against censorship in the arts which attracted considerable media interest and put him in the spotlight.

His weakness for public attention never changed, even when, for reasons I still do not understand, his beliefs were radically transformed. From liberal letter-writer he became hard-line right-wing activist, and in 1977 he launched the South African branch of the National Front, affiliating it to the parent party back in the mother country. It was part of a moderate cross-commonwealth expansion by the British party. Right-wing-inclined émigrés in Australia and New Zealand, who presumably had had some connection with the NF before quitting the UK, also established 'branches' at around the same time. In the long term, none came to very much.

* * *

I was selling insurance door to door. It had not been one of my most successful days, and I stepped into a bar for a drink. I was served by Jack Noble, who paid for my drink and invited me to a meeting of the National Front. This was shortly before I was introduced to the Herstigtes, and while it is true that I was very bitter at the scant attention being paid to deprived whites like myself, I was not, at that stage, mad keen to get involved. Nevertheless, the old tug was there and, drawn partly by that, and partly by pure boredom, I drove into Johannesburg after work one weekday evening to hear what the Front had to offer.

By then, of course, I had been out of active politics for several years, but I had not entirely forgotten just how intensely tiresome meetings of small groups of the political faithful could be. Even so, I was not prepared for what followed: an evening of unutterable tedium.

A couple of dozen members – and myself – sat through two or three of the most acutely sleep-inducing speeches I had encountered in all my many years in the political fringes. After a while, the urge to liven up the proceedings was irresistible and I took to the floor. Within a few minutes I had electrified the entire hall. I was in my element: I ranted and raved, brandishing fists and stamping feet in my customary fashion, and delivered a savage indictment of the apartheid regime's abandonment of its foot-soldiers – the ordinary white working-class Joe like me. To round it off I launched into an impassioned attack on 'the Jewish-controlled press', a tirade which left Ray Joseph, a reporter from the *Johannesburg Sunday Times*, sitting near me, looking distinctly nervous. Several years later, after I 'came out' as a mole, we met in London for a drink. 'Only my laundryman knows how frightened I was that night,' he told me.

When I sat down, the small audience hooted and

clapped wildly. The 'star speakers' on the platform looked, it must be said, just a trifle discomfited at having been so rudely up-staged. As the meeting drew to a close, people seized my hand and slapped me on the back. In the bar afterwards, I was prevailed upon to join the party and, seeing no good reason not to, I signed an application form. It had to be approved, of course, but that was no more than a formality. I was an overnight success, and my rise to NF fame was accelerated by Ray Joseph's lengthy report of the meeting – and my speech – in the following day's *Johannesburg Sunday Times*.

The SANF at that time was neither so big nor so dynamic that it could afford to pass up such an opportunity. At the handful of party meetings I attended during the following weeks, I was invariably invited to the platform to address the faithful and I was received with tremendous enthusiasm. It wasn't that my rhetorical skills were particularly outstanding, although by anyone's standards they were respectable. It was more a simple case of 'In the land of the blind, the one-eyed man is king'. In no time at all, to my surprise, I was offered a senior post – chairmanship of the NF. After only a little hesitation, I accepted it.

Under my stewardship, the NF swiftly earned itself a degree of notoriety simply by mimicking the sorts of publicity stunts I had learned during my days with the British Movement as a lieutenant to Colin Jordan. In anyone else's terms, it was all a bit of political silliness – often no more serious than the daft stunts which the old League of Empire Loyalists pulled off at Tory Party conferences and the like in Britain in the 1950s and '60s. But in South Africa, where politics had for so long followed the staid pattern laid down by the 'reformed' protestants of the National Party, we arrived like a bolt from the heavens and took the media by storm. It was probably the most original thing to happen in political life in the Republic since the Boer War itself.

If I had to be perfectly honest, I would have to confess that it was little more than political tomfoolery which I found difficult to take especially seriously, so no one was more astonished than I by the reactions we provoked.

On one occasion, for instance, a small group of activists managed to gain access to the top floors of the 700-foot-high Carlton Tower building in central Johannesburg, and deluged the city centre with over 10,000 leaflets denouncing the National Party's 'betrayal of the white race'. In Johannesburg, you have to realize, the streets are kept meticulously clean and a pedestrian in the street would not dream of dropping even a used bus ticket on the pavement. On that day, those very city streets were buried in a snowstorm of our SANF propaganda. Like all our stunts, it won us acres of coverage in the newspapers the following day, and applications for membership began to arrive in increasing numbers.

With 'successes' like these under our belt, it was natural enough that there should be contacts between the respective leaderships of the NF and of the Herstigte National Party, both of which were now campaigning against racial sell-outs by the government. I had already written for *Die Afrikaaner* and spoken at HNP meetings when it was proposed that joint leadership meetings should be held from time to time.

At the first get-together, the NF was represented by myself, Jack Noble, and an expatriate Italian called Max Bollo. There was little, if any, disagreement on fundamentals: HNP boss Marais put forward the view that 'English-speaking South Africa has been hijacked by the Jews'. The function of the NF should be to act as a catalyst for anxious white South Africans who were worried by the apparent trend towards liberalization and reform, but who felt out of place with the HNP which was, after all, predominantly Afrikaans. In this way, and working together, we could maximize our appeal in both of these distinct white communities, which traditionally had stood apart from each other, and which were unlikely to be united in support of any single political party.

But it wasn't only in the direction of the Herstigtes that the NF had cast its eye in seeking out alliances with like-minded groups. Through Jack Noble, we had developed an even closer relationship with a group of expatriate Italian fascists who called their small organization UNIDO and who were led by two men: Max Bollo and Fabio Miriello. My experience during this particular phase of joint work convinced me that I was seen by the rest of the NF's leadership as little more than a figurehead; 'good old Ray', who could come up with new ideas for headline-winning stunts, write hard-hitting pieces for the party magazine *Hitback*, or be relied on to take a meeting by storm and whip up the party's followers to new heights of enthusiasm. In our dealings with these Italians, however, I was kept very much at arm's length, and I suspected that something else was going on. At some of our party meetings, in 1978 and early 1979, our English members would find themselves outnumbered by Italian and Portuguese fascists, who conducted themselves in a peculiarly furtive fashion. I was not the only one to feel uncomfortable, but, without any clear suspicions of anything untoward going on, I ploughed on as the party's leading workhorse.

Soon afterwards, we plunged into our first real political campaign. Following several months of rather childish, though successful, publicity stunts, we took on the police and the government over the encroachment of coloured tenants into a white residential area. It was to prove successful beyond our imaginings, but at the same time it was to be, for me, a turning point. I was to find out what, in simple human terms, racism really meant, and where the policies of racism, if successful, could lead.

Hillbrow, a suburb of Johannesburg, was classified as a white area under the iron laws of apartheid. But, unfortunately for landlords in the area, there were simply not enough white tenants around to fill all the rented properties available in the area, and many had been vacant for long periods. The laws of the market, as they often are, were found to be more powerful than the ideological laws of apartheid, and before long landlords were actively encouraging coloured families to move into the area and rent property. To all of this the police, very friendly locally with the landlords, turned a blind eye. They had no intention of letting their own suffer as a result of 'separate development'. Things were, after all, supposed to be the other way round.

Until, that is, just after the New Year in 1979, when the SANF took up cudgels on behalf of the sanctity of apartheid's founding principles. Party activists began leafleting the area, denouncing this 'thin edge of the black wedge' being driven into 'our' white suburbs. Naturally, we blamed the Jews for what was happening. One of our leaflets blamed 'money-grabbing Zionist landlords' for allowing Indians to live in the area, and declared that 'this country is yours, not the Zionists''. Then we toured the area, knocking on doors and pinpointing houses where coloured, mostly Indian, families were living. We approached the police demanding that action be taken to evict them from the area and threatening court injunctions if the police failed to act. Not surprisingly, the police authorities were soon forced to begin turning coloured people out of their homes to preserve the precious white identity of Hillbrow, even if this led to squeals of anguish from white landlords as a consequence.

Although I was chairman of the Front at the time, I had not actually been involved in the decision to begin this particular campaign. That's not to say that I disagreed with it, but I did feel just a little put out at having been excluded from the discussions in the party leadership which preceded it. In public and in my dealings with the press, I staunchly defended what we were doing. It was only when I happened to pay a social visit to the Hillbrow district that my faith in the politics of racial supremacy was shaken. And it was shaken very rudely indeed.

It was a fine, bright Sunday afternoon in late March. With my daughter I drove the seven or eight miles from our home to Hillbrow to see some family friends. We had a couple of afternoon drinks while the kids played in the back garden. Returning home, we stopped off for an ice-cream in a small café.

Directly opposite our pavement table was a truly pathetic-looking Indian family, squatting at the roadside with what few possessions they owned tied up in bundles of blankets. Wandering across the road I asked the husband what the problem was. When he replied that they had been evicted by police from the house they had been living in for the last year, and that the police had blamed the NF, I felt a knot tighten in my guts. How on earth could I begin to tell him that I was responsible for what had happened to him? On one level I wanted to show my sympathy for this poor family, stuck out here in the streets with nowhere in the world to go, but this simple human response was ruled out by the knowledge that I was to blame for their predicament. I muttered something unintelligible, dragged my daughter away from her ice-cream and, almost literally, fled from Hillbrow feeling thoroughly ashamed.

Of one thing I was suddenly sure: never again could I be party to visiting such misery on human beings. It would be difficult enough now living with the consequences of what I had already done, and I could not ever contemplate adding to it. My days as a racist were over.

The whole episode did, in fact, ring a little familiar, and when I got home I rooted through the press cuttings on SANF activities which I had clipped and collected over the past few months. One Sunday paper, a month or so earlier, had published a very similar story. Its significance at the time had passed me by. After that afternoon in Hillbrow I read it again, much more slowly and in a rather different light. 'Pitched into no-home street' told almost exactly the tale which had shaken me in Hillbrow a few hours earlier. In this case, the paper reported, an Indian family of eight had been forced to pitch a tent and live in the street outside the house they had occupied for several years. They were particularly unlucky – only their front door crossed the imaginary line separating the 'coloured' area from the white. But this was enough to have them kicked into the street by police enforcing the Group Areas Act – at the demand of the National Front. And there, right in the middle, was a quote the reporter had obtained from me: 'They may not thank us now but we are doing them a favour,' I had intoned, restating the Front's 'for public consumption' explanation of our campaign. 'We believe the government must provide housing for them, but it won't as long as they can stay in white areas. This could speed the whole process up.'

It was utter cant and I knew it. The reality was that Front members hated blacks and coloureds, cared not one jot for their welfare, and were interested only in maintaining racial separation and white supremacy.

Utterly disgusted with myself, I threw the paper into a corner and went to bed. It was a long time before I was able to sleep.

Dramatic though it sounds – and was – this event was not entirely a 'road to Damascus' conversion. A few things had already happened in my life which, while not themselves enough to shake me out of political habits years in the making, did nevertheless help to tip the balance.

I had, strange as it may seem, already established friendships with a couple of Jewish chaps who had been extremely kind to my family and myself when times had been hard. They knew all about my peculiar political views, but did not seem to hold them against me, and took me at face value as a friend. I spent many afternoons in their company at race meetings at Alberton. I suppose in some ways these sorts of contacts may have softened my belief that other races – especially Jews – were the enemy of whites like myself, but they did not, in themselves, lead to any 'blinding light' revelations. The catalyst was that Sunday afternoon in Hillbrow, which left me shaken, confused and ashamed. At home I was broody and preoccupied that fateful Sunday evening, and eventually I knew that I could not live with myself if I carried on as before. 'No, it's over,' I decided.

This coincided with other developments to make a turning point in both my political and my personal life. My wife had for some time been suggesting that we might do better to return to England. As things stood, prospects in South Africa following my accident were no longer so attractive as to warrant our continued separation from our families and friends back in the old country.

And in the NF itself things were taking an ominous turn. Increasingly, certain matters were being discussed in a tightly-knit little caucus which seemed to be operating like some secretive cell. At executive meetings it was becoming clear that certain decisions were being taken before the official meetings even began. And after executive meetings some members could be found closeted away from the rest of us who were enjoying the traditional post-meeting drink. On one occasion I caught a whispered reference to 'sabotage' but, after all, this is the sort of word often bandied around metaphorically in political circles, especially those where conspiracy theories hold sway. It was some time later, after my return to Britain, that the full horrifying significance of these little bar-corner cabals became clear to me, but even so, at the time, the odd worry was certainly lurking in my mind. I became increasingly persuaded that I was regarded as something of a useful idiot: making the speeches, and fronting for the party, but being kept deliberately in the dark by a group of very sinister individuals who were now firmly in control.

More and more inclined to get out, I told my wife that if she was still keen to get back to England, we would do so as soon as we could sort out our affairs and sell up. She was delighted.

One particular dilemma, however, was still to be dealt with. It would be a few months before we would be able to leave South Africa. In the meantime, what was I to do about the NF? I could, of course, have simply walked quietly away, telling the party I wanted no more to do with it. Or I could have gone in for some public recantation which would, no doubt, have had some damaging effect on the Front, even if only in the short term. But preying on my mind was the conviction that just getting out would do little to repair the damage that I now knew I had inflicted on innocent victims, almost certainly from the day that I had first been baptized into the world of the extreme right. Most of this would never be known to me – perhaps that is what makes such extremism so easy to settle into. For all the time you spend propagandizing, issuing inflammatory leaflets, or organizing provocative demonstrations, you are rarely around to appreciate the consequences. The seed of hate which you plant in someone's mind may only come to fruition years later, when its lineage to your own contribution has been well obscured by time and intervening events. And, while you are located firmly on the fringes, you rarely see any direct consequence of your campaigns for policies rooted in racism and national socialism. In that respect, Hillbrow was out of the ordinary: I was directly confronted with the dreadful playing out of events which I had had a hand in shaping. I had met a family which I had thrown into the streets, and I knew there were probably many, many more. Hillbrow was only the result of my most recent efforts: what of the possible consequences of the previous ten years of political activism? It was not enough, now, simply to walk away, shamed or otherwise. Something in the way of reparation was called for. Weighing up the risks to myself, and to my family, I decided to stay on, acting out the role of dedicated racist demagogue, but using any information to which this gave me access against the Front. I decided, in spy-world parlance, to become a 'mole'.

I made contact with a leading figure in the Jewish community in Johannesburg and, over the five or six months between my change of heart and my departure for England, I fed a steady stream of information in his direction

– lists of NF members, details of high-level party discussions and meetings, and highly secret plans for a major party rally in Johannesburg.

This was due to take place in January 1979. It was generally agreed that some major public event would have to be staged to impress upon the public the more serious and established image that Bollo, Noble and friends wanted to adopt. The Front could not forever go on simply with headline-grabbing publicity stunts like Hillbrow. At some stage it had to begin looking and behaving like a serious political party. A major rally of members and supporters in Johannesburg was planned as the first step in this phase of the NF's emergence as a political force.

But such schemes were not without their problems. As a rule, racist parties like the NF or the HNP had little trouble from opposition in the black or coloured communities. Quite apart from the restrictions which existed to curtail significant political activity within those communities, black and coloured people in South Africa, and their representative organizations, had much greater and more important tasks facing them. Confronted by the apartheid system in all its brutality, they could easily be forgiven for not getting too worked up about the antics of a few racists on the political fringe. In the Jewish community, however, the issue struck a deeper chord. South Africa's Jews, about 115,000 of them, arrived in large part from Lithuania in the late nineteenth century. Their numbers were swelled by an emigration from Israel in the 1970s, but they are still a small minority within the white population of about four million. Many Jewish people, it is well known, are particularly prominent in the fight against apartheid in South Africa, despite, in recent years, the increasing degree of co-operation between the governments of South Africa and Israel; co-operation in both the economic and military spheres.

While on a number of occasions a lurking strand of anti-semitism in South Africa's ruling establishment has been identified, and while Jewish people have often complained that certain careers, professions and educational opportunities appear to be all but closed to them, nevertheless the South African government did sometimes respond to Jewish representations over the activities of anti-semitic and neo-nazi organizations. For instance, some of the 'revisionist' texts, freely sold in Europe, repeating nazi claims that the Jewish Holocaust during the Second World War did not take place, were officially prohibited in the Republic of South Africa.

So the NF, and groups like it, had to be extremely careful if they had any plans to organize public activities likely to cause offence to the Jewish community. In the case of the Front, which by now was making no secret of its anti-semitism, this meant almost any public activity at all. Details of the January rally, therefore, were only in part made public. Important details, such as the actual venue, were a closely guarded secret. Even members and their guests (many Herstigtes were due to attend) were only informed at the very last minute.

As it happened, they found out later than their opponents. As Front chairman, I had been privy to the news that a hotel in Loveday Street was to be the venue ever since the secret booking was made. It was one of the first pieces of valuable advance intelligence I passed over to my Jewish community contact. He didn't waste it: when I arrived that Saturday afternoon to speak at the rally, I couldn't even get near the hotel. Several hundred young Jewish demonstrators had surrounded the building, virtually laying siege to it, and were trading punches with those Front members who had actually got near. The police had sealed off nearby streets, including the one I was trying to use to approach the hotel, and made it very clear to me that, platform speaker or not, there was no way I was getting near that building that afternoon. So, for the next couple of hours, I stood on the other side of the police barricade while the Front got the first dose of real opposition it had seen since it began stirring up trouble less than two years earlier. I must admit, although I had to keep up an appearance of being angry and outraged, that inside I was crowing with delight.

It was as a direct consequence of these events that the government decided, the following month, to stop British NF leader John Tyndall entering the country to address SANF meetings, thus putting paid to further plans for a morale-boosting gathering of all the forces on South Africa's far right. I was beginning to understand just how much of an impact one individual saboteur could have. The Front's best-laid plans were collapsing in ruins, and it was all down to me.

My plans to return to England were not particularly well advanced when, only a few months after the Loveday Street fiasco, events took a rather unexpected turn, and I ended up leaving South Africa in something of a hurry.

I was working at that time as a physical training teacher at St George's, an Anglican boys' orphanage in Johannesburg. It cared for about thirty boys aged sixteen and seventeen, and I was in charge of their sporting activities. In February, a friend had asked me to lend him some money so that he could buy a birthday present for his wife. Not having any cash to hand, and it being a weekend, I rather foolishly handed him my credit card and told him to get what he wanted with it. He could make a reasonable copy of my signature, and pay me back the following week when he received his monthly pay cheque. In very little time at all he had run up a bill of more than £3,000, which I was neither willing nor able to pay. The police visited me, and I was charged with credit card fraud, although I was told, unofficially, that the case was little more than a formality and that after the court had decided I was not liable for these debts, charges could be brought against my erstwhile friend. Meanwhile, I was bailed for the sum of £1,500.

But the wheels of South African justice grind exceedingly slowly, and I was faced with the prospect, having already decided to return to England, of having to sit it out for a year or more in South Africa, after the committal proceedings, waiting for my case to come to trial. Talking the matter over with my wife, I decided that £1,500 was not enough to keep us hanging on for another year. So, having managed to save enough from my job at St George's, I bought air tickets for the whole family and we boarded a plane for England two weeks later, just a couple of days before my first committal hearing was due in Johannesburg.

But no sooner had we arrived back in England than I was astonished to read newspaper stories in the British press connecting me with the alleged embezzlement of over £20,000 from a benevolent society for English-speaking immigrants, called the Sons of England, and suggesting that this had been the real reason for my 'jumping bail'. The Sons of England was a mutual aid society of English-speaking immigrants, a masonic-style outfit which tried to ensure that immigrants from the mother country looked after one another. The National Front, considering it to be an ideal base from which to recruit influential and wealthy members, had infiltrated it and taken it over. I was even made its secretary. But I knew nothing of the vanishing funds and, to this day, I have never been charged with having had anything to do with it. The truth was that the money had been taken by Jack Noble, who returned to England shortly before me, in even greater haste. When we met, after my own return, he boasted to me of having cleaned up almost the entire missing £20,000, a large proportion of which he had donated to the National Front in England.

This was not, however, the only mystery which was cleared up for me after I got back. Light was finally thrown on all that mysterious caballing and furtiveness by some SANF leaders and their Italian comrades which had puzzled me while I was the party chairman. They were embarked, it transpired, on a fully-fledged campaign to achieve their aims by the use of terrorism.

It was in March 1978, only a year or so after he had founded the South African NF, that Jack Noble announced that it would henceforth be joining forces with a right-wing Italian group called UNIDO to beat 'creeping integration and multi-racialism'. It was the formal beginning of a relationship which would lead to terrorism, arrests and a sensational court case which signalled the demise of the party.

UNIDO (International Union for the Defence of the West) had been set up in 1976, with supporters in Pretoria, Johannesburg and East Rand. Later, it claimed to have had up to 500 members, but to my certain knowledge only a few dozen were involved when the merger with the NF was announced. They published a journal called *Noi Europa*, met secretly in a Johannesburg restaurant, and each year held a dinner to mark the 'March on Rome' of 1922 when Benito Mussolini took power in Italy. From the beginning, the organization was firmly controlled by two men: Max Bollo and Fabio Miriello, both of whom were to be guiding lights when the NF/UNIDO alliance began a campaign of terror in 1980.

Bollo, in his mid-thirties when I first met him, worked for a major office equipment firm in Johannesburg. Extremely intelligent, and speaking several languages, he arrived in South Africa in the mid-1970s from Angola, having previously spent time in Mozambique and Kenya. Like other UNIDO members, he was a devout disciple of Mussolini and believed that Hitler had simply plagiarized ideas originally developed by the Italian dictator. He was married, but not much of a family man, and his wife separated from him in 1979, fed up, I was told at the time, with the amount of time he devoted to his fringe political activities. Although we rarely met socially, he and I often enjoyed a drink together after some NF meeting or other.

His partner, Fabio Miriello, lived in a plush country lodge in Orange Grove on the outskirts of Johannesburg, and worked as an engineer. Miriello edited *Noi Europa*, having been kicked off another, more moderate, Italian community newspaper, *Il Voce*, for trying to sneak in articles reflecting his own less than moderate views.

These Italians, much more skilled political operators than most of the Front's English-speaking leaders, quickly launched a campaign to unite the several far-right groups which, until then, were all doing their own separate thing to oppose what they had all identified as 'creeping multi-racialism' in South African society. High on the list of targets which they hoped to bring into a single organization were the HNP and an even more extreme Afrikaans group, the Afrikaaner Resistance Movement, usually known by its Afrikaans initials, AWB. A small group of Ku Klux Klan members in South Africa were also targeted for recruitment.

The AWB, like the Herstigtes, was a white supremacist,

anti-semitic, predominantly Afrikaans-based party. Its flags and symbols bore an uncanny similarity to those of Hitler's nazi party and, indeed, the AWB traced its traditions back to the paramilitary Ossawa Brandwag, which supported Hitler during the Second World War. Some of its supporters – most notably later President John Vorster – were interned for the duration of hostilities as a result.

Anti-semitism was a key feature of its ideology. At a rally in 1977, one speaker claimed that Harry Oppenheimer, of the Anglo American Corporation, and other Jews had stolen the natural resources of South Africa. Its propaganda explicitly accused 'Jewry' of being behind 'South African Leftism' and pressure for reform of the apartheid system.

In 1981 it became clear that the AWB was receiving financial backing from HNP founder Albert Herzog, the former government minister who set up the HNP in protest at John Vorster's 'liberalism' in 1969. By then eighty-two years old, and having dropped out of politics for several years, his reappearance was something of a surprise, but seemed to be linked to efforts to unite several diverse far-right groups. The HNP, it was said, by this time having established itself far more successfully than any of the other fringe groups involved in these 'fusion' negotiations, refused to have anything to do with the idea, considerably disappointing their founder and former leader.

Police raids in December 1982 on the homes of leading AWB members, including its leader Eugene Terre'blanche, uncovered stockpiles of arms and ammunition. Terre'blanche received a suspended sentence, but two other AWB members, convicted of conspiring to cause explosions and assassinate religious leaders, were each gaoled for fifteen years.

Pressure for co-operation between extremist white groups had been growing for some time, and although no formal unification ever took place, joint leadership meetings were held. In November 1978, for instance, plans were laid for a grand joint rally to be addressed by the leader of the British National Front, John Tyndall.

Behind this ambitious plan were the Front, the HNP, UNIDO and the AWB. Had it gone ahead, it would no doubt have given a huge impetus to the Italians' drive for a united party. As it turned out, the event was first postponed until February and then cancelled altogether when the Interior Minister, Alwyn Schlebusch, refused Tyndall an entry visa. Institutionalized racism was one thing, but the South African authorities felt they had troubles enough of their own without allowing some foreign nazi agitator in to make matters worse. Nevertheless, the Front and UNIDO were by now working hand in glove, and shortly afterwards it was announced that the KKK was also joining the club. The two major Afrikaans groups, HNP and AWB, were still doing their own thing, harbouring lingering suspicions about these 'johnny-come-lately' immigrant racists.

When Jack Noble left South Africa to return to Britain in March 1979, his place as secretary of the party was taken by Alan Fotheringham, a former HNP member whom Noble himself had recruited. Fotheringham had been an election candidate for the Herstigtes in Witbank in 1977, winning 600 votes and losing his deposit. According to HNP leader Jaap Marais, he left the party shortly afterwards. It was during Fotheringham's leadership, that some of the National Front were encouraged by Bollo and Miriello to embark upon a new strategy of terror.

They were going to force a halt to 'creeping racial liberalism' with guns and bombs. Carefully screening their most fanatical supporters, they organized them into a tightly knit terrorist cell and embarked upon a campaign of violence whose targets were any public symbols of multi-racialism. They called themselves the 'Wit Kommando', or White Commando.

The first attacks took place in the early months of 1980. Bombs rocked a couple of cinemas in black areas, and the offices of the South African Institute for Race Relations. These were followed by explosions at the home of Natal MP Derril Watterson and at the office of Professor Jan Lombard at Pretoria University. Further attacks took place at the office of the Transkei Consul in Port Elizabeth in October, and at the Pretoria University office of Professor Franz Maritz in December. In all cases, the attacks were directed either at black targets, or at liberal whites who had made public their view that the apartheid system should be reformed. It was a miracle that nobody was killed.

At first it was assumed, not unnaturally, that militant Afrikaaners were responsible, but when the first public claim was made by the 'Wit Kommando', the Afrikaans in which their communiqué was written was poor, and police investigating the attacks began to look in other directions.

In February 1981 they raided several houses and offices belonging to NF and UNIDO leaders, arresting Bollo, Miriello, Alan Fotheringham and several others. Fotheringham was later released without charge. What they found was a horrifying portent of what the Wit Kommando intended for the future: at Max Bollo's house and in a Johannesburg office they uncovered 47 kilos of plastic explosives, mines, two cases of hand grenades, phosphorous grenades, and firearms. Most ominously, perhaps, they soon realized that many of the items were official issue to the South African Army.

They also found a 'hitlist' of future targets, which included the Transvaal's Education chief, Professor J. H. Jooste, and Professor Hennie van der Walt, chairman of the Van der Walt Commission. Also planned, but aborted, had been a bomb attack on Bishop Desmond Tutu, leader of the South African Council of Churches.

Three NF/UNIDO leaders were eventually charged: Bollo, Miriello and Monica Huggett. Huggett, although warned by the trial judge that she might incriminate herself, turned state's evidence against the others when they came to trial in September 1981, and painted a vivid picture of the demented activities of this racially-motivated terror cell.

She revealed that Wit Kommando members had first been recruited by Bollo at a meeting in June 1980 of leaders from NF, UNIDO, AWB and HNP. She herself had joined the Ku Klux Klan in the United States, and her particular early contribution was to present Bollo with copies of *The Poor Man's James Bond*, which explained how to make explosives from ordinary household materials, and *Explosives and Demolition*, which explained how and in what quantities they should be used. The army weapons, she said, came from a sympathetic soldier called Eugenio Zoppis, and she later recruited two other members to the terror team. She also provided a garage where Bollo and Miriello experimented with explosives which they had stolen.

An interesting sidelight on links between the NF and the HNP came on the first day of the trial, when Piet Rudolph, a prominent HNP supporter sitting in the public gallery, stood and applauded as Bollo and Miriello were led into the court. The HNP was singularly embarrassed by the whole affair, not least by its earlier connection with Alan Fotheringham. The party denied that it had ever heard of UNIDO and rushed into court itself in a vain attempt to stop distribution of a paper which drew attention to Fotheringham's candidacy on behalf of the party in 1977.

Max Bollo, the ringleader of the whole affair, was eventually convicted of sabotage, terrorism and house-breaking, and sentenced to fifty-two years' gaol. Miriello, his right-hand man, got nineteen years for the same offences.

Although these events were set in train just after my break with racialist politics and my departure from South Africa, they nevertheless brought home to me the reality of what I had been involved in. These men who had so readily taken to the gun and bomb to achieve their political goals were men with whom I had worked and campaigned closely and whose ideas I had largely shared. They were little different from any of us who went out to campaign for 'white power', and as such, they are themselves clear proof of what I have since come to believe passionately – that it is a very short and easy journey from racial politics to racial murder, and from there to genocide. The liquidation of one's racial enemies is the logical corollary of the philosophy of race war.

3

Back to England

It's surprising how much difference an absence of eleven years can make. As we travelled to Leicester by train from London, having a few hours earlier landed at Heathrow Airport from Johannesburg, I was immediately struck by how strange the English countryside seemed; how unfamiliar it all was after our years of self-imposed exile in South Africa.

With nowhere to live, it was natural enough that we should impose ourselves on my wife's mother in Leicester while we looked for a house and made arrangements to settle once again in the town we had left more than ten years earlier. Her house was not enormous, but there was enough room to look after the four of us until we could find a place of our own. And, needless to say, having more or less reconciled herself to seeing her daughter and her family only rarely, if at all, after our move to South Africa, her mother was delighted that we had returned, and would probably have put up with us indefinitely if it had been necessary.

One thing that had to be sorted out quickly, however, was the outstanding matter of that assault charge which I had given a miss when I emigrated in 1969. At the time, our plans to leave England were well advanced and, rightly or wrongly, I saw no real need to hold everything up to make a brief appearance at Leicester magistrates' court to answer a rather trifling charge and, assuming I had been convicted, be punished with a small fine or whatever. Now it was a little more serious, having been complicated by the fact that I didn't turn up to answer the charge and there was probably a warrant out for me for failing to appear. Before we could settle down and begin to pick up the threads of a normal life in Leicester, I wanted to get this cleared up and put behind me.

I turned to the telephone yellow pages to find a solicitor, and one name that was listed seemed to ring a vague and distant bell. That name was Anthony Reed Herbert, who ran a firm called Reed Herbert & Co., from an address in Humberstone Road in the centre of Leicester. I telephoned his office and made an appointment to see him the following day.

If his name rang only a distant bell with me, mine seemed to have set a whole peal going with Anthony Reed Herbert. He greeted me like a long-lost brother and enthused over my earlier history with Colin Jordan and the NSM. Reed Herbert, of course, was by now the kingpin in the Leicester branch of the National Front, a party which had been set up only shortly before my move to South Africa, but which had, in the meantime, established itself as the primary far-right political party in Britain.

Although I had been acquainted with a few NF activists before I left the UK, Reed Herbert had not been one of them. At that time he had been a dedicated member of the Conservative Party, and especially active in the Young Conservatives. But he had always placed himself firmly on the party's far-right flank, and was especially obsessed, as were many of its supporters in areas with relatively high concentrations of immigrants, with the whole question of race. Like many others, he had taken great comfort from the 1970 election promises of Tory leader Edward Heath that further curbs on immigration would be introduced which would finally put an end to primary immigration. At the same time, the Conservative election manifesto assured voters that the government would give renewed encouragement to a policy of 'voluntary repatriation'. The pledges having been made, Reed Herbert and many others felt utterly betrayed when Heath, as Prime Minister, allowed the 30,000-strong Asian community of Uganda, expelled by President Idi Amin, to settle in Britain in 1972. The fact that such a policy was unavoidable if these people, robbed of everything they had worked for and built up in East Africa, were not to be shunted from pillar to post across the globe, meant nothing to the likes of Tony Reed Herbert. Simple humanitarian concerns had no place in their rigid scheme of things. As far as they were concerned, Edward Heath was simply going to allow yet more 'wogs' to settle in our green and pleasant land, polluting it with their strange dress, food, language and customs. In the pantheon of traitors to white race and nation, the Prime Minister quickly achieved pride of place. Rarely can a party leader have been so deeply hated by so many grassroots members of his own party.

The consequences for the party were fairly serious. Across the country, but particularly in parts of inner London and the industrial areas of the Midlands and the North, there was a sizeable haemorrhage of middle-level party activists. Many tore up their cards in disgust and cast around for another political vehicle which gave truer expression to their views on race and immigration. Almost invariably, that vehicle was the National Front.

The birth of the NF in 1967 marked quite a radical departure for the British far right. Ever since the defeat of Hitler and Mussolini in the Second World War it had been extremely hard-going for them even up until the late 1960s. The 'great man' of British fascism, Sir Oswald

Mosley, had been wholly discredited as the public mind, not unreasonably, identified him with the totalitarian dictators against whom the free world had been forced to go to war, with an unprecedented cost in human life and suffering. It was small wonder that the remnants of the blackshirted Mosley movement made so little headway in the post-war years, and they were certainly not helped by the arrogant, imperious behaviour of their leader, who absented himself to Orsay, in France, to live in luxury while he awaited the call from the British people to return and lead their country once again to greatness. His supporters became not so much a political party, but a fan club, dedicated to keeping alive the quickly fading reputation of the once and future king of British fascism.

With the demise of the Mosley tradition, the reins of the far right were taken over by extremists who came from a quite different tradition. Where Mosley had derived much of his political inspiration and style from the fascist legions of the Italian dictator Benito Mussolini, his rather lesser-known rival, Arnold Leese, drew heavily upon the Germanic national socialism of Adolf Hitler and his followers. A former veterinary surgeon, Leese had developed a peculiar hatred for Jews, rooted, it seems, in an obsession with Jewish 'ritual slaughter', and had the dubious distinction of having put forward gas chambers as the 'solution' to the 'Jewish problem' long before the idea suggested itself to Hitler and the nazis. He became involved with the anti-semitic publishing house 'Britons Publishing' after returning from France, where he served in the British Army during the First World War. Shortly afterwards, as candidate of his own Fascist League, he and a supporter were elected to Stamford Borough Council in Lincolnshire. When he formed the Imperial Fascist League in 1928, he unashamedly adopted the uniform and symbols of Hitler's nazi party, and rebuffed all Mosley's overtures four years later when the nascent British Union of Fascists recruited most of the other small fascist-inclined groups into one catch-all organization under Mosley's personal leadership. Leese publicly baited Mosley as a 'kosher fascist', that is, one approved by the 'Jewish conspiracy' which Leese, like Hitler, believed was plotting to take over the world. Mosley responded in true fascist style, sending squads of blackshirt heavies to physically attack meetings of Leese's Imperial Fascist League and punish him for his sectarian carping. Soon afterwards he was gaoled for six months for 'causing a public mischief' by publishing an article alleging that Jews offered up young gentile children as human sacrifices. Needless to say, given his fanatical devotion to Hitler, he was imprisoned during the Second World War, only being released in 1944 because of his failing health. He emerged unrepentant, publishing justifications for the nazi Holocaust against the Jews, and helping wanted war criminals to escape justice.

In the pre-war years, Leese was without doubt the poor relation of British fascism, which had become personified in the public mind by his rival Mosley. All of this changed in the years after the war. As Mosley's star faded, Leese and his followers became the inspirational starting point for a generation of far-right leaders, establishing a tradition in which the National Front stood in unbroken line of succession. In 1946 Leese recruited a young admirer in Cambridge graduate Colin Jordan. He was, of course, to play a formative part in my own development as a committed national socialist.

At Cambridge, Jordan had formed the 'Nationalist Club' and was quickly invited to join the Council of the British People's Party, a post-war effort of the 12th Duke of Bedford and former Mosleyites who felt that the 'leader' had been too soft. They included supporters of the traitor William Joyce, hanged for his wartime broadcasts from Germany as 'Lord Haw Haw'. After university, Jordan became a schoolteacher in Birmingham but by far his main preoccupation in life was national socialism, and he was taken under the wing of Arnold Leese, who saw in him considerable potential. For ten years, Leese guided the development of the future godfather of British nazism. When Leese died in 1956, leadership of his still small coterie of followers fell to Jordan, who worked closely with Leese's equally fanatical widow, May. She turned over to Jordan free and exclusive use of her husband's large property in Notting Hill (later named 'Arnold Leese House') which gave him the material wherewithal to build up the national socialist movement. On her death, she left the property to Jordan, and it became the headquarters and base of operations for his White Defence League, launched soon after. It was in this period, and in association with Jordan, that many of the future leaders of the extreme right of the 1960s and 1970s initially cut their teeth, and it was within the WDL's ranks and those of Jordan's later grouping that their fanatical devotion to the memory of Hitler was honed.

Among his colleagues in the WDL was John Tyndall, who by 1968 was prominent in the leadership of the National Front and was to shape its growth for the next ten years. The White Defence League lasted only a few years but made a name for itself by its violent intervention in the 1958 'race riots' in Notting Hill.

After this, which they felt was a highly successful episode in the slow process of rebuilding the extreme right as a political force, Jordan, Tyndall and John Bean (another later leader) resolved to launch a fully-fledged party. In 1960, joining forces with the minuscule National Labour Party, they announced the birth of the British National Party. A look at the party's policy statement revealed, however, just how 'British' the organization really was: they wanted to set up 'a racial nationalist folk state . . . embodied in the creed of national socialism and uniquely implemented by Adolf Hitler'.

But it was precisely this hard-line worship of Hitler that led to splits appearing in the ranks shortly afterwards. In 1962, John Bean led a faction fight against Jordan, arguing that his blind adherence to Hitler and the Third Reich was 'a wrongful direction of tactics' and meant that the party neglected 'Britain, Europe and the White World struggle of today and the future'.

The split was not long in coming, but it was the more forward-looking 'British nazis' who had most support in the party. Jordan had no intention of bending the knee and departed to form his own party. Among the Hitlerian fanatics who went with him was John Tyndall.

Together they launched the National Socialist Movement, which made no bones about its total, uncritical admiration for Hitler and all his works. The party was born on 20 April 1962, the anniversary of Hitler's birthday. The theme of its first public rally in London was 'Free Britain from Jewish Control', and its members paraded in uniforms that echoed strongly those worn by Hitler's brownshirt squads. It was Tyndall who provoked a riot in Trafalgar Square by declaring from the platform that 'the Jew is like a poisonous maggot feeding on a body in an advanced stage of decay'.

Three years earlier, a tubby Hertfordshire schoolboy called Martin Webster had joined the League of Empire Loyalists. Largely conservative by disposition, and ex-colonial by background, the League had become a rather blimpish rallying point for Tory opponents of Macmillan's 'wind of change' policy to dismantle the British empire. Its activities were only semi-serious, consisting of heaving flour bombs at party grandees, or interrupting party functions with anti-Macmillan heckling. Martin Webster's politics were right-wing from an early age, and a schoolboy contemporary later told how, during playground war games, Webster always wanted to be the *Luftwaffe*. In 1960 he had joined the League and participated eagerly – at first – in what he called 'enjoyable pranksterism'. Standing in the crowd at Trafalgar Square, listening to Tyndall's anti-Jewish fulminations, he was moved to recognize how juvenile had been his political activism up till then. He signed up for the NSM immediately, and shortly afterwards, the party newspaper carried an article under his name explaining 'Why I am a nazi'.

Later the same year, Webster gave an interview to the *Sunday People*, in the course of which he declared that 'we are busy forming a well-oiled nazi machine in this country'.

What he did not reveal to the *People* was that the NSM was also busy forming a well-oiled private army. Fortunately, Special Branch officers were monitoring the activities of the Spearhead group, and found it to be the paramilitary wing of the NSM. One of its declared aims was to form 'a monolithic combat-efficient international political apparatus to combat and utterly destroy the international Jew-Communist and Zionist apparatus of treason and subversion'. Camps were subsequently raided by police, and Jordan, Tyndall and others received prison sentences for organizing and equipping a paramilitary force.

It was during this period that the history of the NSM began to degenerate into farce. Before going to prison,

Tyndall had become engaged to the wealthy perfume heiress, Françoise Dior, also a fanatical nazi and a leading member of the NSM. For various reasons, some of them extremely personal, Dior became disillusioned with the dour Tyndall, and, soon after his release from prison, took up with his more flamboyant 'führer', Colin Jordan. They were married at Arnold Leese House in a bizarre ceremony which involved each of them shedding drops of their blood on to the title page of a virgin copy of *Mein Kampf*. It was all too much for the extremely vain John Tyndall, who promptly quit the NSM to launch his own party. In May 1964, he set up the Greater Britain Movement. With him in the saddle was the burly figure of Martin Webster.

Again, the British-sounding name could not disguise their Hitlerian inclinations. Tyndall's journal, *Spearhead*, launched at the same time in support of the GBM, announced in its inaugural issue that 'while adhering without fear and without compromise to every essential tenet of the national socialist creed, the GBM will seek to introduce that creed to the British people in a manner more in touch with British affairs and much more in touch with British interests and aims'.

But just in case this might be taken to convey a certain moderation of the beliefs of Tyndall and his fellow nazis, things were spelt out just as unequivocally as in the past in the GBM's party programme. It promised that, under a GBM government, 'racial laws will be enacted forbidding marriage between Britons and non-Aryans: medical measures will be taken to prevent procreation on the part of all those who have hereditary defects, either racial, mental or physical.' And just to make sure that there was no confusion, Tyndall wrote, 'The removal of the Jews from Britain must be a cardinal aim of the new order.'

It was such uncompromising views which kept Tyndall and his party out in the cold when other rival far-right groups began to discuss the possibility of combining their forces.

Prime movers in the amalgamation stakes were the British National Party and the League of Empire Loyalists. After negotiations in 1966, the inauguration of the NF was announced in 1967. The BNP, in the couple of years leading up to this marriage of extremists, had taken some steps at least to conceal the national socialist core of its policies. In ideological terms, of course, the BNP had little in common with the crusted Tories of the LEL, but they were keen to rope them in for the respectability, influential contacts and, above all, money that they could bring with them. One of the conditions of the merger, which was to be led by former LEL leader A. K. Chesterton, was the exclusion of overt nazis like Tyndall and his entire GBM membership. The BNP journal, *Combat*, edited by John Bean, declared that the GBM 'would not be coming into the new movement' and that 'anti-semitism and pro-nazism would certainly not be part of National Front policy'.

A third partner in the merger, which went on to sweep up many locally-based right-wing and anti-immigration pressure groups, was the same Racial Preservation Society whose literature had had such a profound effect upon me in the period leading up to my own political commitment to National Socialism. The RPS could bring to the Front its extensive international contacts, its expertise in producing race propaganda, and, again importantly, a number of wealthy individuals willing to pump their money into promising far-right ventures.

The exclusion of Tyndall and Webster did not last long. There was considerable goodwill towards them among grassroots NF activists, espcially those who had come from the BNP, and pressure built up for them to be admitted. Following signals late in 1967 that they would not be refused individual membership, GBM members were instructed by Tyndall, in the pages of *Spearhead*, that the GBM was being wound up, and that they should all apply to join the National Front. Most of the group's 138 members did exactly that.

Tyndall carried on publishing *Spearhead* as the principal printed voice of the extreme right in Britain but, at last, began to clean up his act. Its more outrageously anti-semitic features were quietly dropped and henceforth, for over a decade, he resorted instead to hints and euphemism to inform his followers that he had not abandoned the true faith. For public consumption, however, he supported the NF strategy of attempting to build electoral success upon the image of a respectable political party determined to do something about immigration, which was being unfairly excluded from the mainstream of political life.

His real intentions were made clear in a letter he wrote to an American nazi leader, William Pierce, at the very time that he was pressing to be allowed to join the NF. This letter was subsequently discovered and made public by *World in Action* when they broadcast a television investigation of the NF in 1978. In it, Tyndall was disarmingly frank about how the future of the Front could fit into his own plans to build a nazi party: 'Our faction – the National Socialist faction – will have the key strategic advantage and will therefore put us in a position to thwart any moves towards a takeover by liberal elements'. His faction, he went on, would 'use the moderate elements, to work behind them for as long as is necessary, but to effectively control them'.

For the first ten years of the NF's existence, this strategy paid off handsomely. From beginnings which were modest in the extreme, the NF successfully used 'moderate elements' and a single issue – immigration – to build a party of probably 20,000 members by 1977, and a record of quite considerable electoral success in many areas, in a number of which they had firmly broken through the 'fringe vote' barrier of 10 per cent and were holding their own, threatening to begin winning seats, at least at local council level, in the very near future.

It is widely acknowledged that this astonishing rate of progress was only broken by the combined weight of a phenomenally successful campaign against them waged in the late 1970s by the Anti-Nazi League, and by the intervention by Mrs Thatcher herself on the race question in 1978, when she declared that people were becoming alarmed at being 'rather swamped' by people of 'an alien culture'. Overnight, this cut much of the ground from beneath the Front, repaired many bridges that had been damaged during the Heath years, and seriously damaged the NF's prospects. In the 1979 general election it became clear just how much damage had been inflicted, as the Front's vote declined dramatically. To this day, their hatred of Margaret Thatcher runs very, very deep.

Leicester, the town I had left in 1969 and returned to in 1980, had been by far the most profitable hunting ground for the NF throughout this period, and much of its success was due to the talented leadership provided by Tony Reed Herbert, who joined after defecting from the Conservatives in 1972, enraged by the Ugandan Asians' 'sellout' by Edward Heath. And the reason his name was oddly familiar when I spotted it in the Yellow Pages while looking for a solicitor was that I had seen it often enough, in print, in connection with the National Front, in the local Leicester newspaper which my mother-in-law had mailed regularly to us during our eleven years in South Africa.

And Tony Reed Herbert had certainly heard of me. In the usual manner of these things, my exploits as a lieutenant to Colin Jordan years before had become magnified and overblown in the small-town mythology of Leicester's extreme right. I had, it seems, gone down in history as one of the most outrageous and outstanding activists that the area had produced. Needless to say, some of the tales upon which this reputation had been constructed were apocryphal, and, in the telling at frequent nazi drinking sessions, had been embellished beyond recognition.

This, it appeared, was going to be my problem. When I outlined my legal problem to Reed Herbert he affected to look extremely concerned. 'The Jews will get you if they can, Ray,' he told me, adding that he did not feel it would be a simple matter to get me out of this little pickle too easily. As things turned out, it could not have been more straightforward. The local police did not seem at all interested in raking up the original complaint, and we ended up with a compromise: I pleaded guilty to common assault and received a suspended sentence. Reed Herbert was adamant that it had been resolved only thanks to his singular legal skills. I was more inclined to chalk it up to the mists of time. In the future, however, it was to stand me in good stead. In *Searchlight*, where I had later to be presented as an incorrigible, hard-line and dedicated nazi, we blew it up into a vicious attack on a Jewish man, a tale which enhanced my standing on the far right considerably, and successfully confused one or two people among my nazi comrades who were a bit doubtful about the strength of my commitment.

It was obvious that Reed Herbert was eyeing me up as a potential prize catch for the local NF, which was then beginning preparations for the run up to the 1979 General Election. He had a large, well-established and relatively prosperous branch under his leadership, but he clearly felt that someone of my proven organizational talents, not to mention my well-known skill for attracting the attention of the media, would be an asset, particularly at a time when they expected the election campaign to be the hardest-going they had faced for years.

I was invited to attend an election meeting in support of local candidate John Peacock, and, although I had already broken in my own mind with their politics and had no intention of becoming involved with the NF, I decided to go, more out of curiosity than anything else, and because I did not want to antagonize Reed Herbert, who still had charge of clearing up those legal loose ends for me, with an outright refusal. The meeting was held in Loughborough, with Peacock and Reed Herbert speaking. I sat quietly in the audience and took no part in the proceedings.

When the meeting ended, and after the ritual couple of last-minute pints in a nearby pub, I was offered a lift back to Leicester by one of Reed Herbert's helpers, a man called Ron Lee. Travelling with us was another activist called Hughie Porter. Both, strangely, committed suicide with drug overdoses the following year. Both were known among NF members to be regular drug users and small-time pushers, and although this would have caused serious embarrassment for the party had it become publicly known, it was tolerated by the NF branch leadership. Shortly before, Lee had pulled off quite a successful coup for the Front by infiltrating the local branch of the Socialist Workers Party, one of the main forces organizing opposition to the NF through the Anti-Nazi League. His friend, Porter, was a particularly unsavoury character with several convictions for child molesting, another fact known but tolerated by the local NF leadership.

That car journey back to Leicester, coming immediately after the Loughborough election meeting, brought home to me just how successful had been the strategy of deception which the Front was practising upon the electorate. From their public platform, both Reed Herbert and Peacock had presented the sweet and reasonable face of the party. How outrageous, they declared, that they should be branded as nazis by their opponents. How unfair that they should so often be denied a public voice. They were as committed to democracy as anybody else. They deplored racial violence, but laid the blame for it firmly at the door of the 'race mixers and the race traitors' who had encouraged massive coloured immigration without ever seeking the views of the British people. They intended no harm to black people – they would repatriate them humanely, not to say generously. Their gripe was not against Jews as such, but only against those who misused their power and influence against the interests of Britain and its people.

It was exactly the pitch that had led to such impressive local electoral advances for the NF two and three years previously, but it contrasted starkly with the private conversations of NF activists. In the car, Lee and Porter recounted with glee what would happen 'when we take power', which would, it appeared, include raping little Jewish girls before they joined their families waiting in line to be shepherded into newly built gas chambers. These men, I concluded, were not just fanatics, they were psychopaths. God help us all, I thought, if the likes of them ever take power. Making the obligatory grateful noises, I got out of the car at my mother-in-law's house and hurried indoors, thankful to be once again in the world of the sane and sensible.

Much shaken by my encounter with the NF, my thoughts turned, against my better instincts, I should add, to continuing the disruptive work I had begun in the later stages of my involvement with the South African National Front. With this in the back of my mind, but without as yet any firm resolve, I decided to tag along with Reed Herbert and his cronies. When I was invited to attend the NF's Annual General Meeting in Great Yarmouth that summer, I went along, keeping my eyes and ears open but playing no active part in the proceedings. For a few months after that my involvement was minimal. The assault case was by now sorted out, I was busy looking for work and, frankly, I was not that enthusiastic about keeping company with the coterie of maniacs around Reed Herbert. Then, towards the end of 1979, Reed Herbert sought me out, and asked me if I was working. I replied that I wasn't. Perhaps I would like to work with him, he suggested. He was trying to expand the legal aid side of his solicitor's practice, and was looking for someone to attend the local court, sitting in the public gallery and touting for business among defendants who turned up unrepresented. There would be a commission in it for me, for every client I brought in. Struggling a little at the time to make ends meet on modest supplementary benefit payments, I took up his offer. I suppose I should have known better: for all the dozens of cases I brought to his office over the next few months I received not a single penny of the promised commission.

My re-involvement with Reed Herbert and the growth of his legal work coincided with him branching out on his own politically. The General Election earlier that year had been a turning point for the National Front. After the spectacular promise it had shown in local elections in 1976 and 1977, and in numerous by-elections since then, its support had collapsed at the polls in the General Election. After stretching its resources desperately to find election deposits for more than 300 candidates in the field, its average vote had come to just 2 per cent. Needless to say, recriminations were quick to follow.

To those hardline nazi critics who had accused the Front of 'selling out' on the basic principles of national socialism, of pussyfooting around, for instance, on the 'Jewish question', the NF had been able to make a powerful response. When was the last time, they would argue, that a 'nationalist party' was regularly polling well over 10 per cent in elections. Their demonstrable success was the most eloquent defence of the strategy they had adopted, in Tyndall's words, of 'working behind the moderate elements'. But as the success began to crumble, the ideological chickens came home to roost, and the hard-liners screamed, 'We told you so.' Inside the Front the election débâcle set off a furious row between those who were convinced that the future lay in 'more of the same', but without former nazis like Tyndall and Webster whose backgrounds had compromised the party's 'respectable' image, and those now convinced of the futility of projecting a moderate image because 'the media is controlled by the Jews and will never allow us a hearing'. For these hard-liners there was now no justifiable reason for concealing what they truly believed. It was time to bring the trappings of hard-core national socialism from out of the wardrobe where they had been mothballed for the last ten years.

In the few months following the election, the Front disintegrated into no less than four separate organizations. The party itself, under the chairmanship of former NSM activist Andrew Brons, and the organizational leadership of Martin Webster, set out to plough a new furrow, drawing heavily on the ideas of the brownshirt Strasser brothers. They had led the 'left-wing' opposition to Hitler in the nazi party before the war, before being purged for their pains. Many of their followers were slaughtered in the 'Night of the Long Knives'. Tyndall, convinced that it was the homosexuality of Martin Webster and his circle of political associates which had led to the demise of the Front, led what he believed to be the more morally upstanding elements into a new group which he christened the New National Front, and which began to adopt a much more unashamedly pro-nazi posture. The pretext for his departure was the refusal of the NF National Directorate to recognize his claim to be the omniscient führer of the movement and to confer dictatorial powers upon him to run the party as he saw fit.

A smaller group of supporters of ex-chairman Andrew Fountaine, preaching a new strategy of respectability, launched themselves as the National Front Constitutional Movement with the specific intention of trying to win support on the far-right flanks of the Conservative Party. Eventually, a number of them ended up joining the Tories, and one, Richard Franklin, was discovered in 1983 to be running as a local council election candidate.

The fourth splinter was led by Tony Reed Herbert and was largely based on the sizeable NF branch which he had built up in Leicester over the preceding ten years. Having first christened his organization the British People's Party, Reed Herbert changed it to the British Democratic Party when it was pointed out (in *Searchlight*) that another organization with pro-German leanings had called itself the British People's Party in the pre-war period.

Like the NFCM, he believed that the Front had come unstuck because of the obvious pro-Hitler pedigrees of so many of its leaders, but particularly of John Tyndall and Webster, the Laurel and Hardy double act who effectively ran the NF in tandem from shortly after its inception until they parted company in 1980. It was, as much as anything, the constant republishing throughout the 1970s of the picture of this ill-assorted pair dolled up in their nazi uniforms and adorned with swastika regalia that had lately done the Front so much damage.

I believed then, and still do, that Reed Herbert represented a particular threat from the right that his rivals did not. He was in a unique position as a fairly well-respected solicitor in Leicester, a former leader of the Young Conservatives, and a man having no overt nazi background who, publicly at least, disassociated himself from those who did, or who embraced Teutonic national socialism openly. In his new scheme of things, the ex-Hitlerites would be excluded from the party, so that, hopefully, the thousands of voters who had supported the NF in the local elections of 1976 and 1977, but who were later frightened off, could be tempted back. His privately expressed hard-line views were unknown outside the ranks of his supporters and associates, so to the electorate he could present what I called 'nazism with a smiling face'. If anybody was going to break through and build upon the successes of the NF's earlier strategy of deception, I was convinced it would be him. And the early signs confirmed my view: in the first local council election which the BDP contested, it walked away with 11 per cent of the vote. This, by any standards, was a very promising beginning.

It did not take a lot of reflection for me to decide that he simply could not be allowed to get away with it. By now I had heard enough about *Searchlight* (not least of all from the monthly venomous outbursts of Reed Herbert as the latest issue came into his hands) to know that if I was going to do anything to thwart the BDP's plans, these were the people who could make best use of the information which came my way. It was only intended to be a once and for all effort, however, so I saw no need to tell them who was providing them with details of Reed Herbert's intentions. I telephoned the magazine's Birmingham office a few times, and, without revealing my name, passed on a list of BDP members and activists, plans for future activities, and general right-wing gossip about who was up to what. It was intended to be my last modest fling before I slipped away from politics and resumed a normal family life. It didn't quite work out like that.

'Don't you think we should meet up and have a drink sometime?', the chap I knew only as Derek suggested one day when I telephoned. I didn't resist too much. As much as anything I was a little curious to find out what sort of people were behind this intriguing little magazine. For, I suppose, fairly obvious reasons, only the editor's name ever appears in its pages and the rest of its sizeable editorial team stay firmly in the background. We arranged to meet a couple of evenings later at the Grand Hotel in Leicester. Over a few drinks we chatted generally about what was happening on the right, without me ever letting on who I was. He didn't seem to mind, and accepted my anonymity in good humour. As we left the hotel, he grinned at me and shook his head. 'By the time we next meet I'll know who you are.'

'Why do you have to know?'

'Natural curiosity.'

'You might as well know now then.' I told him who I was.

He was clearly surprised but recovered quickly and I could see that look in his eyes that told me he was instantly weighing up the possibilities of having such a highly-placed source in Reed Herbert's operation.

'Before you get any grand ideas,' I said firmly, 'understand that there's not much more to come from me. I've told you just about everything I've picked up to date, and I don't intend sticking around with these lunatics. I'm on my way out.'

'Sure,' he smiled, 'I understand.'

We met again a couple of weeks later, this time in a more private setting, and after we had run through the bits and pieces of information I had picked up recently, Derek very gently broached the subject of my future intentions. I have to admit, it was done with consummate skill. How serious a threat did I believe Reed Herbert posed? What would be the consequences if his bid for political respectability paid off? What did I think was the best way of dealing with it? How did I feel about *Searchlight*'s approach to countering the threat from the right by exposing in detail its hidden aims and activities?

By the time I realized where his line of questioning was leading, the outcome was really a foregone conclusion. If my assessment of Reed Herbert and the BDP was accurate, and if I was truly opposed to what he was trying to do, then perhaps, given the unique opportunities open to me, I had something of a duty (although Derek avoided using such a strong word) to stay with him and exploit my connection.

'Think it over,' he said. 'Why don't you give me a call in a few days?'

'You haven't left me a lot of choice, have you?' I answered, a little ruefully. He just shrugged his shoulders and smiled.

4

A Mole in Action

In a modest sort of way, working as a 'mole' in the extreme right gives you some interesting insights into what it must be like to operate at the 'sharp end' in the world of espionage. Just like a spy you have to live, twenty-four hours a day, a false existence. It's not just a case of taking out membership of British Movement or whatever and putting on an occasional performance like some actor on stage. You have to allow it to take over your whole life – just as it would if you were genuinely a top-level activist in one of these groups. Like all small political movements, the nazi grouplets are usually composed of so few hard-core members that the demands made of the truly dedicated ones are enormous – and you don't get to the top without displaying something like that degree of fanatical dedication. Of course, when you are truly 'of the faith' you make such sacrifices willingly. When you are not, the workload and the pressure of constantly endeavouring to give the impression that you are gladly doing it all for the cause can be a considerable burden.

There are certain things that follow from this. Firstly, you begin to understand the deep and lasting relationship which, at any rate according to the books, develops between a 'spy' and his or her controller. There are times when you feel you might go crazy if you did not have one person in the world with whom you could talk freely of your true feelings without having to watch every word or be constantly on guard against letting slip the odd remark that would bury you. Many times, I am convinced, I would have been on the verge of cracking up had I not had the support and encouragement of my friends and colleagues at *Searchlight*. Often, when things were bearing down particularly hard, I travelled to London to meet one or two of them just for a few sociable hours away from the madhouse world I had involved myself in. Over a few drinks, we would chat about cricket, or our families, or any of the million or so ordinary things that other people can chat about whenever they feel so inclined, without having, as I did in my usual company, to make sure that every conversation was peppered with pejorative references to blacks or Jews. Then, batteries re-charged, I would return to Leicester refreshed and throw myself once again into the fray.

But you also come to appreciate, and with hindsight enjoy immensely, those moments so exquisitely laden with irony or contradiction that this time, you are convinced, you are finally going to betray your true feelings and see the whole pretence come crashing around your ears. What can you do, for instance, when, during some disaster which you yourself have brought down upon him, a leading nazi weeps on your shoulders declaring you to be the only truly loyal friend and comrade he has left in the world?

This sort of predicament visited me more than once while I was 'undercover' but never more frequently, nor more hilariously, than during a nine-month spell from mid-1981 until early 1982 which began with Granada Television's *World in Action* team investigating a gun-running racket operated by the BDP in Leicester. Between us, *World in Action*, *Searchlight* and myself ran such rings around the characters involved that they must have believed the gods themselves were conspiring against them. When the dust settled, one of Britain's smaller but more promising right-wing parties lay in ruins and its leader was in exile in Ireland.

During a succession of meetings with Derek in early 1980, we discussed in detail my plan of campaign over the coming months. In addition to working out how best to utilize my connection with Reed Herbert, we talked over the possibility of exploiting my former association with Colin Jordan to forge a link with British Movement, the organization he founded, but which was now led by the former milkman from Liverpool, Michael McLaughlin. As I describe later, I had little difficulty in joining BM – McLaughlin fairly leapt at the opportunity of recruiting an old nazi stalwart of proven ability and approved my application for membership in June 1980 without question. How I was to develop my work in BM without antagonizing Reed Herbert, with whom we were also anxious that I should cultivate a close link, was something of a problem. We decided in the end to try to keep both balls in the air at the same time. McLaughlin readily agreed that it would be useful to have someone in the BDP camp to poach as many promising members as possible. Reed Herbert was a little more difficult to crack, so we approached the problem delicately. Although I joined British Movement I never actually joined the BDP. But I did make myself absolutely indispensable to Reed Herbert and his party, and virtually lived in the Leicester office from which he conducted both his legal business and his political operations. My part-time touting for business on his behalf at the local court provided an ideal pretext for spending many hours on the premises. I quickly became his right-hand man, answering most of the BDP's mail and sending out information packs to enquirers or would-be members. When it came to organizing the highly secret BDP party in April to celebrate Hitler's birthday, I was entrusted with the arrangements, and a jolly '*sieg heil*ing' time was had by Reed Herbert's closet nazis in the highly illegal basement bar at BDP headquarters. If the police had known that illegally brewed beer was being sold on these premises, I thought they would have to act. However, when this particular story was told, through the *Daily Mirror*, no official action followed. Needless to say, all the information I gathered from being close to Reed Herbert was passed back to *Searchlight*. I also ended up producing and editing the BDP's magazine *British News* and organizing the party's filing system. Equally needless to say, these activities also provided rich seams of information which went straight into another filing system – the one at *Searchlight*'s Birmingham office. In the end, I was virtually running the party – and all without ever becoming a member.

At the beginning, Reed Herbert was a little uneasy about my membership of British Movement and badgered me about joining the BDP. I managed to hold him off with a simple appeal to his vanity and his absolutely overweening ambition. Would it not be better, I asked, if the nazi movement could evolve a form of 'pincer strategy', appealing on the one hand as a respectable, 'clean' political party, but still, on the other hand, retaining the capacity for 'underground activities', like attacks on left-wingers and immigrants? In the past, I put to him, the Front had suffered because, all too often, responsibility for violent activities had been pinned fairly and squarely on its members, thus prejudicing its potential popularity. In the near future, I said, I could successfully challenge Michael McLaughlin for the leadership of BM. Then, with Reed Herbert and myself more or less in harness, we could use BDP as the respectable face of the nazi movement and BM as its street army. At the same time, uniting the two groups would simultaneously give us a fair chance of establishing ourselves as the major party on the far right, sweeping the Front and Tyndall's new organization into oblivion.

Reed Herbert jumped at the idea. He could fulfil a life's ambition, commanding his very own brownshirt street army but, if the going got difficult, dump responsibility on to somebody else – me. He was not to know at the time that I also had other plans for British Movement, which far from being taken over lock, stock and barrel, I eventually drove into the ground, fragmented and bankrupt.

Two specific subjects constantly preoccupied Reed Herbert at this time: obtaining weapons to equip his street army for 'the big showdown', in what he believed was 'the coming race war', and setting up illegal television transmissions to break into scheduled programmes with racist propaganda. These particular obsessions were to prove his downfall.

Late one evening in early 1981, I was telephoned by Dave Gagin, a local builder and one of Reed Herbert's BDP lieutenants. He told me that he had just been contacted by an American right-winger asking if he could supply weapons. The American had been vague, but had suggested that he was part of a far-right group at an American military base.

I was not to know, of course, that this American was as phoney a nazi as I was, so naturally I called one of my *Searchlight* contacts to tell him what was going on. By this time, Gerry Gable had replaced Derek as my point of contact at the magazine. He advised me to leave the whole thing alone. It was only later, and not on the phone, that I was told that *Searchlight* and *World in*

Action were working together on this scheme, and that there was no need for me to expose myself to the risk of arrest. If this happened, my only course of action to avoid imprisonment would be to reveal my true activities on the extreme right, and this, obviously, was to be avoided if at all possible.

Searchlight already had bits of information about gun dealing which I had picked up in Leicester: several members including Reed Herbert had boasted to me of having acquired their own illegal guns, which they had purchased from an NF member in Rochdale and brought to Leicester by car – usually Reed Herbert's.

I had also reported back on Reed Herbert's scheme to set up illegal television broadcasts: when a prototype transmitter was tested (with reasonable success, broadcasting to a distance of about 300 yards) I was invited to be present. The BDP now had the capability to beam its racist message to every television set in a block of four or five streets on a council estate, but Reed Herbert was still not satisfied and was searching round for ways of boosting output.

It was probably inevitable that I would get sucked into this affair despite everyone's good intentions at the start. Thanks to my information, *World in Action* knew how to bait the trap which their American impostor was setting: he simply offered Reed Herbert powerful transmitting equipment in exchange for guns and Reed Herbert was hooked.

The American's cover story was ingenious: he told Reed Herbert that with some fellow extremists on a US military base he was planning to raid the base's armoury for weapons. But they needed some weapons to carry out the attack and, assuming that some might actually be used, they did not dare use guns which could be traced

back to American servicemen. It had to look as if outsiders had attacked the armoury. That was where Reed
Herbert came in. The negotiations dragged on for weeks,
but not once did Reed Herbert confide in me about what
was going on – if it hadn't been for that late-night call
from Dave Gagin, I would have been totally in the dark
about the whole thing.

Reed Herbert eventually decided to draw me in when
he needed a favour. He appeared one day on my doorstep
and asked me to drive with him to Victoria Park in
Leicester. I was to watch for anything suspicious while he
met somebody.

Rather nervously he left the car and spent a few minutes
talking to a man seated on the park bench. As we drove
out of the city centre, he told me of the negotiations going
on: how the American wanted to trade transmitters for
guns, and how he, Reed Herbert, was trying to arrange
it.

Reed Herbert held out for as long as possible to extract
the best possible deal from the American, but in the end
'Bob Matthews', as the impostor had introduced himself,
feigned impatience, and told Reed Herbert that time was
running out. He needed a gesture of good faith – and
some proof of the solicitor's ability to supply what he was
looking for. 'My people think I'm wasting my time,' he
said, 'and they want some sort of guarantee that you can
deliver what you say you can deliver.' In the end it was
agreed that, in advance of a full trade of transmitters for
guns, Reed Herbert would supply one gun for £200, as a
gesture of good faith.

Back in Reed Herbert's office it was agreed that the
intermediary was to be John Grand Scrutton, a gullible,
none too bright errand boy of Reed Herbert's, who was
also in the BDP. He would take a Luger which Reed

Herbert had bought for him in Rochdale, leave it at some 'dead letter box' which he would select and which would be known only to him, and then speak to the American from a public call box telling him where he could collect the weapon and where he should deliver the money. None of them knew, at this stage, that every meeting with 'the Yank' was being filmed by *World in Action*, and every telephone conversation carefully recorded. John Grand Scrutton obediently did his master's bidding.

Grand Scrutton could not have done a better job if we had paid him to. After leaving the Luger, wrapped in black polythene, under a bush in a city centre cemetery, he spoke to 'Matthews' from a call box:

'I think I can get hold of about six of the items you require.'

'You're talking about six what? Pistols or what?' asked Matthews.

'Well, yes,' replied Scrutton. 'I don't like to mention too much over the phone because you never know who's listening in. Now what I shall need for two of them will be about, say, two hundred and fifty quid each, about five hundred quid.'

'What time of day should the money be delivered?'

'Well, any time to suit yourself. Make it out to Mr Reed Herbert, 337 Humberstone Road, Leicester. In cash, of course, Bob. Mr Reed Herbert will know what it's all about, of course, and then he'll contact me.'

The conversation was recorded and they were, in police parlance, caught bang to rights. The evidence would soon be presented to *World in Action*'s millions mid-week viewers across the nation.

It would have been pleasing if the fact that they had been so completely caught out could have remained secret until the programme was actually broadcast. Unfortu-

nately, after a confidential viewing for Fleet Street television critics a few hours before transmission, one
journalist broke the embargo which had been imposed by
Granada, and phoned Reed Herbert, telling him of the
programme's allegations and asking for comments. Reed
Herbert's response, after an initial stunned silence, was
by all accounts pure joy to behold. Among others he
phoned *World in Action* producer Geoffrey Seed. When
Seed and I met a few months later he described to me the
speechless, spluttering response from the solicitor. It was,
he said, the 'classic response of someone who realizes he's
just been taken. Venom and nastiness were pouring from
every orifice.' He knew full well his judgement and his
credibility were shot through and, worse, he knew he was
the architect of his own misfortune. There was very little
he *could* say.

Unfortunately I was not present in his office to witness
the screaming fit which greeted the news that he had been
taken for a ride. But I heard about it in all its delightful
detail from an equally stunned John Grand Scrutton who
turned up on my doorstep afterwards.

Scrutton himself was a picture, hopping from one foot
to the other, spitting and spluttering and quite, quite
speechless. All he could say when I opened my front door
was, 'A reporter . . . a fucking reporter . . . a reporter.'
'What on earth are you gibbering about, John,' I asked,
feigning bewilderment but suspecting right away that
things had come to a head. 'The Yank . . . the fucking
yank . . . a fucking reporter,' he stammered on, wholly
incapable of coherent speech. 'Who for?' I asked, 'the
News of the World?' 'F..f..fucking *World in Action*,' he
finally blurted out. These were the last coherent words he
uttered for some time.

I did my best to calm him down. What could they

prove? What hard evidence could they possibly have? Unless, I added, a little mischievously, they had been filming and recording all the conversations between 'Bob Matthews' and the BDP. At this point Scrutton's eye rolled heavenwards, almost as if he were about to break into prayer. 'Oh fucking no', was all he said.

But he did have one consolation: 'Matthews' was to have been told where the gun was after the money had been delivered to Reed Herbert on Scrutton's instructions. But Granada had decided that to collect it would have placed them in a difficult legal situation, so the phone call with Scrutton had been Matthews' last contact with the BDP. The money had never been delivered, so the whereabouts of the gun had never been disclosed. Pulling himself together, Scrutton went off into the night to retrieve it.

This small consolation was short-lived. An hour or so later my phone rang. It was Scrutton, even more agitated than before. 'It's gone . . . it's fucking gone,' he howled. 'What's gone?' I teased him. 'You know . . . the thing I left in the graveyard.' 'You'd better come round right away, John,' I told him, trying to sound deeply troubled. 'Now you really are in the shit.'

At this point I was as bewildered as anyone. I could only assume that *Searchlight* had somehow pulled a fast one and recovered the vital piece of evidence. But how did they know where it was? The answer was they didn't. When I phoned Gerry at the magazine he was as mystified as me. So who had the gun?

Scrutton appeared shortly afterwards in a state of complete shock, and began to tell the rest of his tale of woe. The gun was his. Reed Herbert wouldn't risk his own gun and now wouldn't give Scrutton the £200 which it had cost him, even though he had put it up for Reed Herbert's deal with 'the Yank'. Even so, he sighed, no one could *prove* it was his. 'No,' I replied, 'you did clean the prints off, didn't you?'

'Oh yes,' said Scrutton dismissively, as though to say, 'What sort of idiot do you take me for?'

'Good. What was it wrapped in?'

'A plastic bag.'

'And you did wipe that, didn't you?' Long pause.

'No, I don't think I fucking did . . .'

I assumed a look of horror. 'Oh my God, John, don't you know plastic holds fingerprints better than anything else? You're fucked, mate. You've had it. They've got your bloody prints.'

For a couple of hours we sat in my living room waiting for *World in Action* to appear on the television at eight o'clock. We watched in almost complete silence, only groans and guttural noises from John punctuating the proceedings with increasing regularity and at increasing volume. For poor old John the sting was in the tail: his final giveaway telephone conversation with Matthews was the climax of the show, followed by the narrator's voice announcing solemnly that 'we have given our dossier to the police'.

This was the final straw: zombie-like, Scrutton walked across the room and started to bang his head against the wall. 'My mother always said I'd come to no good,' he moaned.

Still seeking consolation, Scrutton now persuaded himself that some gardener had probably picked up the gun and thrown it away with other litter without unwrapping it. In fact, we knew the following day from *World in Action* that it had been handed in to the police in

Leicester, but as this had not been made public, it was difficult to explode this particular firecracker beneath the hapless Scrutton. The obvious solution would have been to announce it in *Searchlight*, but the magazine was not due to appear for another three weeks. One of *Searchlight*'s journalists solved the problem with a short piece in *Labour Weekly* a few days later, and I was able to phone Reed Herbert and Scrutton, feigning absolute horror, to reveal that the cat was truly out of the bag. Scrutton was dumbstruck, and both Reed Herbert and myself knew that it would take only the most cursory questioning from the police to persuade Scrutton to come clean on the whole episode. Reed Herbert was by now an extremely worried man.

He had, of course, every reason to be. Unlike most of the individuals involved, he had a considerable amount to lose. He epitomized the sort of young, professional, skilled activist who had provided the NF with the respectable, serious image on which much of its success in the mid-1970s was built. A consummate media performer, he ensured that the Front's racist message, dressed up in sweet reason itself, received ample coverage in the local press and on television. As membership in Leicester grew, so Reed Herbert's organizational skills marshalled the party's new support into a well-oiled machine. Election campaigns were fought with a degree of professionalism which left some other parties breathless, and the party even established its first regional headquarters in Leicester. Local members themselves provided the money to purchase a property in Humberstone Road which became the organizational hub of Front work in the city. Small wonder, therefore, that in the 1976 local council elections, the NF had polled around 30,000 votes in this one city and had come within an ace of winning the party's first council seats.

His private life was equally blessed. After leaving a firm of Leicester solicitors in 1977, Reed Herbert set himself up in practice with another NF solicitor, Philip Gegan, at that time working in East Anglia. Together, they set up as Reed Herbert, Gegan & Co. with offices in Berridge Street, Leicester, premises they kept until the Front purchased its Humberstone Road HQ, when Reed Herbert moved in there as well.

Scrutton joined the Front in about 1975 and quickly became friendly with Reed Herbert who used him as an errand boy. When the Reed Herbert-Gegan practice was established, Scrutton was unemployed and ended up hanging around the Berridge Street office doing odd jobs, making coffee, cleaning up, and even answering the phone when both partners were out. Gradually he had taken a greater part in running the office and was even given his own set of keys.

But Reed Herbert had other irons in the fire as well. Leicester, of course, has traditionally been a centre for textiles and knitwear, and it did not take long for the sharp-witted Reed Herbert to become aware of the possibilities for making quick and considerable profits. He set up his own company, Hefstar Ltd, which traded as the Leicester Embroidery Company. With two embroidery machines he undertook contract work from local knitwear firms, taking in their finished garments and adorning them with the small embroidered motifs which had become so fashionable – and which enhanced their sale price quite considerably. As fate would have it, Reed Herbert had asked me to take a paid position with Hefstar as Sales Manager, a role which kept me close to the man still without actually having to join his British Democratic

Party. It was another way in which I was to become indispensable to him and able to prompt him to confide in me almost totally. *Searchlight* and *World in Action* were to take full advantage of the opportunities which such a state of affairs offered.

In the months immediately prior to the WIA investigation, Reed Herbert had been running down the mundane, day-to-day side of his legal work. He had struck up a close working relationship with one of Britain's leading, but most secretive nazis, Les Vaughan, who offered him a much more lucrative outlet for his legal talents.

Vaughan was a member of the underground nazi group Column 88, which specialized in providing paramilitary training for the 'cream' of Britain's nazis, and undertaking 'intelligence work' on behalf of the movement as a whole. Vaughan, its self-styled 'security officer', had been centrally involved in arranging paramilitary training since the early 1970s, and his activities were once the subject of questions in the House of Commons when it transpired that Column 88 'manoeuvres' had also involved a local Territorial Army unit which he and some of his fellow nazis had infiltrated.

A private investigator by profession, Vaughan was now working with a highly reputable London enquiry company called Transnational Ltd, and was in a position to put lucrative legal work Reed Herbert's way. In all, he was prepared to guarantee Reed Herbert work to the tune of £5,000 a year. Vaughan intimated to me that he shared my view about the BDP's potential for success, and saw this financial arrangement as a way of making Reed Herbert beholden to him – thus putting the BDP more or less under the direct control of Column 88.

But between them they hatched even more ambitious plans. Vaughan was scheming to cream off some of

Transnational's highly paid debt recovery work for a new 'private eye' outfit, Bellchamber & Co., which he had set up jointly with Reed Herbert and Steve Brady, an officer of another nazi organization called the League of St George. I was roped in to attend a course being organized at Transnational with a view to getting work there and helping Vaughan to obtain the valuable list of Transnational's clients whom Bellchamber could then approach and, hopefully, poach.

I managed to acquire copies of Bellchamber's letterhead with Brady's name on it alongside Vaughan's, and passed them on to *Searchlight*. Because of their sensitivity they were never published, but Vaughan suspected at one point that some had gone missing. He was furious and told me that if he found out who had been responsible he would 'kill them'. To make the point he told me that he had, only recently, had one dissident Column 88 member 'put in hospital' for eight months, and that the culprit in this case could expect no less. Fortunately for me, his prime suspect was Brighton nazi Tony Hancock, whom Vaughan believed was also trying to exert influence over Reed Herbert, and whom, like Vaughan, the solicitor had invited for shooting weekends on his Welsh farm. Fortunately for Hancock, Vaughan never carried out his threat.

Set all of this together, and it becomes clear fairly quickly that Reed Herbert had a considerable amount to lose after the *World in Action* fiasco. And small wonder, therefore, that the schemes he hatched to keep the lid on the affair – and in particular to keep Grand Scrutton out of the hands of the Leicester police – took on an increasingly desperate note.

He decided that Scrutton had to leave the country, so he was put on a ferry to the Irish Republic – and, as luck would have it, I was asked to travel with him as his nursemaid. Reed Herbert was leaving nothing to chance.

The action in this increasingly hilarious saga now moved across the Irish Sea to a lonely corner of the Irish Republic.

Scrutton, ordered to report to Reed Herbert's office in Humberstone Road, was immediately driven by the solicitor to Liverpool. At first he was hidden at the home of a Merseyside NF supporter until the intentions of the police investigating the case became a little clearer. Although Reed Herbert claimed to have 'friends on the force', the police were clearly under tremendous pressure locally at least to make a show of probing the gun ring. About three weeks later, Reed Herbert asked me to accompany him to Liverpool to break to the helpless Scrutton the news that he was going into exile – temporarily at least – 'across the water'. Until now, Scrutton's flight had cost Reed Herbert only the fifty pounds or so which he had earlier given the fugitive as pocket money. Now the costs were to rocket and were, needless to say, an increasing source of anguish to the penny-wise solicitor.

We told Scrutton it was now clear that the police had found his fingerprints on the Luger's plastic wrapping, and he should be on the next ferry from the Pier Head to the Irish Republic. Such was Reed Herbert's state of panic at this stage that he would not even let Scrutton return to the house where he had been hidden to collect his belongings. Always watching his own back, he did not want to be seen by the NF members who had been helping him out by sheltering Scrutton. Scrutton was given about £100 and told in no uncertain terms not to phone anybody, or write or talk to anyone about the affair. He was simply to vanish from view till the heat died down, and Ireland, from where extradition was difficult in cases which had a political dimension, was the obvious place to go to ground.

But Scrutton was an unpredictable fugitive, and certainly did not relish the idea of rotting away on his own over in Ireland. After a couple of weeks in Dublin, virtually penniless and thoroughly miserable, he returned to Merseyside, to the home of the NF members who had previously looked after him. He got in touch with Reed Herbert but was angrily told to get on the next ferry back to Eire. An associate of Reed Herbert, George Faulkner, was deputed to acompany him across the water on the jetfoil, but Scrutton, with another £200 of Reed Herbert's money in his pocket, managed to persuade Faulkner, after only a couple of days, that they might as well return to England where he could find cheap lodgings and lie low.

So, without telling Reed Herbert, Scrutton went to ground first in Chester, then in New Brighton, and then in Wrexham. All this time, Reed Herbert was having to pay out for Scrutton's keep – supposedly in the Irish Republic.

Somehow, however, Reed Herbert found out that Scrutton was ignoring his instructions. I was packed off to Wrexham to collect him, and, by the scruff of the neck if necessary, escort him to Ireland and stay with him, keeping him out of further mischief. We took the jetfoil to Dublin and booked into a cheap hotel.

After a couple of weeks we moved on to Limerick, again staying in cheap hotels and boarding houses, funded all the while with sums of money sent over by Reed Herbert. I opened a series of Building Society accounts to clear the cheques he sent over, but also as preparation for another venture Reed Herbert had in mind.

Realizing that the Scrutton bolt hole could become a

bottomless pit into which he was pouring money, the solicitor planned to extend his hosiery business to Ireland. I began collecting sizeable consignments of knitwear from Leicester and carrying them to Ireland. Through advertisements in local papers we recruited housewives to hold sales parties in their homes. They would sell jumpers to their friends and neighbours and, after paying them a small commission, we would walk away with the profits. In this way, Reed Herbert could finance Grand Scrutton – and myself – hiding out in Ireland indefinitely. Not long afterwards, Reed Herbert came across the water himself. Awash with money from the sale of the NF's headquarters building in Leicester (which he had astutely purchased in his own name) he spent £17,000 on a small cottage and some land at Curailly, near Ballydavid, in Dingle Bay, on the windswept western coast.

But at a meeting in a pub in Cork, Scrutton's dream of going home to his mother was rudely shattered when Reed Herbert told him he would probably have to stay in Ireland for two years until the fuss had completely died down.

Scrutton's hysterical response, not to mention the prospect of financing him for so long, forced Reed Herbert to re-think, and soon afterwards, during Christmas 1981, one of his BDP associates from Leicester arrived at Curailly with several hundred pounds and a letter instructing me to put Scrutton on a plane for South Africa – far enough away, presumably, that he couldn't ever return on some spur of the moment whim. I was to accompany him, and assure him that Reed Herbert would continue to provide him with funds. Had this little gambit succeeded, it would have eased the situation considerably for Reed Herbert. Scrutton was by far the weakest link in the chain of contact with *World in Action*'s American investigator. His resistance would collapse rapidly under any sort of police questioning and Reed Herbert understood this only too well. Scrutton was also the person against whom *World in Action*'s evidence was most damning. If Reed Herbert himself was to be netted, Scrutton had to be prevented from fleeing the coop.

I contacted *Searchlight* giving them all the details of our planned flight from Dublin, via Paris, to Johannesburg. Using contacts they had in France, they were able, indirectly, to inform the French authorities of our plan to change planes at Paris.

As a result, our brief spell at Orly Airport was spent in locked rooms, in the custody of French police who seemed remarkably well-briefed about the whole affair.

In my case, they appeared a little too well-briefed. From, I can only suppose, contacts with the British security services, they clearly knew that I was not the dyed-in-the-wool nazi I pretended to be, and I was made an oblique but pretty obvious offer of 'someone to talk to in London'. Feigning puzzlement I declined the approach as politely as I could and a couple of hours later I was reunited with a trembling John Grand Scrutton as we were put on a plane back to Ireland. The tickets which I had bought to take us to South Africa were now useless, of course, and Tony Reed Herbert was to bemoan the loss of a further several hundred pounds in his now desperate efforts to keep the law from his door.

At this stage, some of those involved began to consider even more drastic options to the problem which Grand Scrutton posed. Two firm proposals – from nazi supporters in Liverpool and Rugby – were actually put forward for murdering him, but while he deserved his come-uppance, I could not stand by while people plotted his death. The idea was still being discussed when it was exposed in *Searchlight*. That quickly put an end to it.

Back in Dingle Bay, Scrutton felt helplessly trapped. He believed, not without some justification, that he was taking the can for Reed Herbert's gun-running adventure while the solicitor and others involved were leading relatively normal lives back in Leicester. He began talking about making a clean breast of things and throwing himself on the mercy of the authorities. Very carefully, for I did not want him at some later stage to tell Reed Herbert I had put him up to it, I encouraged him to do so.

After writing one or two madcap letters to *Searchlight* and to Leicester's Chief Constable, he finally contacted Geoffrey Seed, the Granada producer who had made the *World in Action* programme. With a colleague, Seed travelled to Ireland to meet Scrutton, and there began one of the most hilarious episodes of the whole saga.

For three days, Scrutton tried to get his visitors to use their best offices on his behalf with the police. He was advised that his best course of action was to make a full and frank statement about everything he knew of the gun deal and take it to the police in Leicester. Of course, he tried to minimize his involvement, and had already pre-pared a story which conveniently left out key people and events.

The three days he spent in their company were possibly the most bewildering of his life. Every so often he would be left alone with one of the reporters while the other 'went out for some air'. In fact, they would rendezvous with me in a pub around the corner from their hotel and together we would go through the latest line of defence Scrutton was offering. Since he was rehearsing these tales with me each evening at the cottage, I was able to advise them on the best line of attack to break down his story, and soon he was in a corner with little option but to come clean. He wrote and signed a lengthy statement implicating a number of his 'comrades' in the affair.

When he returned to the cottage that evening, having promised to follow his inquisitors back to England a couple of days later, he was a miserable and mystified man. 'I just couldn't pull the wool over their eyes, Ray,' he told me. 'You've got to give it to those Jews – they're fucking clever.' As it happened, neither of the reporters was Jewish, but in the paranoid fantasies of a nazi mind like Scrutton's, there was no other possible explanation.

It was only later, when I met Geoffrey Seed again in England, that I found out that Scrutton had held out on them in just one respect: he steadfastly refused to incriminate me by naming me in his statement. 'I'm not going to drop Ray in it,' he told them, 'he's the only friend I've got left in the world.' I didn't know whether to laugh or cry.

In the end, however, for all this, our efforts came to little. Scrutton returned to Leicester as agreed and, armed with his signed confession, presented himself at Leicester police station. But to this day, despite all the evidence, there has been not one single prosecution arising from the entire affair.

5

Burying the Phoenix

With the enactment of the first Race Relations Act in 1968, the days of self-proclaimed black-hating, Jew-baiting groups like Colin Jordan's National Socialist Movement were numbered. For years they had had things their own way. Unless catch-all provisions of common law, like creating a public mischief, could be successfully invoked, there was no real limit on what they could say or do to advance their aim of heightening racial tension. And this was reflected in the crudely offensive nature of much of their propaganda and public activity. As it turned out, with the unsuccessful prosecution of the Racial Preservation Society in Lewes under the Act soon after its passage, the new law did not provide quite the weapon against incitement to racial hatred that many had hoped it would. But when it initially passed into the statute book, it seemed threatening enough to some nazi groups to persuade them that a more cautious approach would be advisable.

It was for precisely this reason that in May 1968 Colin Jordan formally wound up the National Socialist Movement. The organization which, against the stream on the far right, had remained ostentatiously loyal to the swastika, the jackboot, and all the other trimmings and symbols of Hitler-style national socialism, gave way to a new group called British Movement. Even with the choice of name, Colin Jordan was buckling under to the inevitable.

It was intended that British Movement would remain

more or less in the same mould as NSM. It still publicly defended Hitler and either denied, or excused, the murderous policies of his regime. It still believed that Jews were at the root of all evil to be found in the world and that coloured immigration was part of a Jewish-sponsored plot to dilute the purity of the white race and undermine its fundamental superiority. In this respect, it remained considerably more hard-line than the NF with its recently adopted 'softly softly' approach. But it sought to be so without trangressing the boundaries which the law had recently established. With only a few dozen activists and a couple of hundred paid-up supporters, it could not afford to see its most capable members regularly locked away for infractions of the Race Relations Act. Instead, it would chance its arm by operating as near as possible to the limits of the law.

Jordan wrote in private correspondence at the time that

'It is certainly our aim with British Movement to present a strong line on paramount issues of the day, but equally certainly to do so on a broader basis (that of our 12 principles) than that of the old NSM, recognizing that the form, details and methods of the old NSM are not those which will facilitate mustering the maximum patriotic support in the short time available to us in the face of the desperate situation of our race and nation. Our principles are in harmony with the essence of National Socialism, but we have discarded the mistaken tactics of overtly emulating the form, details and methods of the particular application of the creed to Germany thirty years ago.'

In order that other activities should not suffer, however, an underground outfit, called the National Socialist Group, was established under the leadership of David Courtney in Blackheath, South London. The NSG was to handle, for instance, contacts with hard-line nazis overseas which had previously been the responsiblity of the

NSM but which were now judged to be 'too sensitive' to acknowledge openly. Notionally independent of BM, the NSG was nevertheless set up with Jordan's approval and he regularly passed on to Courtney the names of enquirers, particularly from overseas, whom he considered to be useful contacts for the British nazi movement.

Jordan made the link he wanted clear to Courtney when he wrote to him in July 1968:

'It is essential to have the most friendly and helpful relations to mutual advantage and at the same time to keep the two bodies firmly and distinctly separate and *formally* [my emphasis] independent, and the mutually supporting good connection an informal one. For this reason it is desirable that a prominent official in one should not be a prominent official in the other.'

Jordan and Courtney conferred at 'private' social evenings organized by BM. One of these, which I was told of, was held on 27 September 1968, at a secret venue near Notting Hill Gate Post Office. Publicly, however (for instance to the *Sunday Telegraph* only a month later), Jordan flatly denied there was any connection between the two groups. He endeavoured to cover the tracks of their secret meetings in London by assuming the false name 'Roger McDermott' whenever he had dealings with Courtney.

As it happened, NSG did not last long after the police Special Branch began to take a look into its activities in 1969, and Courtney and his associates vanished from sight for more than ten years. Special Branch had almost certainly become worried about some of the 'outdoor training' held by NSG in Scotland in 1968. It worried Jordan as well, for he wrote to Courtney warning that 'you will need to be careful that nothing . . . can be construed as an offence under Section 2 of the Public

Order Act'. This was the very law under which Jordan had earlier been gaoled for organizing his own paramilitary force, Spearhead.

The 1968 launch of British Movement had coincided with my own recruitment by Colin Jordan, itself followed only shortly afterwards by my appointment as Leicester BM organizer with general responsibilities for the whole of the East Midlands. As such, I attended monthly meetings of the national directorate and had a voice in all the major decisions taken, even though Colin Jordan, as 'Leader', always had the final say.

When, as BM candidate in the Birmingham Ladywood by-election in June 1969, he polled 3½ per cent, fighting on the sort of unequivocally racist platform that would have made even the NF cringe with embarrassment at the time, it was widely seen on the right as a vindication of the 'no surrender' brand of British fascism.

Jordan was without doubt the most talented, intelligent and charismatic of all the pretenders to the role of führer of the extreme right. Neither Tyndall nor Webster in the NF, nor anyone else, enjoyed quite the standing that he had achieved over the years as mentor to a whole generation of activists. But none of this could save him when, several years later, he fell foul of the law.

His arrest in Coventry in 1976, while I was in South Africa, had nothing to do with the race laws, nor the Public Order Act. It was a simple case of shoplifting. Worse, he was caught stealing from the 'Jewish-owned' store, Tesco. Worse still, he was caught pinching a couple of pairs of bright red ladies' panties. It was not exactly the sort of criminal conviction of which political martyrs are made. Jordan made some ritual noises about being framed by 'the Jews', but he knew, and the rest of the BM knew, that he could not carry on as leader if the organization had any pretensions at all to being taken seriously.

He duly resigned the leadership and announced that, for the time being at least, he would be taking a back-seat, advisory role in the movement's affairs. His appointed successor was the considerably less charismatic Liverpool British Movement organizer Michael McLaughlin, a former milkman whose political beliefs had broken the heart of his father, a lifelong socialist, Irish republican, and veteran of the Spanish Civil War, who fought against Franco with the International Brigades.

McLaughlin joined BM soon after its inauguration in 1968. No one doubted his zeal nor his organizational abilities, but there were few around who were prepared to take him seriously as a possible 'führer'. It was clearly intended, so I was later told by other key BM members of the time, that he simply keep the driving seat warm for Jordan to return when the fuss about his shoplifting exploits had died down.

But McLaughlin had other plans. He soon made it clear to his lieutenants that there was no way he was going to relinquish control of the party to Jordan, whom he variously dismissed as 'a has been', 'a clown' and 'a Hollywood nazi'. Jordan was never allowed to perform the behind-the-scenes, elder statesman role he had fore-seen for himself, and was quickly frozen out of the day-to-day life of the organization. Seething with anger and resentment, he sold up his house in Coventry and retired to a small farmhouse in Pateley Bridge, Yorkshire, pub-lishing an occasional broadsheet called *Gothic Ripples* (after a pre-war journal of the same name edited by Arnold Leese) in which he fulminated bitterly against the young upstart who had usurped his throne.

The contrast between the styles of the two leaders could not have been more pronounced. Jordan had, and still has, an unshakeable belief in the almost mystical qualities of his own charisma. He honestly believed that in the right circumstances, presented with him as leader and the right set of national socialist policies, the mass of 'white Britons' would flock to his banners. Quite mistakenly, he read the Ladywood election result in 1969 as proof of this conviction. McLaughlin, on the other hand, had no such charismatic personality upon which to pin similar hopes. True, he suffered from a massively over-inflated ego, was pompous in manner and arrogant in dealing with those he considered his lessers, but he understood all too well the need for painstaking organisational effort if the movement was to grow.

Under his leadership it had switched its orientation dramatically. Its publications and propaganda were now geared almost exclusively to the young, white working class. There, he believed, he would find an audience immediately receptive to the much cruder race-hate message which his journals like *The Phoenix* and *British Patriot* now propagated. And, he was convinced, there he could recruit the sort of members who would give BM the image of aggressiveness and excitement that could create a bandwagon effect among working-class youth. In short, he wanted to go into the council estates, schools and youth clubs, and make British Movement fashionable.

In this, he came very close to success. By the time I rejoined in mid-1980, membership had risen considerably and now numbered more than 2,000, almost all of them young white skinheads. Unemployed, often unemployable, they snatched at the scapegoats which BM offered as the causes of their own plight. And such was the depth of their bitterness at having nothing at all in life, that it took very little to get them to take out their resentment, often with great violence, upon the blacks and Asians they believed had deprived them of work, homes – even girlfriends. Nothing got them more worked up than the idea of black men going out with 'our women', and mixed couples who happened upon BM supporters at night frequently had a very hard time of it.

British Movement members were known at this time to be even more involved in random violent attacks against black people than NF supporters. The viciousness of some of these incidents was beyond belief, but it was all connived at and quietly encouraged by the party leadership, who saw the heightening of racial tension as a necessary condition for the popular acceptance of racial political parties.

With growth came benefits. Not only was membership rising steadily, but with it came much increased subscription income and a boost in literature sales. Possibly for the first time, British Movement as an organization was generating enough income to keep the leader in some sort of comfort. He moved the headquarters from Coventry, where it had been based under Jordan, first to his home on Merseyside, and then to premises over a shop in Chester. There a few BM volunteers serviced the party machine, such as it was, and raked in the money from lucrative merchandising pitches to the members. Local units were required to take bulk orders of the movement newspaper and all its literature. Then they had to purchase uniforms and regalia. Members were also expected to purchase nazi books from the BM bookclub. All of this, of course, included a stiff mark-up which went straight into party funds – in effect, to provide a hefty salary for the leader. It was supplemented by fund-raising events organized by party units, and the collections which were taken up at all BM events. Michael McLaughlin was beginning to discover that the life of a führer, even of a comparatively small and insignificant political outfit, need not necessarily be one of sacrifice and self-denial.

In all of this, McLaughlin was riding the crest of a wave which had been set up by forces quite outside his control. Jordan had pulled out of British Movement in 1975, a year which turned out to be the starting point for a dramatic upsurge in right-wing activity and support fanned by a number of events which received massive amplification in the news media. There was the episode of the unfortunate Asians who were expelled from Malawi. Following the fury over the Ugandan Asians' exodus to Britain only four years earlier, it was in every respect a powder-keg issue – and one which was whipped into flames when newspapers discovered that some of these refugees had been temporarily housed in four-star hotels by local authorities on their arrival. Then followed the leaked Hawley Report into pending immigration to the UK from the Indian sub-continent, and another inflammatory speech from Enoch Powell.

It was, by all accounts, an exceptionally hot summer in 1976, and the hysterical news reports of these issues did nothing to cool the situation as far as race relations were concerned. Many a nazi activist I met on my return had treasured the screaming Fleet Street front pages of that time as an object lesson to themselves and others of how little it might take to spark off a fully-fledged race war.

But the climax, and the event into which racists and fascist activists could throw themselves with a vengeance, was the trial and imprisonment of race rebel Robert Relf from Leamington.

Relf was gaoled for contempt of court after refusing to obey the law – the Race Relations Act – by removing a sign which advertised his house 'For sale – to a white family only'. His case was eagerly taken up by the press who quickly dubbed him a race martyr, and considerable public sympathy was aroused for this apparently courageous man who courted imprisonment by exercising, as it was seen, his right to free speech. In gaol, he heightened the tension of the situation by going on hunger strike, though I heard later that sympathetic warders were keeping him going with a secret diet of Complan. Certainly when he was released, after a weary court decided that gaol would not force him to purge his contempt, he looked only a little the worse for wear, and certainly not like a man who had been refusing food for weeks.

Of course, everyone on the far right tried to claim him for their own. The National Front quickly adopted him as a 'race martyr' and organized demonstrations – including a considerable one at Stafford prison where he was gaoled – demanding his release.

Relf had earlier, however, been a member of British Movement, and McLaughlin was quick to cash in. He installed himself on a more or less permanent basis at Relf's home, working closely alongside the 'race martyr's' wife, Sadie, to present Relf to the world as a victimized man of principle.

For a while it worked, but support began to fall off quickly after reporters began to nose into his real background. When the *Sunday Times* published letters sent by Relf, full of hysterical and filthy abuse of immigrants and signed 'come back Hitler, all is forgiven', even some of his most vocal supporters – outside the realm of the far right – began to lower their voices. Then it was revealed that he had tried to launch a Ku Klux Klan group in Britain and had served as bodyguard to Colin Jordan.

Nevertheless, the damage had been done. The Relf case had been the high point of a summer when little but race seemed to feature on the front pages or the news bulletins, and rarely in a form which seemed likely to strengthen race relations. It was some considerable time before the damage was undone. In the meantime, both the NF and BM were cock-a-hoop. Both had noticeably increased their membership and support over the year, with the Front building gleefully upon its successes in local elections the year before and looking forward to more dramatic growth in the near future. With hindsight, we can see that it was a high point from which the Front's electoral support, and subsequently its membership, went into decline, never to recover. But at the time their high hopes seemed more than justified.

On a more modest scale, some of the success of that year rubbed off on BM. Its membership, like the Front's, rose, although it tended to recruit either the more violently-inclined young racist thug, or the more ideologically hard-line national socialist. Not for them striving after a respectable image in the manner of the NF. As a consequence, over the next three or four years, BM did not follow the NF into decline. Just the reverse in fact. As the Front dwindled, torn apart by a debate over the best road to power after its pathetic showing in the 1979 election, BM was ideally placed to pick up those for whom the lesson of 1976–9 was that 'nationalists' would never, ultimately, win power through the ballot box. As they became disillusioned with the NF's election strategy, so many of them became recruits to McLaughlin's nazi orthodoxy. From a group only a few hundred strong when he took it over from Colin Jordan, McLaughlin transformed BM into an organization of 3,000, largely street-hardened, uncompromising nazi activists.

It was in mid-1980 that, at the behest of *Searchlight*, I made my first overtures to McLaughlin. No one was very surprised. People on the far right who had known me before my time in South Africa knew that I had been as hard-line a national socialist as you could find. It was extremely unlikely that anyone as outspoken as I had been would have seen much future in the NF, nor, for that matter, in the long term, in the BDP, which was simply taking one step further the NF's respectability strategy. For those who knew me, BM was my natural political home.

Writing to McLaughlin I told him that since arriving back in Leicester I had become a bit involved with Reed Herbert's BDP, but that I realized that, if I were serious, I should consider rejoining British Movement. After all, I said, it was still the only truly authentic voice of the aspirations of the white British people. McLaughlin knew of me by reputation and could clearly use a good organizer. He wrote back almost immediately welcoming my application to rejoin BM and inviting me to his North Wales headquarters, at my convenience, to discuss the particular contribution I might make.

It was a couple of months later, in August, before I had the opportunity to see him. With my family, I spent a short summer holiday with friends in Lampeter, mid-Wales, and I took advantage of a day when the rest were off on a trip to the coast to drive to Shotton, in Clwyd, where BM's headquarters were situated and where McLaughlin held court.

When Colin Jordan had led BM, he had run and administered the organization from the front room of his terraced house in Coventry, where he also devoted himself to the care of his elderly mother. McLaughlin, hailing from Merseyside, had moved the party centre to North

Wales, where he had set up in a two-room office suite above a mini-cab firm on Chester Road East. It was in the heart of an area which had been massively depressed by the rundown of the local steel industry, and BM head-quarters, which I entered up a stairway tucked away in a back alley, exuded the same atmosphere of depression and squalor. It was a pig-sty; uncleaned, furnished with junk furniture and decorated only, but predictably, with portraits and busts of Hitler and other nazi heroes. Clearly little of the frenetic fund-raising going on in the BM branches was being invested in the fabric of the party. Security precautions were virtually non-existent, and the place was ankle-deep in unsold nazi literature.

I was shown into McLaughlin's seedy office by a BM member, Sue Hayes, who was later to become his wife. With pomposity bordering on the absurd he rose to greet me with the words, 'Mr Hill, I presume. I'm Mike McLaughlin – the Leader.' The last word was delivered wih some emphasis. 'Pillock,' I thought, as I took his hand and shook it warmly. Almost without pause he launched into a bitter tirade against the police. He had recently lost his driving licence, an event which had confirmed his belief that the police were now 'the puppets of a treasonous regime'.

We spent the next couple of hours discussing the work that I might do for BM in Leicester and the East Midlands generally. I raised one or two ostensible reservations that I had about joining and allowed him to persuade me that they were really without foundation. In the end, he could have been forgiven for concluding that he had talked me into rejoining, which was rather more satisfactory than my appearing over-eager. He was much preoccupied with the splits which had opened up in the NF, and the recruitment opportunities which this presented to the BM.

My task, as Leicester organizer (no sooner had I joined than I was promoted to 'Area Leader') was to sweep up the remnants of the NF in the East Midlands, who had for the most part lost faith in the Front's leadership but had not yet been targeted for recruitment by any of the warring factions other than Reed Herbert's BDP. This was doomed, McLaughlin had concluded, as a locally-based flash in the pan. British Movement, if it played its cards right, could clean up.

There was, however, little to start with. He supplied me with the names of two or three inactive members, who, it seemed, represented the entire BM strength in Leicester. Armed with these, and a pile of BM literature, I was despatched to build a solid BM presence in the town. Typically, McLaughlin made no mention whatsoever of meeting any expenses I might incur in the course of all this.

In fact, it turned out to be easier than I had imagined. In a short time I had gathered in a couple of dozen of Leicester's former hard-core NF activists. All had long track records of commitment to right-wing politics and were, with the demise of the NF, almost looking for a new home. Most of them readily accepted my invitation to join British Movement.

In the normal course of events, this would have been greeted with bitter opposition from Tony Reed Herbert. On this occasion, his support for my efforts had already been enlisted. Having persuaded him of the value of the 'pincer strategy', in which he would control BDP, the respectable political party, and I would control the BM street army, with the two of us informally acting in concert, I now had his blessing to go out and recruit for British Movement. In this way, I hoped to be able to keep a foot in both camps for as long as possible – and play both sides against the middle at the same time.

The perennial dilemma attached to this sort of 'undercover' activity, I came to realize, was drawing a line which clearly distinguished what could contribute to outwitting your opponents from actions carried out on their behalf which might, your own longer-term intentions notwithstanding, actually help them.

For instance, you would not survive long as a city organizer if you did not attempt to recruit members and develop the organization in that city. And if you wanted to work your way up the party hierarchy, to be even better placed to obtain information which might damage the organization, you really had little choice but to chalk up a few local victories upon which your credibility could be built. In the course of this, it can be rightly argued, you may well contribute to damaging race relations in the town where you are active. If you achieve a position in the party of any real prominence you might even have an impact which is felt outside your own locality. In the end, however, if you honestly believe that by infiltrating groups like BM you can put yourself in a position to inflict damage upon them which far outweighs anything you might rather not have done in the course of getting there, you leave yourself with little choice.

There is, you keep telling yourself, a greater good to be achieved. One line which I did always draw concerned violence. I was not prepared to protect my 'cover' to the point where I became involved in racial violence carried out by BM members or other racists. Nor was I prepared to get stuck in against anti-fascists who were, although they were not to realize it for some time, really fighting my side of the fence. And where I knew with certainty of fascist involvement in violence or planned violence, I tried, wherever it was possible, to see that this information was communicated to the proper authorities. As far as I could, I tried to ensure that any little victories which built up my reputation as a fascist leader were of the propaganda or speech-making variety.

It was such an endeavour that won me my first spurs from McLaughlin and impressed upon him that here he had an organizer who could grab headlines for BM. After a riot in the Highfields area of Leicester in 1980, I organized a number of telephone calls from BM members (who did not admit to being such, of course) to the local paper, the *Leicester Mercury*, claiming to have received a leaflet alleging that the *Mercury* had tried to cover up the fact that a riot had taken place and demanding to know if the allegations were true.

The leaflet had never actually been published but the *Mercury* rose to the bait splendidly. Two weeks after the riot it devoted its entire editorial column to defence of its low-key reporting of the riot and to an attack on BM. Naturally it brought our allegations and our name to the attention of a far wider public than we could ever have done on our own, and the members were delighted with my little ploy.

So was Mike McLaughlin. I quickly posted him copies of the follow-up leaflet which replied to the editorial, and the cuttings from the *Mercury* (which we had now christened the *Mockery* in our leaflets). He wrote back with a glowing tribute to my abilities: 'It's gratifying to know that in Leicester we have someone who can be left to get on with the job and do it cleverly and with competence. Your quick reaction to the *Mercury*'s blackout and the subsequent excellent content of the leaflet "The *Mercury*

and the Highfields riot" must have had a marvellous
effect.'

Bemoaning the lack of resources BM had at a national
level, he nevertheless promised that he would 'put your
activities and your response to them to the best possible
use in the coming weeks'. This was the sort of empty talk
designed to encourage young enthusiasts who knew no
better; I certainly wasn't taken in by his exhortation that
'in the immortal words of Adolf Hitler, in their greatest
hour of need, the people will grasp the hand of national
salvation'.

But his letter of congratulation was useful. I was able
to read it out at the next meeting of the BM branch and
use it to good effect in enhancing my own standing both
as a successful local leader and as someone held high in
the esteem of 'the Leader'.

Shortly afterwards I was invited by BM's Birmingham
organizer, Peter Marriner, to put in an appearance at a
BM film show and social which he was holding at the
Centre Hotel. He had arranged for Steve Brady, of the
League of St George, to bring a film of proceedings at
that year's international nazi rally at Diksmuide; the
intention was, I suppose, to enthuse Midlands nazis with
images of their comrades from many different countries
coming together to show the world that a movement
honouring the ideals of Adolf Hitler was still alive and
well.

The hotel conference room had, as usual, been booked
under an entirely fictitious name. Hotel managments had
a habit of refusing or cancelling bookings for their premises if they discovered their guests to be a gang of nazis.
On this occasion, despite the secrecy, news of the planned
event had apparently leaked to local NF members, who
had sneaked into the meeting room earlier in the day and

painted the walls with pro-NF and anti-BM graffiti. The management, needless to say, were not best pleased and tried to cancel the booking. Only some forthright talk from Marriner, threatening legal action for breach of contract, ensured that the meeting went ahead. The organization, however, was pretty typical of what you might expect from a fringe political group. Brady was two hours late in arriving with the film and another had to be cobbled up at short notice to plug the gap in the proceedings. I was invited to speak and addressed the assembled faithful on the rightness of our struggle, insisting that our day would come. They were impressed and I received enthusiastic applause.

Afterwards, I lost no time in using the incident to ingratiate myself further with McLaughlin, writing to him warning of a security leak in the Birmingham branch and drawing attention to the fact that Brady, a non-BM member, had, alone of those present, been told the details of the venue. The rest had been redirected from a meeting point at New Street Station. I left McLaughlin to draw his own conclusion.

McLaughlin fell for it. His reply invited me to take charge of a new 'anti-subversion unit' he was setting up in the party to foil infiltrators and informers. Of course, this would have given me much increased access to details about BM members on the pretext of policing the movement internally. It would also have given me the perfect excuse to pry to my heart's content into the affairs of particular members and the right to insist on co-operation from others in doing so. It might also have provided me with wonderful opportunities to have thrown out members who I could persuade McLaughlin were security risks. All of these possibilities might have presented themselves: unfortunately, like so many of McLaughlin's bright ideas, it remained empty talk. The unit was never set up and I was never put in charge of its work.

Nevertheless, I wrote back, making further observations about Brady's presence and hinting, in a very veiled fashion, that maybe the League of St George was trying to sabotage BM. It was classic example of sowing a bit of enmity between friends, and, once again, McLaughlin fell for it. He wrote back, thanking me for my 'candid letter', assuring me that 'your views have been very helpful and appreciated', and extending my field of responsibility across the whole of the Midlands. Marriner, who had covered Birmingham and the West Midlands, had just resigned on health grounds, and I was the obvious choice to keep an eye on his patch. I was also asked to 'see that incompetents and malcontents are gently pushed out whenever it is necessary'.

All of this was less than a month after I met McLaughlin at his office, and only about two months after I applied to join the party. So far, it was all progressing far better, and far more quickly, than I would have believed possible, and says much for the gullibility and judgement of the putative führer, Michael McLaughlin.

It was beginning to dawn, both upon myself and upon my colleagues at *Searchlight*, that my astonishing rate of progress opened up remarkable opportunities. If we played our cards cleverly enough we might, in a very short time indeed, be able to foment enough internal strife in BM to take it to the brink of collapse. The strategy we adopted envisaged that over the next few months I would endeavour to establish myself as a rival to McLaughlin for the party leadership. As long as I recruited enough support, the plan could not fail. Either I would depose McLaughlin and then allow BM to collapse under leadership the like of which they would never have seen before, or McLaughlin would be forced to expel me, in which case I would split the party, taking as many members as possible with me. Once we had decided to go for broke, McLaughlin was in a no-win situation. Unwittingly, he helped me lay the basis for the whole thing.

In October 1980, a BM demonstration was planned in Welling, Kent. Organizing it was Kent leader Nicky Crane, who had only recently been arrested on charges of riot in Woolwich, following an incident outside a cinema where members of the public had been violently attacked and a policewoman seriously beaten. To British Movement, of course, he was instantly elevated to the status of a racial Audie Murphy and the stops were pulled out to bus maximum numbers of members to the Welling march. However, for whatever reason, McLaughlin himself could not attend and he phoned me to ask if I would stand in for him at the head of the demonstration. I told him I would be honoured.

The march went well. I was photographed at the front giving nazi salutes, and I made a rip-roaring speech which was met with delirious applause from about 200 or so racially-inclined skinheads who had marched behind me. In private conversation with activists, however, I missed no opportunity to make guarded suggestions that while I was out there 'on the front line' with them McLaughlin was comfortably esconced in North Wales 'raking in the membership fees'. In fact, it was largely true, but it did no harm to ram the point home and encourage members to look upon me as the *de facto* front-line leader. In the following BM organizers' bulletin, McLaughlin commended me for taking charge and closing the meeting 'with a speech that not only put fire into the members and supporters but also told the police what white patriots thought of them'.

The event also demonstrated just how successfully I had managed to wed Tony Reed Herbert to the idea of the two-party 'pincer strategy'. As a rule, members of one right-wing group would court expulsion if they turned out to support a march organized by another. In Welling, however, the BM ranks were swollen by members of Reed Herbert's BDP, who attended with his express permission. Among them were Chris Newman and BDP election candidate Jim Taylor, who both played a prominent role in the proceedings. McLaughlin, of course, knew nothing of this until he heard it later from his own members and saw it reported in the subsequent issue of *Searchlight*. He was, so I was told, more than a little perplexed at the presence of his rivals on a BM demonstration. Several Leicester BDP members, like Chris Newman, Mick Harrison, Jack Munton and Dave Gagin, were simultaneously members of BM. McLaughlin would have had a fit if he had known.

One of the major points of contrast between BM under the earlier leadership of Colin Jordan, and later under McLaughlin, was its attitude towards unifying the fragmented forces of the extreme right. It was an ideal to which Jordan had always subscribed although, ironically, it was essentially only his own embarrassing reputation as a swastika-clad führer which represented the main obstacle to such unity. But this did not stop him trying.

His burning ambition was to link BM to the growing forces of the National Front, with himself being appointed to an important leadership function as part of any deal. Throughout the early 1970s, he published a series of leaflets and appeals aimed directly at winning support within the NF for such a merger.

In 1970, a BM leaflet appeared called 'Nationalist Solidarity in '70', which was 'a call for unity now to

members of all patriotic organizations'. The lack of unity
on the right it attributed to 'lack of perspective concerning
minor differences, untimely and invalid notions of
"respectability", petty vanities, and personal hostility in
the course of which past politics are held against some by
others who shared those politics'. Mostly true, up to a
point, although the last observation is a transparent lie.
Neither the BM nor the NF had in essence jettisoned
those 'past politics' as the secret correspondence of Tyndall and Jordan referred to earlier makes clear. The Front
had simply gone a little further than Jordan in attempting
to draw a discreet veil over their core beliefs.

Another appeal issued by Jordan at the same time
called for 'nationalist unity now' and warned that 'this
decade may well be your last chance of success . . . with
unity [nationalists] would today be strong and effective,
and right now on the road to power. Instead you are weak
and ineffective through division into numerous competing
organizations. Thereby the enemy is delighted, the public
is deterred from giving support, and you are doomed to
defeat.'

A year later, he organized a 'conference for solidarity'
in Birmingham to which other right-wing groups were,
through a direct appeal to their leaders, invited to take
part. It was largely a waste of time. Jordan's personal
ambitions and his desire to use merger to win for himself
a louder voice than he had leading the diminutive ranks
of BM, were quite obvious to other groups, including the
NF. They had nothing to gain from unity with Jordan, but
he had plenty to gain from unity with them. Most did not
even bother to reply to his letter.

Michael McLaughlin's approach to unity stood in
marked contrast to all of this. By the time he took over
he could see the larger NF starting to slip and BM

beginning to pick up momentum. He predicted that the boot might soon be on the other foot and that BM's best prospects lay in continuing to distinguish itself from the 'kosher' NF and recruiting its disenchanted hard-liners. He saw no future, especially at this time, in sinking differences with a fading force.

And anybody who dared raise their voice in favour of the 'principle' of nationalist unity, as opposed to any temporary tactical alignment, risked the full withering scorn of McLaughlin's tongue. When the NF stopped hiding their politics beneath a bushel and conducted themselves in a principled national socialist fashion, he argued, then we could talk about a 'principle' of unity. The sooner the Front was finished off the sooner would rise 'like the Phoenix' a party truly dedicated to constructing a national socialist folk state. He had in mind, of course, British Movement, led by Michael McLaughlin.

But such an attitude could prove to be his undoing if the very genuine desire for unity in the far-right movement could be properly exploited. With *Searchlight*, I came to the conclusion that if I could present a challenge to McLaughlin, and strongly make a case for unity, we could both tempt him into expelling me, in which case I could not be accused of splitting the movement, and prepare the ground for a significant number of BM members to leave with me, encouraged by the prospect of unification with another organization.

For the moment, I concentrated on building myself up as an alternative leader, assiduously cultivating activist members at every opportunity. I used the same old theme that the movement's leadership was stale, tired, lazy and probably corrupt and that change was needed. Without actually putting myself forward as his replacement, I did make the point strongly that leadership required someone who was prepared to 'lead from the front'. The point was not lost. Some members even started muttering about having an election for a new leader. So much for the 'führer principle'.

When BM organized its next national outing, it was intended that both McLaughlin and myself would address a march and rally in central London. It took place in Paddington, and about 500 crop-headed BM members and supporters had a very hard time of it at the hands of a police force who seemed to take inordinate delight in harassing marchers and generally making life difficult.

The event was actually filmed by a television team from the current affairs programme *TV Eye*, and the images of *sieg-heil*-ing skinheaded hooligans stamping through west London which were beamed to the general public the following week, did little to enhance BM's pretensions to being the government of the future.

In particular, they discomfited Albert Chambers, the imposing and violent head of the 'leader guard', a hand-picked élite team of members who were supposed to act as bodyguards to party leaders. Faced with persistent questioning from *TV Eye*'s reporter now the Labour Party's election mastermind, Bryan Gould MP, he turned his back and fled into the crowd.

McLaughlin first got wind of the mood of many members at the rally which concluded the march. Public speaking was never his particular forte, and no matter how excited he became, the impact was always obscured by his pompous, nasal style of delivery. He spoke, rather optimistically, about BM's future, replete with references to 'the Phoenix', a metaphor which seemed always to feature in his thinking. Then I spoke. Putting aside any grandiose visions of the future, I launched into a bitter attack on the police, who had, I said, exposed themselves as the allies and bootboys of the race-mixing establish-

ment, victimizing and harassing well-intentioned nationalists who were seeking only to save their country from
ruin. This sort of vituperous assault on the police invariably guaranteed rapturous applause from skinhead audiences, who hated the police pathologically. This occasion
was no exception. McLaughlin had been received with
steady, polite applause. When I finished my address there
was a roar of approval, and many even began clapping
and chanting 'Ray Hill, Ray Hill' in unison. Clearly, in
their eyes, I was the star of the moment. I glanced towards
McLaughlin; he glared furiously at me. A falling out
would not be long in coming.

His position was a little precarious because he had only
recently come under fire from his predecessor and former
leader Colin Jordan, whom many BM supporters still
listened to with great reverence. When Jordan handed
over the reins in the wake of the panty-theft fiasco, he
had assumed that when the dust settled he would be
welcomed back like some leader from exile. McLaughlin
had other ideas, based on the quite different assumption
that Jordan was gone for good. It was a couple of years
before this sank home to Jordan, by now living in his
remote Yorkshire farmhouse, caring for his increasingly
elderly and infirm mother. Perhaps it was his overweening
belief in his own destiny which precluded for so long any
suspicion that he was being frozen out permanently.
Anyway, in 1978 he issued a bulletin to BM members
repudiating McLaughlin and urging them to reform BM
by restoring the party constitution which McLaughlin had
treated as irrelevant ever since taking office.

I opened up correspondence with Jordan who was, after
all, my old mentor and 'führer' from the 1960s. Writing
to me, he was quite frank (as I invited him to be) about
what should be done with BM and he seemed delighted

to find in me someone who appeared to be thinking along similar lines. I told him, in confidence, that I believed BM had to be reformed radically if anything at all was to be salvaged from the visionary movement he had created back in 1968. Jordan could not have agreed more, but warned me against being too optimistic:

'McLaughlin has demonstrated his alacrity in expelling people galore for stepping out of line in the sense of appearing to him to be some present or future critic of his divine right to rule despotically and for evermore . . . my bet is that these days as soon as anyone – whoever he is – shows signs of doing anything about it, namely criticizing his lordship or calling for a constitution or for leadership elections, he will be branded as some foul monster of subversion, probably an agent of the hideous Colin Jordan who is supposed to be an agent of something else and so on, and summarily expelled; so that all his work in BM up to that point will have been to the benefit of McLaughlin, and he will have nothing to show for it.'

Two months later, I wrote to him again, explaining that I had given his thoughts careful consideration and that I still felt that priority had to be given to reforming the movement before one would be justified in precipitating a split, or even, at this stage, challenging McLaughlin for the leadership.

Jordan agreed that this course was, in the short term at least, preferable to either a palace revolution, or allowing things to drift, but he counselled that:

'McLaughlin will fight tooth and nail against any move designed to replace his absolutely despotic rule with constitutional government for the movement . . . such power as he has had has very definitely gone to his head to the extent of veritable megalomania, so that whatever his talents . . . are cancelled out by the fact that he is a menace in the consequences of his illusions of self-importance.'

And he strongly encouraged me to 'take advantage of one's moral strength' by appearing to give McLaughlin the chance to see reason before launching an all-out attack.

Jordan suggested to me a complicated and escalating campaign to bring pressure to bear upon McLaughlin. In the end, this particular advice became academic. McLaughlin's paranoia had already got the better of him and only a few weeks later I was summarily expelled from the party. He clearly believed that by quick and ruthless action he could save himself. The truth was rather different: he had walked blindly into a rather carefully-laid trap.

My expulsion caused a furore among the membership. In London, Tony Malski (at that time a BM organizer, though later to form his own National Socialist Action Party and dabble in terrorism) pledged his support for me against McLaughlin. And in Leicester the branch I had established and quickly built up was, predictably, solidly behind me. At the next Leicester meeting, the members unanimously agreed that I should ignore McLaughlin's edict and carry on, as before, as local BM leader. As far as they were concerned, they no longer accepted the leadership of Michael McLaughlin. I was also backed by former 'race rebel' Robert Relf and his Leamington chum Mick Cole. Both had left BM in disgust at McLaughlin's actions but told me they would rejoin if I wrested the leadership from him.

From around the country came similar declarations of support from groups of activists who resented McLaughlin's overbearing and dictatorial approach. To all intents and purposes, BM was split down the middle.

Other problems were piling up for McLaughlin at the same time. In January, three of his Birmingham members,

Rod Roberts, Robert Giles and Harvey Stock, were convicted on weapons charges at Birmingham Crown Court. Police who raided a farm belonging to Roberts's parents in Worcestershire found an astonishing stockpile of machine guns, rifles, pistols and ammunition. Incredibly, whilst on bail for these charges, Roberts was allowed by McLaughlin to attend BM marches and even stand as a BM candidate in local council elections. He had been a key member in the Birmingham area, so highly regarded that he was chosen to safe house American Ku Klux Klan leader David Dukes when he toured Britain in 1978, and later the fugitive German nazi Manfred Roeder. He also hosted the 20 April celebrations to commemorate the birthday of Adolf Hitler, possibly the most important date in the national socialist calendar. At this particular event in 1979, police raided Roberts's flat in South Birmingham after weapons were produced and handed round among the BM and NF members present.

Roberts, along with Stock, had first been arrested over a year before their eventual conviction when they tried to burn down the Birmingham race relations offices in revenge for the conviction and gaoling of McLaughlin under the Race Relations Act. In the event, they set fire to a job centre by mistake and were caught red-handed. Subsequent police enquiries led to the arms haul in Worcestershire.

Roberts ended up getting seven years. Stock and Giles, charged with lesser offences, both got suspended sentences, as did local NF activist Harold Simcox, for arms offences. Two local arms dealers were also convicted.

If McLaughlin had had any reservations about this sort of activity he would, of course, have suspended Roberts from membership as soon as the charges had been laid a year earlier. The fact that he not only chose not to, but permitted him to represent BM as a local council election candidate, says much about the organization that McLaughlin was trying to build, and of the lengths to which some were prepared to go in fighting the race war.

It was at about this time that I learned the identities of two prominent BM members who had carried out a near-fatal assault on a black 'Rasta' on the underground at Bromley by Bow station. He had been battered senseless with a fire extinguisher after being literally kicked out of the carriage. Their names were passed on to the authorities.

In the crescendo of press interest that followed the Roberts/Stock trial, McLaughlin tried to create the impression that Roberts was an insignificant member, generally thought to be a little odd. I knew the truth to be different. He was a trusted, dedicated activist who was prepared to take considerable risks when asked to – or ordered to – by others.

I gave the knife a further twist by issuing my own statement about McLaughlin's behaviour and distributing it to all BM members. Comparing the validity of his edict expelling me to that of a letter from him to the Queen telling her he was dissolving Parliament, I announced that the Leicester branch was refusing to recognize his authority and had endorsed me as its local organizer. I stressed, as I had in the past, that I had 'no ambitions in respect of the leadership of BM', which must have raised the odd wry smile, and I hinted that if 'the leader' did not see reason I might be forced to begin legal proceedings against him challenging his right to expel me for no reason when I was a member of good standing. 'When Mr McLaughlin learns the consequences of refusing to recognize an injunction his attitude will change and he will once more acknowledge that I am a rightful member of the Movement,' I declared.

It closed with, though I say it myself, a masterly piece of mischief-making:

'I do not intend to foster or take part in any 'split' of the Movement. I do not aim for the leadership of the Movement. I do, however, insist upon justice and further insist that I am, and shall remain, a member of the BM who is entitled to all the rights and privileges of such membership.

'Finally, when Nick Crane, Tony Lawrence and the rest of the lads were in custody over the Woolwich disturbance, I asked our gallant leader if he would stand bail for them if necessary. His answer was "no". In the event, it did not turn out to be necessary but it might be well worth asking those concerned just who it was who DID offer to stand bail for them should they need it. Perhaps it was Mr McLaughlin's long history of such disloyalty to the ordinary members that led the man to believe that a replacement, any replacement, would be welcomed by the membership.

'Whoever the leader may be, however, I, Ray Hill, will remain in the British Movement.'

BM members still in touch with McLaughlin told me later that it had driven him into a frenzy. He knew, as well as I, that I was issuing a direct challenge to his leadership and he was extremely concerned that I might succeed.

He immediately sent out instructions that any members in London (where much of BM's support was concentrated) who associated with me would be expelled forthwith, but it was an empty threat, impossible to carry out. The way that BM was structured at that time conferred enormous power and influence upon local organizers and these were the very people who were encouraging me most strongly to take on McLaughlin. The majority of London organizers, hard-core activists like Mark Thomas,

Nicky Crane, Steve and Matt Morgan, Glen Bennett and John Barton, adopted the same attitude as members in Leicester and simply ignored McLaughlin's missives from North Wales. I still regularly attended functions held by London units, thus presenting McLaughlin with a challenge he dared not acccept. If he tried to discipline people for associating with me he would himself split the movement. In the end he did nothing.

I now had the support of Colin Jordan, most BM organizers and about half of the membership. To this could be added the moral support of a significant section of the League of St George, whom I had also been cultivating, and who had much influence with key activists in BM and other groups. McLaughlin, on the other hand, was under pressure from his supporters to make his peace with me, but, his vanity apart, he knew quite well that any rapprochement would lead quickly to my supplanting him as leader. All I had to do was lead my followers off somewhere else and BM would collapse. He could not sustain a full-time operation with only half as many members as it had been built upon.

And he knew that waiting in the wings was former NF chief John Tyndall, still lording it over his own modestly-sized New National Front, and desperately casting around for new forces with whom to throw in his lot. If I could offer BM's dissidents a new home, they would leave in droves and all would be up for McLaughlin. This was the strategy which, after long discussions with *Searchlight*, we decided to adopt.

It took almost two years before this game was finally played out, but there can be no doubt that BM's slide into oblivion, with its disbandment formally announced by McLaughlin in September 1983, began at this point. True to my word, I issued a writ against McLaughlin alleging that my expulsion was invalid and in breach of the rules and constitution of British Movement. In preparing all the legal papers for the case I received tactical advice from Colin Jordan, and considerable practical assistance from solicitor Tony Reed Herbert, both unwittingly doing their bit to advance the ultimate demise of BM.

McLaughlin, on the other hand, was forced to take expensive legal advice. In December 1981, soon after the writ was served, he tried to wriggle his way out by changing BM's name to the British Nationalist and Socialist Movement, claiming that BM, from which I had been expelled, no longer existed, so I could hardly be reinstated into membership. At the same time, he launched a campaign to vilify me in BNSM's internal bulletins. Foolishly, in making claims that 'not a single sympathizer' had taken my part against expulsion, he only ensured that he was even further discredited in the eyes of a growing number of members who knew this to be an outrageous falsehood. There are some circumstances where you have to treat Dr Goebbels's advice about 'the big lie' with a degree of healthy scepticism.

Two things were clear: BNSM, as it was now called, was drifting quickly into financial chaos, and members were leaving in droves. Important national and local functions were being taken over by inexperienced, and usually uneducated, younger members. Leicester branch stayed intact under my guidance, but played no part in the national life of the movement and certainly contributed nothing to its upkeep.

From then on, only the occasional demonstration and a series of minor exercises in pulling the wool over the eyes of journalists kept BM in the public eye. Press releases would be issued in any town where a couple of BM members could be gathered together, declaring that a

'White Power' march, or something similar, would take place a couple of weeks hence. Needless to say, there was never any intention, nor the wherewithal, to organize such an event, but local newspapers, as often as not, leapt at the bait and accorded the story front-page treatment.

But these were the dying splutters of a movement which had been young, healthy and growing when I signed up in June 1980. When, in September 1983, two years after I left, McLaughlin forlornly announced that BM was being closed down, he paid a bitter tribute to my work by singling out the enormous legal bills that my injunction (which had never even gone to trial) had cost him, and the terminal drain they had put upon BM's resources.

By this time, however, I was firmly established in quite another organization. Now I was deputy leader to Tyndall in the newly launched British National Party.

6

Out-foxing the Fuhrer

In the New Year of 1981, I sat down for several hours with a couple of *Searchlight's* staff writers to take stock of the situation. British Movement, as an organization, was clearly on the skids and no useful purpose would be served by devoting time and energy to a protracted struggle with McLaughlin for readmission or for the leadership. Perfectly good results could be achieved from the outside by allowing the legal action to take its course and by prising away as many members as could be persuaded to follow me. It was this that would give me clout in the movement as a whole.

When you are in a position to deliver a couple of hundred members – we are, after all, talking of a political movement where groups may as a rule count their membership in hundreds, or a very few thousand at most – then you can drive a hard bargain indeed as the price of your involvement.

The obvious target was John Tyndall. His New National Front, not helped by a singularly unimaginative change of name, had been floundering ever since he quit the NF the year before, protesting about the 'homosexual clique' which controlled the party. Always holding an extremely high opinion of his own talents and popularity in the movement, Tyndall had imagined that it would only be a matter of time before the far right as a whole saw the light and rallied once more to his leadership. Unfortunately, things had not worked out quite so inexorably and he found himself leading only a couple of hundred faithful admirers, and depending financially upon the largesse of his father-in-law, former NF official Charles Parker.

We decided that I should, very tentatively, establish contact with Tyndall. At the same time, I still had a good relationship with Tony Reed Herbert and the British Democratic Party in Leicester with increasingly useful access to the office from which he conducted both his business and his political affairs. The 'pincer strategy' was still intact as long as I kept control of British Movement in Leicester, and he could hardly blame me for being expelled by McLaughlin. Reed Herbert, we decided, should be kept on good terms, but on a back burner until something concrete had been established with Tyndall. As things turned out, and as I described earlier, we were very soon presented with an excellent opportunity to finish off the BDP as well, but that lay in the future and was not, at that time, part of our scheme of things. For the moment we set ourselves two objectives: to speed BM into decline and to use the support I had among its former and present members to win for myself a position of some importance in John Tyndall's organization.

In January I wrote to Tyndall at his home in Hove, Sussex. Anticipating that he would have been well aware of the chaos into which the South African NF had been plunged in the months leading up to my return to England, I decided to take a fairly bare-faced approach. I raised the matter myself, but pleaded that my name had been unfairly blackened by being linked to the Sons of England affair, and blamed it all on a media smear campaign. Tyndall, claiming so often to have himself been the victim of such tactics, would find it difficult to reject such a defence.

Nor could he resist an appeal to his own self-importance, so I stressed the central role that a man of his 'moral authority' would have to play in reunifying the fragmented forces of nationalism.

For almost two months I had no reply, and was ready to conclude that, for whatever reason, Tyndall was not interested. In March I attended a demonstration organized by his New NF, but quite deliberately adopted a low profile. Having made sure that Tyndall himself saw me in his ranks, I engaged Parker, his father-in-law, in conversation, chatting generally about the state of affairs on the far right and offering the view that McLaughlin's declining position would probably lead to some sort of informal alliance between BM and the NF. Both were in trouble, and both attracted similar skinhead support for their public events. Co-operation was the logical next step, although it would have to remain more a backstairs agreement than an open declaration. This, I knew, would be fed back to Tyndall.

Sure enough, within a few days I received, with appropriate apologies, a delayed reply to my letter. And a friendly, constructive reply it was. About South Africa, he admitted he was not closely acquainted with the facts (although there had, he said, been some dark rumour-mongering on the NF directorate by, of all people, 'that utterly treacherous creature Reed Herbert') and he was prepared to give me 'the benefit of the doubt over such matters'.

But his letter confirmed our assessment that an approach from me based on the absolute necessity for unity under his leadership would pay dividends. He wrote:

'I am at the moment trying to make possible a movement towards greater unity among nationalists. In 1967 we achieved a tremendous breakthrough in this regard with the formation of the NF. Now we are back to the retrogressive pre-1967 era of splitting and in-fighting. This is the work of a few well-placed plants who have done a magnificent job (from the point of view of their paymasters) in dividing us all against one another. I am dedicated to seeing to it that we get back together.'

His view of his own place in the scheme of things was quite uncompromising:

'I have many enemies in the camp of nationalism. Some simply hate me because my achievement is greater than that of any post-war nationalist leader, and jealousy in politics is just as corrosive a factor as it is in the world of opera singers, ballerinas or chorus girls – particularly where the disease of homosexuality is present. Others hate me because I am a rather uncompromising personality, not always best equipped to engage in the game of cajolery and flattery that seems to be a part of the political art. Yet more work against me simply because they have been briefed by the enemies of nationalism to do so.

'At the moment I head a faction which represents but a minority in the broader wing of nationalist politics. This will change in time, but it must be recognized as a present reality.'

Concluding, he asked me to provide confidential information about particular individuals in BM – I assumed so that he could assess them as possible recruits from McLaughlin – and this I happily sent him. We were off to a reasonably good start.

This breakthrough coincided with one of the more difficult decisions I had to make during my time 'undercover' on the far right. Should I blow my cover and expose my true role in order that a particularly vicious example of racial violence which I witnessed should be properly punished?

It was late in the evening after a Leicester British Movement branch meeting. Despite the breach with McLaughlin I was trying to keep the city's branch intact as it was the core of my 'dowry' in the hopefully forthcoming political marriage with John Tyndall. With me, travelling home in a car, were BM members Bill Bentley and Bill Hawes, both in high spirits after the meeting, and fuelled by the several drinks they consumed when it was concluded.

Suddenly, one of them yelled to the driver to stop. Before I realized what was happening, Bentley and Hawes were out of the car and walking towards an elderly Asian coming down the street. Holding up a cigarette, Hawes asked him for a light. As the man fumbled in his pockets, Hawes produced a police truncheon from beneath his jacket and delivered a sickening blow to the side of the old man's head. On the ground, he was repeatedly kicked and punched by both men.

The whole thing had taken only a few seconds and the man had already had a terrible hiding by the time I gathered my thoughts and leapt out of the car yelling 'Coppers'. I grabbed Hawes and bundled him to the car screaming, 'Let's get out of here.' There was nothing I could do for the unfortunate Asian.

The car dropped me off at my home shortly afterwards. Waiting a few minutes for them to leave, I raced back to the spot where the attack had taken place. The Asian was gone, so at least I could assume he was either getting home under his own steam, or he was being taken care of. When I got home the second time, although it was after midnight, I telephoned Gerry Gable. 'I'll happily go public to finger the bastards who did this,' I told him. We decided that the police should be informed, and Gerry told me he would take care of it without mentioning my name. There was, of course, a risk that I would come under suspicion as only four people, all BM members, had witnessed the attack, but in the circumstances this was a risk that had to be taken.

Bentley and Hawes were both arrested for the attack shortly afterwards, but it became clear that without my evidence it would probably be impossible to secure a conviction. Much soul-searching went on as we discussed whether I should reveal myself by offering to testify. In the end, we concluded that on balance more might be achieved by my remaining undercover. Events, especially later that year, proved how right we were, but among *Searchlight* staff and myself there was a deep anger that they were going to get away with this.

But not for long, as things turned out. Both Bentley and Hawes were arrested only a few weeks afterwards to be charged with assaulting a fifteen-year-old Asian boy and possessing offensive weapons. Hawes, it transpired, had also been carrying a flick knife with him. Incredibly, the two of them were again arrested during a riot in Leicester while out on bail a few months later. Both were wearing SS badges at the time, and Hawes had a swastika on his arm. When the judge sent him to prison for four years, I had to feign outrage along with the other BM supporters present at the court, but inwardly I was delighted that this young animal had got his deserts. At least one thug was off the streets for a good stretch. Bentley, remanded for social enquiry reports, was later sentenced to eighteen months for actual bodily harm, and six for possessing an offensive weapon. He too was out of the way for a while.

That particular case did not come to court until October 1982. The intervening months had witnessed what was until then one of the most concerted efforts by racists to move into a specific area with the deliberate intention of sparking off bloody racial clashes. It happened in Coventry in May and June, and I happened to get caught up in it all.

In the first half of the year, the town had suffered from

a veritable spate of racially motivated attacks. One young Asian, Satnam Gill, had been killed, many had been stopped and beaten in the street simply because they were black, and the homes of black people in some areas were virtually under siege. They had to live with nightly assaults on their property, with windows being broken, graffiti being sprayed on doors and walls and cars vandalized. Behind it were young white street gangs, as often as not including National Front or BM members who egged the others on. It had all reached very ugly and worrying proportions.

By way of response, various organizations representing the black and Asian communities, along with trades unions and church groups, decided to hold a march through the city on 23 May. Its object was to protest peacefully against racism, and especially against the attacks which were taking place. It was due to assemble and march in the city centre in the early afternoon.

The temptation was too much for some of my colleagues in the West Midlands. First on the telephone was Robert Relf, the 'house for sale rebel' and would-be race martyr who then lived in Leamington. He was no longer a member of the NF, having quit in disgust, not long after joining, following his release from prison in 1976. He discovered that only a small part of the money which had been collected to support his wife while he was locked up had actually reached her. Nor was he particularly impressed at the way the NF seemed to want simply to milk an association with him in his hour of 'glory', without offering him the position of importance in the party which he felt he had earned. Now he was a political 'freelance', publishing the odd leaflet or sticker in co-operation with a few long-standing nazi chums of his from the Coventry and Leamington area. Among these was Mick Cole, a rabid Hitlerite who had been in and out of more nazi organizations than he could recall.

Relf was bubbling with excitement. Word was already out, he told me, that gangs of white skinheads would be turning out to abuse and harass the march. If we played our cards right, we could not only address ourselves to a sizeable captive audience on the day, but, with luck, we could direct things so that the 'reds and niggers' were given a bloody nose to remember. Relf's only political affiliation at the time was with the Danish-based World Union of National Socialists to whom the National Socialist Movement under Colin Jordan had, years before, been linked. His spiritual home in the UK, for all the arguments, was still BM, but he could not bring himself to rejoin. Like many others, he depised the antics of 'the milkman', Mike McLaughlin. On the other hand, he was impressed by my stand against the BM leader, and had, he made clear, no objections if I wanted to try to recruit BM members in Coventry and form a pro-Ray Hill branch in the city.

Of course, I had to appear enthusiastic at such an opportunity and I pledged to bring some Leicester BM members to Coventry for the 23 May march.

But it wasn't only veteran hard-liners like Relf who had plans. The next person to call me was the Coventry organizer of the New National Front, Alan Stewart. He too was trying to organize a racist counter-event in Coventry on the day of the demonstration, and, he told me, his leader John Tyndall had approved an approach to me to suggest that the NNF and BM forces that I controlled should combine forces for the day. The co-operation would, for the moment, remain an informal understanding between us, with both groups free to distribute their own literature and approach recruits.

There was to be no sectarian sniping and, as a body, our respective memberships would present a common front.

With a couple of dozen assorted BM members and BDP hangers-on, I travelled by train to Coventry on the Saturday morning. In the city centre the atmosphere was already tense with many more police on duty than you would ever expect to see on a normal weekend shopping day.

Leaflets produced by right-wingers had already been distributed earlier in the week, urging opponents of the anti-racist rally to assemble beneath Lady Godiva's statue in the city centre. When I arrived there with Relf in the late morning, there were already a couple of hundred gathered: a racist street army, itching for a scrap, and just waiting for leadership. We handed out literally hundreds of leaflets, some imported by Relf from the US and Denmark and flaunting the pro-nazi, 'nigger-hating' politics with which Relf himself had always been associated. By comparison, the BM leaflets I had brought from Leicester might have been considered tame, although such a comparison must be kept in perspective. At the same time, we collected the names of kids interested in joining NNF or BM, or keen to receive more information. In all, more than 150 signed up, showing dramatically how easy it might be to capitalize and recruit among disadvantaged white youngsters in a situation charged with racial tension.

My hope had been to persuade those assembled to hold their own march, preferably in the opposite direction to that organized by the anti-racists. I argued that we could better present the people of Coventry with the message of racial nationalism by having our 200 or so newly found supporters organized into a 'white pride' march, issuing our leaflets to the hundreds of shoppers in the city centre.

But the mood was rather different. These skinheads were there for a scrap, and when Bob Relf told them to spread themselves out in the area between the theatre where they were gathered and the opposing rally and to harass Asians and left-wingers trying to attend, they were off like dogs from a trap.

Relf did not have to spell out that they should attack any opponents they came across. That much was understood. In the end more than seventy people were arrested after a series of running battles, and all I could do was watch proceedings from the steps of the art gallery.

Later, Relf boasted of his involvement to the local newspaper: 'We were surprised at the number of youngsters there. They were just waiting to be organized – and they were looking for leadership. So we gave out the leaflets, hundreds of them, and they seemed really interested . . . we told them to get organized around the area from Coventry Theatre to where the rally was going to be, to spread out to show their disapproval.'

To me, at the end of the day, he put it rather more bluntly: 'We've started a fucking race war, Ray. They can't stop us now!'

Happily, 'they' did, but not before more blood had been spilled. I tore up all the lists of recruits which BM brought back from Coventry and the promised branch was never established. The New NF tried to organize a march three weeks later, to coincide with an anti-racist festival of rock music, but were prevented from doing so when the chief constable applied to the Home Secretary for powers to impose a ban. The festival, happily, passed off without incident.

But in the intervening fortnight, given impetus no doubt by the events of 23 May, racial violence reached new levels. At least two Asians were seriously wounded in knife attacks by skinheads, others were savagely beaten in the streets. And later on a Sunday night, outside a fish and chip shop, Dr Amal Amaranagh Tilak Dharry was fatally stabbed, to die from his wounds in hospital several days later. *Searchlight* at the time chronicled an almost daily catalogue of brutal incidents, which did not die down until after the setback received by the NNF when their intended march was banned. The scars inflicted on Coventry's Asian communities during those dreadful weeks were the result of a carefully-planned intervention by racists intent on stoking up a race war in an already tense situation. They cared not a jot about the dead or broken bodies they left behind. Many of the young skinheads they incited to attack innocent people ended up in the courts and received stiff sentences. Some, it transpired, were to be defended by solicitor Philip Gegan – formerly the NF organizer in Leicester. But of Relf, Mick Coles, Alan Stewart, and the rest of the agitators who stirred so much of it up, not one faced charges of any description.

John Tyndall, who had given the green light to the Coventry events, was very much more at home in his New National Front than he ever had been in the NF itself. Although he still looked back longingly at the days, at the peak of the NF's popularity, when he could count the party's votes in tens of thousands, and march at the head of NF demonstrations thousands strong, he had always resented two things. First, he chafed at the bit to be able to give freer expression than the NF's popularity strategy would allow to his unbridled admiration for the achievements of the Third Reich and the policies of Adolf Hitler. Secondly, he had always found it more than a little irksome to have to work as chairman of an elected national directorate when instinctively he was as committed as had been Hitler himself to the 'führer principle', and he had an abiding conviction that if there was any leader who should enjoy the unfettered powers implied in that principle, it was John Tyndall. This belief had sustained him ever since the day in 1964 when he parted company with another self-appointed führer, Colin Jordan, and launched the first of his very own groups, the Greater Britain Movement. Having, in 1981, quit the NF arguing that only his own unencumbered powers of leadership could have resolved the crisis into which the Front had plunged, no one expected for one moment that Front-style democracy would select the leadership of the NNF. From day one it was firmly under the unchallengeable leadership of John Tyndall.

Although I had seen him, heard him speak, and heard a great deal about him, I had never actually met him until April 1979, shortly after my return from South Africa, when the NF marched through Leicester and precipitated some of the worst political violence in British election history. Outraged anti-fascists ended up fighting a pitched battle with police to prevent the Front from rallying and many were arrested. Police dogs were turned loose on the crowds. Seeing Tyndall perform that day I had a strong instinctive feeling that, while here was a man who very successfully conveyed an impression of strength, even to his political opponents, it was largely an illusion that he had managed to create. I sensed some indefinable weakness well hidden behind the rhetoric, the iron jaw, and the rather too firm handshake. Unfortunately, on that day I rather sullied my copybook by roundly abusing Tyndall's lieutenant, Martin Webster, who told me to 'piss off'. From Webster such behaviour was far from unusual. He only had to suspect that someone not under NF discipline was floating around an NF march or function and he would be provoked into the most outrageously abusive response.

But when he swore at me, I lost my temper, calling him a 'fat loud-mouthed bully and an obese obscenity' and threatening to 'knock your head off your bloody shoulders'. Webster clearly thought twice about taking matters further and quickly found some urgent matter to attend to at another part of the march. Needless to say it was all reported back to Tyndall. Had I been seeking to work with the NF at that stage this would doubtless have been a serious obstacle, but, following the bitter split between Webster and Tyndall, it was turned to my advantage, and Tyndall reminisced gleefully about the episode at our first meeting in 1981 which followed our exchange of correspondence.

We met at the St Ermin's Hotel in London in May. It was all a little tentative, and Tyndall arrived with his wife, Valerie, and his father-in-law, Charles Parker, a Brighton businessman whose funds were keeping Tyndall's political efforts ticking over. Over a couple of drinks we chatted generally about the depressing condition of the British nazi movement, the demise of the Front and the split in BM. I didn't argue when Tyndall tried to persuade me that the primary cause of the split with Webster had been his recent discovery of the latter's 'moral depravity', by which he meant his homosexuality. It was a ridiculous claim. If Tyndall had not been aware of it until shortly before the split, he must have been the only nazi in the western hemisphere who had not. But even this could not be the case. The two men had actually shared accommodation in the 1960s and had been the closest of friends ever since their days together in Jordan's NSM. It was not just an open secret on the far right; it was universally known and frequently referred to by the NF's further-

Above: Ray Hill leads a British National Party march in
London with party leader John Tyndall *(left)* and Charles
Parker *(David Hoffman)*

Below: League of St George leader Mike Griffin in uniform at
the annual nazi gathering in Diksmuide

C. JORDAN
Thorgarth
Greenhow Hill
Harrogate
N. Yorks. HG3 5JQ
Tel: Harrogate 71 11 13

30th August

Dear Ray,

Thank you for your further letter, and the enclosures from which I see that with the passing of the years you have not lost your old touch.

As you remark, I did in my first circular concerning McLaughlin urge BM members to work for the reform of the Movement by restoration of its Constitution which is their safeguard. However I must say that since then, nearly two years ago, there has been to my knowledge no sign of any substantial and concerted move amongst the membership to put things right, and while McLaughlin has demonstrated his alacrity in expelling people galore for stepping out of line in the sense of appearing to him to be some present or future critic of his divine right to rule despotically and for evermore. From his "Organisers and Activists Directive" of the 18th June 1980, a copy of which is in my possession, he has now even formed an "antisubversive group" to counter those who challenge his illegitimate authority, this being announced in the course of a denunciation of "subversion" against him. My bet therefore is that these days as soon as anyone - whoever he is - shows any signs of doing anything about it, namely criticising his lordship or calling for a constitution or for leadership elections, he will be branded as some foul monster of subversion, probably an agent of the hideous Colin Jordan who is supposed to be an agent of something else and so on, and summarily expelled; so that all his work in BM up to that point will have been to the benefit of McLaughlin, and he will have nothing to show for it.

I recall the similarity of the situation with Walter Carr and the NF several years ago. Then Walter put it to me that he would be doing a wise thing in going into the NF to spread the good word and put things right. I put it to him that the clique in power were too firmly entrenched, and that all would happen would be that he would pay an inordinate price for whatever he gained by the contacts he made: in other words he would do a lot of work for the NF which would in effect help the position of the clique in power. Well, Walter went ahead in the NF, and no doubt he met plenty of people and no doubt he passed the good word with at least some of them, but where was the adequate pay off? He could, as I told him beforehand, have met more or less as many NF people without actually joining the NF and doing a great deal of donkey work for them. As it was he did all that donkey work, but the NF still remained the same sort of NF until the time of its recent split.

The whole problem in short is how to help the true cause in these situations without at the same time helping as much if not more the elements who are acting contrary to the true cause.

Well, I have said my piece, and, as you are going ahead, it is a matter for you to see for yourself, and we have to wait and see how things turn out - whether you are able to improve things or whether you find you have either to toe the McLaughlin line or get out.

Incidentally McLaughlin, hot on the heels of his attack on me on the 1st June, issued on the 20th a special 4-page onslaught of abuse and lies about me, in case you have not yet seen this plum. I shall be demolishing this edifice in very much less space in the next "GR".

Enclosed some literature for you, not needed back.

Best wishes,

Colin Jordan

Tony Malski, the National Socialist Action Party 'field marshal', persuaded by French nazis to organize an attack on the Notting Hill Carnival in 1981 *(Evening Post-Echo)*

Below: Colin Jordan *(left)* and John Tyndall at a 1962 (?) camp organized by 'Spearhead', the paramilitary wing of the British National Party. Both were later gaoled for their 'Spearhead' activities

Marital bliss: Adolf Hitler looks down on Colin Jordan and Françoise Dior on their wedding day, October 1963 *(Daily Mirror)*

Below: Expelled from the National Front in 1985, Martin Webster arrives to sign on at his local Unemployment Benefit Office *(David Hoffman)*

bove: Mike McLaughlin, who succeeded Colin Jordan as
ader of British Movement. After an unsuccessful internal
attle with Ray Hill, he was forced to wind the organization up
1984 *(Laurie Sparham)*

pposite top: Oumow and League of St George International
fficer Steve Brady leave Anthony Hancock's Brighton home
1981

pposite bottom: Right-wing publisher Anthony Hancock
ith French nazi contact man Alex Oumow, pictured in
righton, 1981

British Movement   1970

YULETIDE GREETINGS FOR
A NATIONALIST BRITAIN

from   *Colin Jordan*

Nationalists of Britain !
Unite and win !
Disunity means defeat !

Printed and published by British Movement
42 Tudor Avenue, Coventry CV5 7BD

COPY

Tel: Mr. R. Relf,
                              29, Cowbray Close,
0926 - 32436   LEAMINGTON SPA,
                              Warks. CV31 1LB

                                        1st April 1984

R. Hill,
273, Green Lane Road,
LEICESTER.

Hill : You obnoxious traiterous cowardly bastard, I have
always thought that there was nothing lower on the face of
the earth than the evil stinking Jew. However, you have
proved me wrong you have achieved what I thought was
impossible, you have sunk even lower than those hooked nosed
deformed bastards.

I don't know what the N.o.W. or the T.V. producers paid you
to betray your friends, but whatever it was, I somehow feel
its not going to be worth your while.

It's said that you are about to write your memoirs, I would
hurry up if I were you, you,stinking bastard,because somehow I think that it's your obituary that will soon be
written.

Yours in Disgust,

                              ROBERT RELF

COPIES T.
N.o.W
CHANNEL 4. TV.

Altefeld, the 28 februry 1982

Alex Oumow
St. Georg Strasse 16
3443 Altefeld-
        Herleshausen
West-Germany

                Dear Ray,

            .... Receiving this letter,you must think
    what the hell is going on whith on whith Alex and the mad
    frogs ! As you can have seen last you where in Paris, The
    F.N.E. was on a bad slope and only a shadow of the F.A.N.E.
    So I decided to build something on my own, you know, the
    old printing project. I think we can't build anything without
    a good propaganda base. Ihad the opportunity to travel a
    lot these last eight months and to make a lot of contacts
    especially in Spain and in Germany. I am quite desapointed
    to see how things are developping in Euope and really think
    a new impulse has to be given. For this, Ray, I'd like us
    to keep aclose contact. Why wouldn't you come to visit me
    here in Germany ? I live here with a comrade who has bought
    a very big stud and it is the ideal place to meet people .
    I am triyngat the moment to get a financial base for my pro-
    -paganda machine. Everything to come has to be build around
    this. By the way the person you met in Paris-the one Tony M.
    had to meet, he has been arrested and some others too.
            I hope everything is goig all right for you lot in
    England and please, Ray, write me back, I will soon have
    interesting things for you.

            All the best and '88!"

    P.S.   If you needany information about doubtful elements on
           the continent, we can help you as we have build a count
           er-infilt ation service with pretty nice files

---

above: French nazi contact man Alex Oumow writes to
ay Hill

opposite above: Festive greetings to Ray Hill from his British
ovement führer and mentor Colin Jordan

opposite bottom: 'Race Martyr' Robert Relf writes to Ray
ll after Hill had confessed his role as a nazi 'mole'

The cottage at Dingle Bay, County Kerry, which served as a bolt-hole in Ireland for Hill, John Grand Scrutton and Tony Reed Herbert after the gun-running plot had been exposed by Granada's *World in Action*

Below: Stranded: John Grand Scrutton in Tralee ponders his uncertain future as a fugitive. He later returned to England to confess his part in the Leicester gun-running conspiracy

above: Ray Hill *(right)* stands in for British Movement leader
~~M~~ike McLaughlin on a march through Welling, Kent in 1981

below: The British National Party is launched at a press
~~co~~nference in London in 1982. *(Left to right)* Ray Hill, Charles
~~Pa~~rker, Kenneth McKilliam, John Tyndall, John Peacock

Above: Right-wingers assemble in Coventry town centre, May 1981 and, despite Ray Hill's efforts, go on to attack an anti-racism march through the town. Hill *(centre in white jacket)* is accompanied by Leicester activist Bill Bentley *(on Hill's right, smoking cigarette)*

Left: Ray Hill, flanked by Union Jacks, addresses a British National Party rally in London

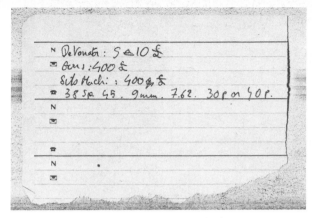

A terrorist's shopping list: this price list for weapons, written in his own handwriting, was given by Yann Tran Long to Ray Kill when they met in London in 1981

Kill meets Yann Tran Long in King's Cross, London, 1981

Diksmuide, Belgium, 1981: Ray Hill links up with
Alex Oumow

Free in London with not a care in the world, convicted Italian
terrorist Roberto Fiore shows tourists around the capital's sites
for a NF-run guide agency, 1983

Italian terrorist suspect Serina Depisa is extradited from London, accompanied by Scotland Yard officers

Below: A Hitler birthday gathering organized by FANE in Paris, the year before a similar event was attended by Ray Hill

WOEDE teen die Amerika-
ners se besluit om Kallie
Knoetze se visum in te trek,
het gister tot 'n uitbarsting
gekom. 'n Protesbrief teen
dié besluit is gister by die
Amerikaanse konsulaat in
Johannesburg ingelewer
deur die konserwatiewe
Nasionale Front. Hier staan
'n woedende mnr. Ray Hill
van die organisasie met die
brief voordat hy dit by die
konsulaat ingelewer het.

Ray Hill as agitator for the
South African National
Front

right competitors like British Movement. Whenever Webster rose to address a Front rally some wag was bound to call out 'silence for the Queen's speech'. But, if this was the way Tyndall wanted it, I was certainly not going to argue with him at this early stage in our relationship. We parted having reached a limited agreement that we would co-operate against our mutual enemies. Whatever help he could give me against McLaughlin, he would. In return, I would do whatever I could to sustain him in his battle with Webster and the NF leadership.

Tyndall revealed that he too had been giving thought to the future in the light of the NF's electoral collapse. We had to recognize, he argued, that nationalism 'was never going to make it through the ballot box', and the aim had to be, in the medium term, to build an organization of 5,000 'solid types' which could be put out on to the streets at any time. The NF, he thought, were moving in the direction of trying to provoke a military coup by fomenting disorder and inter-racial violence, but their waning significance made this unlikely and, anyway, he did not believe a *coup d'état* was possible in Britain without foreign help, and industrial breakdown, rather than a collapse of law and order, was the only thing likely to bring this about.

His NNF had about 1,200 members who would form the basis of a reorganized nationalist party, if that could be achieved. His plans were ambitious: he wanted to buy property in the party's name all over the country to provide it with an infrastructure and set up nationalist bookshops in major cities to break 'the left-wing monopoly of political literature'. None of this was possible, however, unless some successful initiative could reunite the far right. He suggested we meet again to discuss how this might be done.

Shortly afterwards, he visited me in Leicester, again accompanied by his wife and Charles Parker. I had arranged for a few of my supporters to be present, to convey the fact that I had more to offer than my own individual talents. Among those present were both BDP and BM members; I was keen to demonstrate the scope of my influence.

It was at this meeting, in my own front room, that we resolved to constitute a new party. Tyndall would deliver the NNF, I would bring in my BM supporters and whatever I could rustle up locally from the declining BDP. We would also begin approaches to smaller fragments of the 1979 NF break-up, like the NF Constitutional Movement, and we would seek endorsement from the League of St George to get the international seal of approval which they could confer.

A plan of campaign was carefully worked out. Over the next few months, a group was launched calling itself the 'Committee for Nationalist Unity'. In the beginning, none of us were openly identified with it. Its public appeal for a unification of the far right was signed by a number of 'front men' all of whom were well-known and highly regarded activists. Among these were Geoff Dickens, a Rugby businessman and long-time supporter of Colin Jordan, Robert Relf and Glen Bennett, a BM organizer from East London who was later gaoled for attacking an Asian man with an axe. Two NF members, Malcolm Skeggs and Fred Shepherd, also added their names.

When it was published and distributed to 200 leading nazis the statement was, of course, welcomed by both myself and Tyndall, and we declared our willingness to become involved in any merger proposals which grew out of this 'splendid initiative'. Tyndall had already been preparing the ground: in July he held an NNF rally on the theme of unity, declaring that it was essential to put an end to the divisions 'that had weakened nationalists over the past two years'. A debate had been opened up in his magazine *Spearhead* to discuss unity, and I contributed a major article along with Tyndall. Readers could not have been in any doubt that the two of us were collaborating closely.

But Tyndall still stood aside from the public activities of the CNU. Even when, before its appeal, and calling itself the White Nationalist Crusade, it had organized a public rally at Smithfield the previous October, he was absent. Instead, the calls for unity came from myself and people like Robin May, a former NF East End heavy and national officer who had spent the previous couple of years in the wilderness with the NFCM. Robert Relf also endorsed the mood of unity with his presence. (The 'unity' theme was taken a stage further at the end of the rally when many of the participants – myself and Tony Malski included – travelled across to Victoria to attend a meeting of WISE, a vehemently anti-immigration group with links to some Conservative MPs. Addressing us that day was the right-wing MP for Basildon, Harvey Proctor.)

Welcoming the committee's appeal in *Spearhead*, however, Tyndall went just a little overboard in declaring that it would be wrong to view the committee as 'a guise for the NNF to absorb other groups under the leadership of John Tyndall'. In fact, it was precisely that, as Tyndall had made quite apparent to me in all our discussions. Clearly apprehensive in the early stages that I might be trying to manoeuvre myself into the leader's role, he made it plain that the price of his involvement in this regroupment was that he should be undisputed leader, although I would be his *de facto* deputy. Having no intention of actually leading a nazi outfit of my own, I loudly protested my admiration for his talents and my loyalty to him as leader of the new party.

Ostensibly at least, the appeal was to the honest intentions of Britain's nazis, and both the National Front and Michael McLaughlin tumbled into the trap that they knew full well was being laid for them. Martin Webster, to all intents and purposes leading the Front at the time, and worried that two NF members had signed the appeal, immediately issued a circular to his members declaring that the Committee for Nationalist Unity was just 'another attempt by Mr Tyndall to try and "poach" National Front members' and revealing that the CNU's post office box contact address was in reality 'controlled by Tyndall and [his South London organizer] Richard Edmonds'. All of this was quite true, but it looked to many like the sectarian carping which had divided the right for several years. Michael McLaughlin, keenly aware that he stood to lose heavily if a new party was launched, was even more scathing in his attack on the committee which, he wrote, consisted of 'seven totally insignificant rejects from existing or former organizations of the Right'. Tyndall was behind it all, he said, and was hiding behind the names on the appeal leaflet. 'How sad it all is. It must be the ultimate humiliation for a political leader to disguise his participation in a new enterprise knowing that without his name, it will probably be stillborn . . . and with his name it will definitely be stillborn. What a pair of sad sacks Tyndall and Hill have become.'

He rounded off this fairly accurate assessment with the equally accurate observation that I was probably working for *Searchlight*. By linking it with his attack on the CNU, however, he ensured that it was just seen as another smear to damage a unity project which would undoubtedly hurt British Movement seriously.

All of this was grist to the mill. Behind my involvement in the whole enterprise was the certain knowledge that as long as the process of splitting and fusion and then more splitting could be prolonged, no far-right group would be in a position to look outwards and project itself as a serious political force. At that time, we anticipated that we would later be in a position, if BNP began to grow, to split it down the middle by provoking a life or death leadership battle between myself and Tyndall, and then begin the cycle of internal war all over again. As it happened, the BNP never even began to show potential for growth, a factor which helped our later decision that I should go public.

Over the next few months Tyndall and I travelled the country addressing meetings of nazis. Our audiences were a mixed bag: members of other groups like BM, the BDP, or the NF itself. On tour with us was Keith Thomson of the League of St George, with whom we regularly shared our platform. His endorsement, which he told listeners was the endorsement of the League even if it could not as a body say so, was particularly valuable. Hard-liners understood it to be the endorsement of international neo-nazi networks of which the League was the British representative.

In March, an inaugural meeting to discuss the new party was held at the Charing Cross Hotel in London. About fifty people attended, most of them organizers or officials of some far-right group. Tyndall led the New NF delegation, while I turned up with a British Movement group including Bennett, Martin Haine from Brighton, a couple of Leicester BM members, and the Peterborough organizer, Paul Gallagher. Also with me was Birmingham BM fanatic Edith Glastra, who had only recently been exposed in the *News of the World* as 'Evil Edith', indoctrinating youngsters with her Hitlerite beliefs. The British Democratic Party was represented by John Peacock and Dave Gagin from Leicester, and a small group of NF Constitutional Movement members led by Robin May were also in attendance. John Wood, from Sheffield, announced that he was 'representing the League of St George', although at the time that organization was so racked with internal divisions that he could not realistically claim to speak for it at all.

They knew what they were there for and the meeting quickly resolved to form a new party to be called the British National Party. Tyndall preferred the title National Party but was clearly outnumbered on this and did not choose to make an issue of it. The constitution adopted was based almost entirely on that of the New NF (giving the leader the powers that Tyndall held to be so vital) and it was agreed that Tyndall himself should be the leader.

Two weeks later, the party was publicly launched at a press conference in a hotel in Victoria. On the platform, I sat alongside Tyndall and his benefactor Charles Parker, fielding questions from the small gathering of reporters who had seen fit to attend. Tyndall told them that the BNP would be 'the SDP of the far right', with people flocking to it as the only real alternative to the old groups and parties.

The comparison was unfortunate. Also at the Charing Cross Hotel meeting had been a long-standing nazi called Joe Short, well known on the far right as a former NF student organizer and disciple of the occult. He had been convicted of arson in 1969, after a synagogue was firebombed in Sheffield. Over a drink after the press conference, Tyndall confided in me, with a grin, that Short was currently infiltrating the Liberal Party in Croydon, where he had established himself so well that he was due to contest a council election on behalf of the Liberals a few weeks later. Tyndall had learned this from Eddie Morrison, another veteran nazi who had been drawn to the BNP, and who was due to be Short's scrutineer at the poll.

I passed this information on to *Searchlight* and within days Short had been suspended from the Liberal Party while his membership was investigated. That was the end of that little scheme.

Morrison, in fact, had been thrown out of more right-wing groups in his time than most people would realize exist. Extremely violent, with a number of convictions to his name, he had set up a group of his own in Leeds which soon made a name for itself by its violent attacks on political opponents. He had now moved to London where he worked for a travel firm in – of all places – Brixton. Telling me all this, Tyndall also revealed some weeks later that Morrison was to be put in charge of a BNP publicity stunt, during which banner-waving members would invade the pitch at Lord's during a forthcoming Test Match against the Indian cricket team. Both pieces of information were passed on to *Searchlight*. When details of his workplace were published, his employers quickly transferred him to another office in a less sensitive part of London. And when he tried to lead his young BNP followers on to the pitch at Lord's, he found the police ready to deal with their incursion before they had travelled more than a few yards. (Only shortly afterwards, Tyndall expelled him from the BNP, and published a lengthy denunciation in *Spearhead*, in which he accused him of being a hostile agent, working to subvert the numerous nazi groups to which he had belonged.)

But just to keep myself in the eye of the membership, I

accompanied a small group of BNP activists to the transmission, one evening in June, of the BBC radio programme *Any Questions?* We submitted the question, 'Who does the panel think is the person best qualified to lead the country?' As it was read out on air, I leapt on to my seat and bawled, 'John Tyndall, leader of the British National Party.' The impact of such nonsense is, of course, nil, but Tyndall was beside himself with pleasure. At least it had helped assuage any doubts he might have had about my loyalty.

On 24 April, the BNP held its inaugural public demonstration through London. All far-right groups have tended to organize events around this date because of the convenient proximity of St George's Day (on the 23rd), which they can claim to be commemorating, Hitler's birthday (on the 20th), which to national socialists is more important than Christmas and the New Year rolled into one. At the head of about 400 marchers strode Tyndall, Parker and myself, en route from Marble Arch to the Embankment. There I would address a rally before Tyndall's concluding speech. Again, it was a measure of the trust and confidence that Tyndall had in me that I was able to take so prominent a role. He had publicly welcomed me into the party as an able organizer and a 'forceful speaker'. He knew how I had up-staged McLaughlin, but clearly believed that I had recognized his divine right to rule the BNP and would do nothing to undermine his authority.

The march was, in fact, testimony to the extent to which leading members had been prised away from other organizations by the BNP. But as well as the BM and League of St George members who turned out, the march was graced by the presence of the Dowager Lady Jane Birdwood, a veteran racist campaigner who had not been averse to marching openly with the NF in previous years. A woman wholly obsessed with 'the race question', she nevertheless mixed in solidly middle-class racist circles, such as the far-right Conservative groups pressing for repatriation of black and Asian people. Tyndall had assured her that BNP would have none of the unruly roughneck elements which had brought such discredit on both the NF and BM, at least as far as their public images were concerned. The British public were unlikely to accept that the future of 'race and nation' lay in the gangs of booted, tattooed skinheads who made up the bulk of their marches, raising their arms in nazi salutes and screeching '*Sieg Heil, Sieg Heil*' as though at a football match. But Tyndall had reckoned without the quality of the supporters I was bringing into the BNP from BM, and, in the event, he looked decidedly uncomfortable on realizing that something like a quarter of his marchers were the same unkempt skinheads that he had railed against after he quit the NF.

But there was another shock in store. After Kenneth McKilliam had delivered the rally of his stock fiery-eyed monologue about 'race traitors and Kazar Jews', the chairman, David Bruce, called me to the microphone to speak. The first part of my speech was directed against the police, and I told those present that they were not paid to 'withdraw when sub-humans riot in our streets', which, I alleged, they had done recently at Notting Hill. Then I attacked those who still believed that nationalists should court respectability. 'It's time to stand up for what we believe in. I am a national socialist. I have never denied it and I never will.' No matter what image a party is trying to project at a particular time, a speech such as this would always bring the true character of those present bubbling quickly to the surface. I was applauded wildly,

not least by the former BM skinheads present, but Tyndall
squirmed visibly at this rather too open embrace of the
ideology that we both knew he shared.

Birdwood, in turn, was more than a little upset at my
remarks about the police. Speaking immediately after me,
she stressed that the police were not to blame. 'It's all the
fault of Willie Blacklaw and the rest of the cabinet
traitors,' she assured us. This, it must be said, met with
less-than-enthusiastic acclaim from the virulently anti-
police skinheads.

The tactic of using extreme language to smoke out
extremism paid off even more handsomely at the BNP's
next major function, an indoor rally at the Caxton Hall in
London the following October. The venue was secret,
having been booked under a false name, so members
were told to meet at the South African Embassy in
Trafalgar Square, from where they would be redirected
to the meeting hall. About 250 supporters turned up,
again something like a quarter of them skinheads who
had defected from BM. Despite this, however, it was
clear that Tyndall was having some success in appealing
to the more up-market, middle-class fascists who have
been utterly alienated from the NF by their Strasserite
turn.

I spoke first. As luck would have it, Michael
McLaughlin, furious at the swathe of members I had
poached from him, had published an anonymous leaflet
accusing me of any number of crimes, including working
for *Searchlight* and having a conviction for violence. This
was a reference to the fracas I was involved in just before
my spell in South Africa. Indignantly, I denied the
contents of the leaflet, putting it down to the spiteful
rantings of a failed tin-pot leader. One thing, however, I
did own up to: the conviction for 'violent assault'. I had

nothing to be ashamed of, I declared. The victim was 'a communist Jew. I just defended myself too well.' If the perpetrator of the smear was in the hall and had the guts to declare himself, I added, 'I'll soon have another conviction.' Thunderous applause followed, and my skin-head contingent stamped their feet in appreciation. Winding up, I poured scorn on the idea that six million Jews had been murdered by the nazis and brought the house down.

The response to my final contribution clearly tempted Charles Parker, Tyndall's father-in-law, to let his hair down a little as well. Usually one of BNP's more 'moderate' speakers, he abandoned all pretence on this occasion, clearly looking for the same sort of audience reaction that I had received. During the great depression of the 'thirties, he told us, 'all the pawn brokers were Jews who traded on the misery of our people.' He added, 'I detest them as a race.' Turning to black and Asian immigrants, he attacked bitterly 'the mongrel invasion', and declared, 'They can never be British. I am British, they are coons.' His new approach certainly seemed to find favour with his audience and he got much more applause than he was accustomed to at such occasions.

Departing from usual procedure, the entire audience was then asked to stand and sing a couple of 'stirring' songs which had been specially composed for the BNP. One of the most hilarious moments I experienced in all my time on the right then followed: dozens of skinheads solemnly singing, to the tune of 'Keep right on to the end of the road', charming little ditties like:

> 'Let the reds and traitors tremble with fear
> As we march down the streets proud and sure
> For the time is near when those streets we'll clear
> Of those foes . . . of our race . . . evermore.'

And to the tune of 'Hearts of Oak' they sang:

> 'They shall reap as they sow
> And their blood will then flow
> Now we are coming
> See them all running.'

After this somewhat embarrassing interlude, Tyndall
himself took the microphone. No moderation for him
either, as he lashed out at the whole array of far-right
hate figures. Particular venom was directed at those who,
not without reason, had been trying to warn him that I
would challenge his leadership just as I had challenged
McLaughlin, and most likely with similar effect. These
'rumour-mongers' he denounced as typical of those who
had sowed so much suspicion and dissent in nationalist
groups in recent years. 'Those who try to create division
between Ray Hill and myself are doing our movement no
service at all. There is no disagreement between us.'
Given my much more outspoken attachment to national
socialism, this endorsement spoke volumes about the
ideas that really lurk in Tyndall's mind, but which he does
not have the courage to give expression to himself.

The following month he placed himself even more
firmly on the record in proclaiming the unity of purpose
between the two of us. In his newspaper he published a
statement declaring flatly that 'there are no serious disa-
greements between us' and blaming talk of a split on
mischievous rumour-mongering by *Searchlight*. In this,
for once, he was almost right.

At this stage, although it was all to change soon
afterwards, Tyndall was making the running on the right.
He was slowly building up the new party's infrastructure
and was beginning to sweep up a number of NF branches
around the country who had become disillusioned by the

Front's new 'radicalism' and who were really only waiting for a new political home to appear before they defected. The successful launch of the BNP tempted both them and former NF activists who had simply dropped out. Oddly, however, activists in London had been among the most reluctant to back Tyndall. The NF itself at that time was in deep crisis, with its membership at an all-time low, and considerable resentment building up over the leadership being provided by Martin Webster.

This had one dramatic effect which gave us serious cause for concern. Tyndall contacted me to tell me 'in strictest confidence' that he had received an approach from Joe Pearce, the young NF leader and editor of its youth magazine *Bulldog*, who had considerable influence over the Front's many younger members, most of them London skinheads. He had proposed to Tyndall that he should join the BNP, publicly denouncing the Front at the same time, and, hopefully, bringing the bulk of the Young National Front's membership with him. In return he would want a paid full-time post of some significance with the BNP.

Had such a plan succeeded, it would have been a major step forward for the right and would have provided a significant new block of support for Tyndall, not least in London where he was weak. The NF would have been, to all intents and purposes, finished, and Tyndall would have succeeded in rebuilding the coalition which had brought the NF so much success in the 1970s. Both *Searchlight* and I were naturally anxious that this initiative should fail and that the right should remain divided. It was all very well trying to cause as much failure and chaos on the right as we could, but if the result was to unite them all in one party, it would be rather counter-productive, Luckily, Tyndall, who was keen on the idea, had met resistance from Charles Parker who was, after all, paying the piper and calling the tune. I lined up with Parker, warning Tyndall that an influx of 'crazy Strasserites' would once again alienate the middle-class support he had worked hard to win back, and adding that Pearce was known to be ambitious and would, in all likelihood, soon launch a bid for the leadership of the party. For good measure, I also indicated that I had heard that Pearce was, in any case, plotting against Webster and seemed to be trying to back a second horse in case he came off worst in a bid for power in the Front.

The 'wiser counsels' from Parker and myself did the trick and Tyndall rejected Pearce's overtures. And indeed, not long afterwards, Pearce was central in orchestrating the coup which toppled Martin Webster and launched the NF on its new 'Third Position' road, which I describe later.

Working so closely with Tyndall over many months, as his right-hand man and, increasingly, as his confidant, I came to realize just how small and petty a man he was under the austere, Mosley-like exterior which he presented to his followers. Seeing him from a distance, on a public platform or leading a demonstration, one could be forgiven for thinking that here was a man who, even if not over-endowed with intellectual qualities, nevertheless had much of the stuff of which leaders are made. He looked at least decisive, firm and clear in his intentions, and resolute in his pursuit of them. And his self-confidence could convey itself to others, leading them to believe that they were indeed embarked upon an enterprise to reshape the destiny of a nation. The reality was very different. In our utterly contrasting ways, we were both just acting out parts on a political stage. His only redeeming feature was his obvious and, I believe, genuine devotion to his young daughter Marina, born of a marriage in mature age to Charles Parker's daughter Valerie, herself a long-standing far-right activist. This said, he was actually a weak, vacillating, pompous and arrogant man, quite incapable of taking advice or even considering that his own prejudiced reasoning might be something less than unerring. If anything went wrong, when the party suffered setbacks or failed to accomplish some task it had set itself, you may be quite sure that nowhere in the catalogue of blame would the name of John Tyndall feature. The 'führer principle' to which he was so devoted had been elevated into something resembling papal infallibility.

His grossly inflated estimation of his own importance was never more vividly demonstrated than in his boasts to me of 'friends in high places'. In 1982 I was staying with Tyndall and his wife at their home in Hove. He had invited me there to discuss the BNP's political strategy over the forthcoming few years, and, as was quite usual, could not make up his mind on alternatives. As he saw it, the BNP could either continue to fight elections in its own right and under its own banner, or it could concentrate its public efforts on building up a 'street army' and conduct its more directly political activities covertly, through a policy of infiltrating key activists into an established political party with Parliamentary representation. The Conservative Party was the obvious choice. Colin Jordan, with whom Tyndall had become on increasingly good terms since the partially successful unification of the right into the BNP, was strongly recommending the latter course. Tyndall was undecided. Infiltration had its attractions, particularly if there were the chance that BNP sympathizers could thereby be elevated into positions of power and influence. The drawback, as he saw it, was that potentially valuable activists who were 'needed in the field' would be lost.

'And anyway, Ray,' he volunteered, 'there are some already in very high places in the political establishment who will come over to us openly the moment that we get our first parliamentary electoral breakthrough.'

'Is that just your suspicion, John, or do you know it for a fact?'

'Oh, it's a fact all right,' he told me.

'Well . . . who?'

After a moment's pause, he replied, 'Alan Clark, for one.'

I was flabbergasted. Clark was indeed well known for his forthright right-wing views, but he was at the time a junior defence minister. The idea that he was a closet admirer of John Tyndall was mind-boggling.

He went on to tell me that not only had he met Clark, but that they had dined together and that they shared common views on many questions. Clark, he added, was one of the very few establishment politicians he could trust.

I pressed him for more names, but he clammed up. Hinting that there were others he could not name, he said, 'It's not that I don't trust you, Ray, but I really shouldn't even have told you about Clark. I trust you'll respect the confidence.'

This was clearly out of the question, but I assured him I would. When I passed this fascinating claim to my colleagues at *Searchlight* they were equally incredulous. There had been no other evidence to suggest that Clark was a fascist sympathizer, so the 'fact' of his relationship with Tyndall was simply filed away. There was clearly no way in which it could be made public without the risk that

I might have to reveal my true role by helping defend a libel action.

Three years later, as it happened, the truth came out. Clark, who had since moved to the Department of Employment, got himself into hot water by referring, at a departmental briefing meeting, to black people as coming from 'Bongo Bongo Land'. Fittingly, the story was first reported in *Searchlight*, but was eagerly taken up by every Fleet Street paper except, for some curious reason, *The Times*. *Searchlight* reporters tried to put the Tyndall matter to Clark but he steadfastly refused to comment. In private briefings to journalists, however, he did outline his version of the story Tyndall had intimated to me earlier. Tyndall had been writing a regular series of articles in *Spearhead* about the defence of Britain, and had contacted Clark to suggest they meet to discuss matters of common interest. Somewhat intrigued by the idea of meeting the leader of a self-proclaimed nazi sect, Clark agreed. They met once, in a third-rate Italian restaurant selected by Tyndall, and Clark quickly concluded that his dinner companion was 'a bit of a blockhead'.

So if Clark's story is correct (and there can be no reason to doubt the word of a Member of Parliament holding high office in the service of the Crown) a relatively inconsequential – and inconclusive – dinner engagement had been exaggerated in Tyndall's hyper-active ego into a fully-fledged endorsement of his own leadership qualities. Of the two, I confess, I am more inclined to believe Mr Clark.

By the time that I suggested to Tyndall, a couple of months later, that the BNP should set itself a target of contesting fifty seats at the next General Election, I already knew that my days with the BNP were numbered.

Arrangements with Ludi Boeken to make *The Other Face of Terror* were by now well advanced. A certain amount of soul-searching had been involved, but we knew from my close contacts with Tyndall that things were not going well. The split with the NF was terminal so there was little chance of the nazi movement presenting fewer than two faces to the British public for some time. At the same time, BNP's membership seemed to have reached a plateau at around 2,500 and it did not appear imperative that I stay in to put a brake on any explosive rate of growth. Most significantly, perhaps, Tyndall's marriage to Valerie Parker was far from happy, and it was clear that if they parted he would lose the financial support of her father upon which he depended. In the event, this is precisely what happened.

Other financial problems had continued to dog Tyndall from the days of his leadership of the NF. When it split in 1979, there began a series of court actions over control of NF Properties Ltd, a company which the party had set up to control its headquarters building in the East End of London. After the NF was forced out by the local council for breaches of planning regulations, a series of legal tussles led to Tyndall being declared bankrupt, so that, when I came to suggest fifty election candidates, although he supported the idea, he knew he would not be able to contest a seat himself. The law forbids undischarged bankrupts from standing for election.

Even so, he had already decided to fight the election along the lines I proposed. Fifty candidates was the minimum number that a party had to field to be guaranteed radio and television party political broadcasts during an election campaign, and previous experience in the NF suggested that there was no more cost-effective way of recruiting new members. I imagined, however, that it might be difficult for BNP to raise the £7,500 necessary just for candidates' deposits (quite apart from the additional costs of campaigning). I was most surprised when Tyndall simply said that the money would be 'no problem'. He had already decided that I should fight the constituency of Leicester East, held by Labour MP Greville Janner.

For Tyndall, Janner was an obvious target, being then chairman of the Board of Deputies of British Jews. Tyndall was anxious that the main thrust of my campaign should be to question, by smear and innuendo, Janner's basic loyalty to his country. It is commonly held in national socialist circles that anyone who is both Jewish and holds public office must owe their first loyalty to Israel, and be in all likelihood a paid agent of 'Zionism'. This absurd notion, in Tyndall's mind, undoubtedly applied to Greville Janner, and it would be my task, he said, to expose his 'treason' to the people of Leicester West.

So, May 1983 found me trudging the streets of that constituency trying, in a fairly half-hearted fashion, to drum up support for the BNP's election drive. For the television programme, it could not have happened at a better time. When Tyndall, myself and Kenneth McKilliam announced the party's fifty-candidate campaign at a London press conference shortly after the election was called, Ludi Boeken's film crew had an ideal opportunity to film me as Tyndall's right-hand man, sitting next to him on the platform. In the weeks that followed, the same film crew followed me around Leicester, as I knocked on doors and campaigned in shopping centres. None of it, of course, was particuarly revealing, but it did enable us to show, in pictures, just how involved, and how senior, I was in the BNP. Certainly it made it difficult, later on, for Tyndall to dismiss my involvement as unimportant.

I ignored Tyndall's tactical advice that I should focus the campaign on Greville Janner, and instead plugged the repatriation theme that everyone expected from a BNP candidature. And, it must be said, I did play it very low key. By now I knew I would be 'out in the cold' in a few months' time, so I had little enthusiasm for an over-the-top performance which could only have been justified by some long-term gain. At this stage it might only have done damage. But (and this probably says something for the latent racism that exists in a place like Leicester) I still ended up polling the second highest BNP vote in any of the fifty seats we fought.

I got 469 votes, approximately 1 per cent of the vote. As a share of the vote it is, of course, insignificant. But it does mean that there are almost five hundred people in that one constituency who feel strongly enough about race and immigration to be prepared to vote for an unashamedly nazi party. Across Leicester as a whole, where BNP contested three of the city's four constituencies, more than a thousand people in all cast their votes for the BNP. It's a far cry from the days when the National Front could count on thirty or forty times that figure, but it is still a deeply worrying bedrock level of support for the policies of race hatred.

The election campaign, however, signalled the beginning of my withdrawal from BNP. Apart from a meeting with the right-wing historian David Irving, which I describe in Chapter Nine, I adopted an increasingly low profile with the party. The reason for this was simple: on the schedule now was a series of meetings with extremely hard-line nazis in the UK and abroad which would be filmed and recorded for the television programme. Tyn-

dall already knew of earlier contacts of mine with terrorists, and although he did not disapprove, it had made him
extremely nervous, in case publicity about it was used to
damage the BNP. Further contacts, were he to find out
about them, would cause unnecessary complications.
Better to withdraw quietly and concentrate on gathering
the evidence we needed to expose definitively the undercover activities of the British and foreign nazis we had
targeted. In particular, we wanted to probe two areas of
illegal activity: the networks which provided shelter for
right-wing terrorists on the run, and the conspiracies they
had hatched to carry out terrorist attacks. But even before
we began work on the programme, there was much that
we already knew.

7

Safe Housing Conspiracy

With my return to Britain from South Africa, and with the subsequent demise of the South African National Front, I could have been forgiven for believing that particular chapter of my life to be more or less closed. True, after my re-involvement with the far right in England, I was occasionally asked to explain the somewhat odd circumstances surrounding the Front's collapse and my sudden re-appearance in Leicester. South Africa and its affairs, however, were now sufficiently distant for me to be able to offer reasonably plausible explanations without any undue fear that someone might begin digging over events there and suspecting that my role was anything other than as I claimed.

So I was a little surprised, not long after I had thrown myself back into political activity, to receive a phone call from an Italian, whom I shall call Paolo, who used by way of introduction the name of one of my old South African NF colleagues – the Italian immigrant Max Bollo. Paolo asked to see me, and when we met he revealed that Bollo had been an important contact of the Swiss-based nazi international grouping, the New European Order, run from Lausanne by Gaston Amaudruz. Paolo was also connected with the NEO, and was in England, having been sent by his employers, Olivetti, to attend an IBM course in computing. It was not long before he got round to his true purpose in contacting me. He had been told by NEO to put a proposition to me: that I should help arrange safe houses in Britain for right-wing fugitives who might have to escape from the police in Italy.

At the time, of course, the Italian authorities were looking for members of the far-right Armed Revolutionary Nuclei (NAR) who had carried out a series of murders and bombings in Italy, but it was only later that year, after the horrific attack at Bologna railway station when over eighty people were killed by an NAR suitcase bomb in a waiting room, that I realized why Paolo had made his request. The Bologna outrage was followed by an exodus of wanted NAR members, many of whom fled to England.

But Paolo's approach was significant for another reason: it pointed clearly to a relationship between the New European Order and active right-wing terror cells in Europe, a relationship which many had long suspected but never clearly established. Based in Lausanne, Switzerland, and led by Gaston Amaudruz, NEO has worked since its inception in 1954 to link up hard-line nazi organizations throughout the world. Many of the most notorious right-wing paramilitary groups in Europe are believed to be national sections of NEO.

At first Paolo seemed to be asking me to make my own house available for fugitives, but I quickly pointed out that I was well known on the British far right, and was almost certainly under some sort of observation by the authorities. On this inconclusive note our meeting ended, with Paolo promising to give the matter more thought. A week later he got in touch again, suggesting another meeting. By this time he had found lodgings, a first-floor flat in Well Walk, Hampstead, where I met him, and where we discussed the problem at length. If pushed, I told Paolo, I could arrange safe houses through my personal contacts, but I could not vouch for their reliability in matters such as these. It might, I suggested, be worth making an approach to the League of St George, whom I knew to have extensive contacts already with far-right groups in Europe. The man to contact would be Steve Brady, at that time the LSG's International Liaison Officer. Paolo had already heard of the League, and asked me to make the necessary introductions for him. Having only comparatively recently arrived back from Johannesburg, my contact with the League was limited, but I knew enough of them to know that they were the people to go to.

After his ignominious defeat in Notting Hill in the 1958 General Election, Sir Oswald Mosley had finally quit Britain and taken up permanent residence at Orsay, near Paris, where he set himself up as Britain's fascist saviour-in-waiting. Until his death in 1981, he anticipated that at some crisis-ridden stage the British people would finally turn to him, calling him back to greatness.

His supporters, needless to say, remained in Britain, under the declining leadership of Mosley's secretary, Jeffrey Hamm, organized under the banners of the Union Movement and later the Action Party. But it was clear that men and women who had cut their teeth on the streets of London's East End before the war, or in Notting Hill in the fifties, were not going to be happy for long constituted into a political fan club for an elderly expatriate failure, and in 1974 some of them formed themselves into the League of St George. The League called itself a non-sectarian political club, and recruited members from other existing extreme right groups without prejudice to their membership of these other groups. Through book sales, film shows and social events, and not least of all through its journal *League Review*, it set itself the task of keeping alive the spirit of genuine national socialism. This was considered all the more necessary in the mid-1970s when the country's most successful right-wing party since the war, the National Front, was drawing a discreet veil over its own commitment to national socialism and anti-semitism in an energetic effort to drum up votes from a wider electorate. At the same time, however, the League kept alive two basic tenets of Mosley's own philosophy which had been entirely discarded by what was now the mainstream of the British far right. These were a commitment to Europe and a break with 'narrow' British nationalism; and a belief in a united Ireland coupled with support for Irish Republicanism.

But the League also set itself one other key task: it would, unlike many other groups on the British right, take seriously the job of maintaining relationships with nazi organizations and parties in Europe, America, and indeed the rest of the world. From the start it was well equipped to do this. Mosley himself had worked enthusiastically to build a pan-European fascist party, and in 1951 had joined with the German Reich Party, the Italian MSI, Nation Europa and others to launch the 'Malmo International' uniting all of these fascist parties, where each agreed to function as a national chapter of a European Social Movement. It was a split from this Malmo International which in 1954 gave birth to the New European Order, with a more open commitment to national socialism and anti-semitism. The League still saw itself as being very much in this internationalist tradition, and through Steve Brady, who took over as International Liaison Officer from Owen Masters in 1978, it set about assiduously renewing contacts with nazis abroad.

In some ways, Brady was an odd choice for such an important role. His commitment to nazism had never been in doubt, although in 1975/76 he joined with a 'Strasserite' grouping which split from the NF to form the

National Party. Although coming from an Irish Catholic background, he was a staunch anti-republican and, indeed, boasted of his contacts with Protestant paramilitary groups in Northern Ireland. He even, at one stage, acted as adviser to the Ulster Defence Association when it was toying with the idea of establishing its own contacts with far-right groups in Europe.

It was to Brady, who had suggested in June that I should join the League, that I now turned on Paolo's behalf. We met at a League of St George meeting, where I explained the problem and gave Paolo's London telephone number to Brady. Brady indicated that the matter would be taken care of. When we met again shortly afterwards at a League social evening, Brady confirmed that he had been in touch with Paolo. 'Things are in hand,' he told me, but suggested that it would be better, at this stage at least, if I had nothing more to do with the affair. There were, after all, clear and traceable links between myself, Paolo and Max Bollo which, if uncovered, could jeopardize the security of the whole operation. Better for me to drop out. Unfortunately, I had to agree.

Despite this, subsequent events convinced me that arrangements for safe housing had begun. When I attended an LSG meeting at the Oak Tree Tavern in Acton, West London on 27 February 1981, I was surprised to find a small group of Italians present. They were kept on one side in the company of Brady and League leaders Mike Griffin and Keith Thomson, and were not generally introduced. Later in the evening, however, one of them made a short speech in English, thanking their 'English comrades' for their hospitality. Another of them, later identified on Granada's *World in Action* as Alessandro

Alibrandi, wanted in Italy for the murder of a judge, sat in prolonged conversation with leading British Movement official Peter Marriner.

It was at this meeting that I briefly met Alex Oumow, a French nazi introduced to me by Steve Brady as the French group Faisceaux Nationalistes Européens liaison officer for Britain and the USA. I did not appreciate how significant he was until I gained entry a few months later into the world of French right-wing terrorists.

On other occasions I asked Brady if things were all right. Usually, he answered guardedly, or said simply, 'Enrico sends his regards', but it was becoming clear, certainly in my mind, that Italians were being brought over and sheltered.

It was only at the end of 1981 that the scale of the operation became clear. Acting upon requests from the Italian authorities, police in London raided addresses in Harrow, Pinner and Brixton, and arrested seven Italians. All were wanted on terrorism-related charges in Italy and extradition proceedings began. All were members of NAR cells and had been active in FUAN, the youth wing of the MSI. Among League of St George leaders there was panic.

Shortly after the arrests I phoned Brady. 'I hear you've had a bit of bad luck,' I said. I had heard from other sources that 'Brady is flapping', and now I could almost feel him sweating on the other end of the phone. 'For Christ's sake, no,' Brady squealed. 'We can't talk now – I'll see you when I see you,' and he put the phone down.

Other League officials were also having a hard time of it. Mike Griffin and Keith Thomson in particular had been obvious targets for journalists investigating the scale of the safe housing operations. They flatly denied everything, although Thomson did admit at one point to having found a hotel in London for an Italian fascist recently arrived in the country.

He also admitted that the same character had later turned up at a League of St George social evening – the same event, in fact, that I had attended in Acton, where I knew the Italians present to include the wanted killer Alibrandi.

As it was, things did not turn out too unhappily for the League, or for their Italian visitors. After a bungled case was presented to Bow Street magistrates by the Italian authorities, the request for their extradition was refused and they resumed their lives in London, some working as waiters in pizza restaurants and living on a right-wing commune in Brixton, some disappearing from sight altogether. The League breathed a sigh of relief.

Later events confirmed, however, what I had been given to understand by nods and winks from Brady. In 1980, police began investigating the appearance of a nazi 'comic', *The Stormer*, which was being distributed outside schools. Virulently anti-semitic, it carried no publisher's name or address, but the artistic style was unmistakably that of Bob Edwards, a cartoonist who worked for *League Review*. At the same time, responsibility for publishing it was claimed by Robert Relf, already twice gaoled for offences under the Race Relations Act and still determined to become a martyr – the Horst Wessel of the British far right.

But I had already learned that one of the men behind it was Jimmy Styles, an East Londoner who had been active in the National Front before joining the breakaway NF Constitutional Movement in 1979. It wasn't long before police picked up this information and paid Styles a visit. Styles telephoned me. He was extremely frightened and asked if we could meet. He told me he had been turned over and that the Yard wanted to interview him about *The Stormer*.

Between us we cooked up an ingenious little scheme. Suspecting that the police had little to go on apart from unsubstantiated rumours, we decided that a bare-faced, indignant response was appropriate. Together, we went to Scotland Yard, Styles as the suspect, me posing as his solicitor – Joe King (!) It worked perfectly.

I sat there in my pin-striped suit, saying, 'I shouldn't answer that if I were you, Mr Styles', and generally defying the detectives to do their worst. In the end they could do nothing, and when we left the Yard, Styles invited me for a celebratory drink. In an understandably elated and grateful mood, Styles sank a few pints and talked freely.

Soon he was telling me about two Italian house guests who had been staying with him at his flat in East London. He did not disclose their identities to me, but he did reveal that they had been introduced by the League of St George. Unlike most of the Italians who came over, this pair did not exactly keep their heads down, and Styles retailed with glee how they had given him a 'going-away present' before they moved on to new safe accommodation.

Over a meal and much drink, Styles had moaned to them about a nearby bookshop run by left-wingers, which he claimed was a focus for much left-wing activity in that part of the East End. The Italians looked at one another, and one told Styles that they would see what could be done. The next night the shop was gutted by fire in an arson attack. Styles was laughing his head off telling me about it. He thought it was hilarious because the way the Italians had done it had been so casual. He called it a going-away present.

Another nazi who told me that he had been involved with the Italians was Francis Forsyth. A regular at LSG functions, Forsyth ran his own small group called Teutonic Order, linked to the German organization Teutonic Unity, led by gaoled terrorist Manfred Roeder. In June 1980, he revealed to me that Paolo had been staying with him, and that there was an agreement between militants of the MSI and the British far right to exchange personnel to carry out operations. He mentioned one attack which had already allegedly been carried out by Italians – the petrol bombing of a left-wing bookshop in London. I came to wonder if this was the same one which Jimmy Styles later told me about in detail.

The story of the Italian fugitives did not end with their success in the extradition case. Some of them, including Marinella Rita, Massimo Morsello and Amadeo de Francisci, settled into a relatively quiet life in a Brixton hideaway. Others vanished from sight. They resurfaced, however, in September 1982 when police in London swooped on a flat in Chelsea to arrest one of Italy's most wanted right-wing terrorists, Luciano Petrone.

A warrant had been issued for Petrone's arrest several months earlier, following the murder of two policemen in Rome. Petrone, sitting in a car at night with three of his comrades, had been approached by the police officers who wanted to check their papers. The police were disarmed, forced to kneel in the road, and executed with a bullet in the back of the head.

The search for Petrone intensified at the end of the year when a group of men used the Christmas holiday period to break into the Bank of Andalucia in Marbella, Spain, emptying the vaults of ten million pounds. Unfortunately for them, their visit had been recorded on a closed-circuit television camera, and they were quickly identified as members of the NAR from Rome. Italian police moved quickly to arrest several of the gang, but others, including Petrone who was suspected of having masterminded the operation, avoided capture.

Before long, it became clear that he was in London, having travelled on the passport of another known right-wing activist who had reported it lost (several times!) to the Italian police.

During one of his frequent visits to Marbella, he met an English girl, Imogen Lucas-Box, and soon they were lovers. When she returned to London he joined her, and together they set up home in her flat in Chelsea's Walton Street. Following a request for his arrest from the Italian authorities, Special Branch and Anti-Terrorist Squad officers observed the flat for several days before an early evening raid on 21 January when Petrone was arrested in the street outside. He was held in custody and produced at Bow Street magistrates' court for remand a couple of days later.

At this stage it became clear that Petrone had established close contact with the wanted NAR members who had successfully fought off extradition requests earlier in the year. In court to witness his remand was his girlfriend, Imogen Lucas-Box. When she left, she was escorted through the crowds of waiting journalists and film crews by a group of unidentified young men and women, who put her in a car and drove her away. On the way to the car, inquisitive camera crews were physically prevented from filming by people described on news bulletins as 'unknown Italians'.

But they were not entirely unknown. Among those later identified in the group were Massimo Morsello, Amadeo de Francisci, and Marinella Rita – all suspects in the earlier extradition case. Journalists who visited Ms

Lucas-Box at her flat later found Massimo Morsello in attendance, fending off questions and preventing anyone from noting her telephone number. Ms Lucas-Box has said she had no idea that Petrone or his friends had been involved in terrorism.

I heard it persistently rumoured in right-wing circles at the time that Petrone had brought a sizeable portion of the proceeds of the Marbella raid with him to London. None of it has yet been found, but it was suggested that it had found its way into right-wing hands to finance some ambitious propaganda projects. Petrone himself was sentenced to twenty-two years when he stood trial in 1986.

Later events involving another of the wanted Italians confirmed both that he had been in contact with the London NAR cell, and that he had brought funds with him.

In July 1983, *Searchlight* began an investigation, quite independent of information which I had been providing, into a tourist guide company called Heritage Tours, based at 50 Warwick Square in London. Run by two known National Front members, Michael Walker and Nick Griffin, it was suspected of raising funds for right-wing activities. Its publicity material had immediately intrigued *Searchlight* researchers by advertising that Italian-, German- and French-speaking guides were available. *Searchlight* brought in an Italian investigator and booked him on a personal tour, having briefed him beforehand with details of known wanted Italians, and shown him their photographs. He phoned Heritage Tours to make the arrangements, and was told that he would be shown around London the following day by 'Roberto'.

At 9 o'clock the next morning the two men met outside the investigator's South London hotel and took a train from Forest Hill to Charing Cross. There was no doubt by now that the Italian was Roberto Fiore, a well-known NAR activist who had trained in Falange camps in the Lebanon, and was still wanted by the Italian police for attempted murder, firebomb attacks, and a raid on a weapons store in Rome. He was easily identified by a large mole on his right cheek.

They began the tour, ironically at what Fiore called 'the famous Bow Street Magistrates' Court' – where only months earlier he had sat in the dock while Italian requests for his extradition were considered.

Without admitting that he had been involved himself, Fiore told his companion about the case – of how several young Italians had been held on trumped-up charges, but had been freed by 'the wonderful system of British justice'. Soon he came to talk about Petrone. Had he heard that there was, at that moment, another young Italian facing extradition? Yes, the visitor replied, he did remember having read something of it. Such a pity, said Fiore. Petrone was 'so young, with a beautiful girlfriend and lots of money' – and now he might have to spend much of his life in gaol. The reference to money prompted the investigator to push things a little further. They both knew that Petrone was accused of being at Marbella, but, he asked with a nod and a wink, 'was he really there?' Fiore grinned back. 'Of course he was,' he replied.

The Heritage Tours story later broke on the front pages of the national press, principally because the flat from which Heritage Tours operated, and where Fiore lived for some considerable time, was directly above that of then Conservative government Treasury Minister Nicholas Ridley. Quite apart from the revelations about Petrone, the episode was significant for another reason – Nick Griffin and Michael Walker, who ran Heritage Tours, were editors respectively of *Nationalism Today*, the self-styled theoretical journal of the National Front, and *National Democrat*, a lavishly produced though small-circulation independent right-wing journal linked to the French new right movement GRECE. Once again, members of the British right were finding work and accommodation for their fugitive comrades from the continent. Indeed, another inhabitant of 50 Warwick Square, a Young Conservative officer called Gareth Light, later told a national newspaper that Luciano Petrone had also stayed for a while at the flat.

At around the same time that Paolo and Brady were working together to bring wanted Italians to safety in Britain, I became aware of other safe housing schemes operated by, or at least under discussion by, members of the League of St George.

In June 1980, as part of a League delegation, I made the annual pilgrimage to the European nazi rally held in the small Belgian town of Diksmuide, where each year nazis from all over Europe gather to pay homage to nazi war dead.

It was a journey I was to repeat each year until my 'coming out' in 1984. Much of the time British nazis found themselves in bar-room brawls with right-wing militants from other countries. As often as not, the cause was Northern Ireland. Many nationalist groups in Europe supported the aspirations of the Provisional IRA, and could not understand why the British extreme right – with the exception of the League of St George – was so fervently loyalist. On one occasion, British nazis got off their ferry at Ostend to be greeted by Flemish nazis distributing leaflets commemorating the 'martyrdom' of hunger-striker Bobby Sands, who had died earlier in the

Maze prison. A pitched battle was sparked off immediately.

But while younger enthusiasts got drunk, were arrested, or brawled with their 'comrades', nazi leaders often used the occasion to hold highly secret meetings to discuss strategy and joint activities.

Only shortly before the 1980 trip, having impressed people with my obvious leadership qualities in Leicester, and revelling in the status of something of an elder statesman on the far right, I had been invited to join the League, who were traditionally the organizers of the British nazi contingent to Diksmuide. During the festivities I spent most of my time in League company, sharing the welcome that this highly-regarded group received from its European counterparts.

From the moment of our arrival in Belgium the League representatives enjoyed the best in hospitality. Steve Brady joined me and several others at the Pacific Hotel, owned by an ex-SS member, but operated through a front man. On the first evening the whole party adjourned to the 1302 bar in Ostend, owned and run by Bert Erikson, a leading figure in the Belgian VMO (Flemish Militant Order) – subsequently outlawed by the Belgian authorities.

The evening was marked by much drinking and several severe beatings: Diksmuide always seemed to be seized upon as an opportunity for settling old scores.

Among others, LSG member Tony Creese was brutally beaten by a group of British Movement skinheads on the instructions of Steve Brady, who suspected him of selling inside information to the Press. It was five o'clock in the morning before the drinking, singing and fighting subsided and the revellers made their way to bed.

The following day Brady and myself were flag-bearers

at a ceremony at the British war cemetery, where the address was given by ex-major Ian Souter Clarence – a name which will crop up again later. But the important discussions of the weekend were held behind closed doors in the café Den Anker in Bruges, on the Sunday. Attended on behalf of the League by Steve Brady and Mike Griffin, the discussions involved Dr Ed Fields from the American National States Rights Party, leaders of the VMO, and delegates from the Italian terror group New Order. High on the agenda at the get-together was the predicament of NSRP leader J. B. Stoner.

Stoner, an attorney from Alabama, had recently been convicted in the United States on charges of dynamiting a negro church in Birmingham, Alabama almost twenty-two years before. His National States Rights Party was violently opposed to both blacks and Jews and had frequently been linked to the Ku Klux Klan. Although on bail awaiting appeal as his comrades discussed his plight at Bruges, he was unwilling to abscond while there was still a chance of the appeal court freeing him. But if he lost the appeal and faced a hefty gaol sentence, things might be different.

Discussions in Bruges revolved around the possibility that the conviction would stick, and there was general agreement that, in this event, an attempt should be made to free him. League of St George representatives were heavily involved in discussions about which country he should flee to after his escape.

As it happened, three years later Stoner did unsuccessfully exhaust the appeals procedures of the American legal system – and promptly disappeared. Unfortunately, in the meantime the arrests of Italian and German nazis in England had put the spotlight firmly on the safe housing operation and forced it to close down. Stoner was left with nowhere to go and in July 1983 gave himself up to law enforcement authorities in the United States.

A similar predicament faced French nazi leader Mark Frederiksen in 1981. Just before the bombing of the synagogue in Rue Copernic in late 1980, his organization FANE (Fédération d'Action Nationale Européenne) had been banned by the French authorities. Frederiksen promptly reconstituted the party as FNE (Faisceaux Nationalistes Européens), but soon found himself facing criminal proceedings. Plans immediately began to be discussed to deal with a situation in which he might face a substantial gaol sentence.

I was personally approached by one of his lieutenants who asked me to find safe housing for him in the Midlands should the need arise. Naturally, I said I would help if I could, but in the event the matter was taken no further.

One man who very definitely was helped by British nazis was Willy Kraus, a fanatical young nazi from West Germany. He had come over to the UK in 1979 on the run from serious criminal charges back home. His initial contact was through the Belgian nazi leader Roger Spinnewijn who gave him the names of League of St George members in Britain who would help him. Kraus has said himself that his first port of call was the League's leader Mike Griffin, who put him up at his West London home. From there he was passed on to members of British Movement in the West Country who found him lodgings and work as a chef in South Wales and Bristol. All the while, however, he carried on as an active nazi with his newfound British comrades. Kraus's luck ran out in 1982 when he was arrested for theft. After serving a prison sentence here he was deported back to West Germany where the grateful authorities arrested him.

Two other German nazis on the run were arrested by

British police in 1983, hiding out at the home of a veteran British right-winger, former Major Ian Souter Clarence, who lived in Poole, Dorset. Clarence has been ever present on the nazi scene for years. In the early 1960s he was running a Viking Commando youth corps from the school where he worked as a teacher, but, as he inadvertently told a journalist, his aim was as much to indoctrinate young boys in the ideology of national socialism and anticommunism as it was to provide a more exciting alternative to the Boy Scouts. He had been involved with the Hancocks in the Racial Preservation Society for many years, and had been a local organizer for the National Front. Later in 1983 I was to be present with him at Diksmuide when, as part of a League of St George delegation, he delivered a speech at the war cemetery. From his home in Dorset, drawing on his experience as a former soldier and an SAS operative during the last war, he organized survival and paramilitary training for young nazi activists. At one point he was given charge of the British Movement's 'Leader Guard' heavies, with a brief to turn them into something resembling an efficient paramilitary unit. His training courses were regularly advertised through the LSG's *League Review* and would-be participants applied through an LSG box number.

It was only in February 1983 that the Major's less than salubrious activities received the public attention they deserved. Again acting on a request from the continent, CID officers from Poole burst into his home early one Saturday. They arrested two young Germans, Walther Kexel and Ulrich Tillman, and narrowly missed apprehending a third, Odfried Hepp, who had apparently popped out to buy a newspaper. All had belonged to a small nazi cell in Frankfurt.

The police in West Germany wanted them in connection with a series of bomb attacks which had been carried out against American army personnel and establishments in the Federal Republic, but which had previously been blamed on the extreme left 'Revolutionary Cells'. A week before their arrests, three of their Frankfurt comrades had been detained by West German police.

They had also been closely associated with the Hoffman Group's military instructor Arndt Heinz Marx with whom they had been members of a small, violent nazi cell called Sturm 7 in Frankfurt. Marx was also a key link-man between German nazis and the League of St George, with whom he had made contact in 1978. On a trip to the UK he was taken by Brighton nazi Martin Haine to a League meeting to establish contact with the group's leaders. The liaison had been maintained ever since.

Marx and Odfried Hepp had trained together at a PLO camp in the Lebanon, although Marx admitted later that they had not dared to tell the Palestinians that they were from a German nazi organization. Marx also held the dubious distinction of having trained Gundolf Kohler, the young Hoffman member who blew himself up carrying out the bomb attack on the 1980 Oktoberfest in Munich.

The exact circumstances in which Clarence came to be sheltering Kexel and Tillman are unclear, although he claims that it was only after a request from Tillman's father, who was an old friend, that they came to be staying with him for, as far as he was concerned, a short holiday. In order to test Souter Clarence's knowledge of the safe housing scene, and his willingness to help fugitives, I travelled to Dorset to meet him in October 1983. Arriving unannounced, I turned up at Clarence's house one morning just as the Major was about to go out. The conversation was brief but instructive. On a recent trip to Paris, I told him, I had been asked to arrange safe housing for an Italian extremist. Clarence immediately wanted to know 'Who is he? What is he wanted for?' Fortunately I had already been well briefed with a cover story by colleagues at *Searchlight*. I gave him the name of a lesser-known Italian fascist, Cirio Lai, currently sought by police for questioning about terrorism.

Could the Major give me advice? His advice was straightforward. Find him a cheap hotel, where there were many tourists and where he would be inconspicuous. 'For God's sake don't put him in anyone's house,' he urged. 'Look what happened to me.' This, naturally enough, brought the discussion on to the arrested Germans, Kexel and Tillman, with whom, it seemed, the Major was less than pleased.

I indicated that I had heard rumours that Odfried Hepp, who escaped arrest, was hiding in Belgium. 'No chance,' replied Souter Clarence. 'He'll be in Spain by now. If not in Spain,' he added mysteriously, 'then he'll be behind the Iron Curtain.'

In fact, some months later, he was arrested in Paris at a safe house controlled by an ostensibly left-wing terrorist group, the Lebanese Armed Faction and he was subsequently extradited to West Germany for trial.

For European nazis, Britain had been regarded as the perfect safe haven: EEC laws gave them the right freely to live and work here, while our particularly strict extradition rules made it extremely difficult to get them out.

Within the network of Europe's criminal nazi groups, the role of British nazis was seen as being to keep their heads down and make sure that safe housing, and whatever other help was necessary, was available to any continental comrades who had to flee from their own countries. They even had a name for it: the shelter network was called 'Brown Aid' after the brownshirt uniforms worn by Hitler's SA troops. While their comrades in France, Italy and Germany were causing mayhem in the early 1980s, Britain's nazis did nothing to draw unwarranted official attention to their vital role in the movement as a whole.

But this could not go on forever. Some foreign nazis, especially in Germany and France, began to resent the fact that they were taking all the risks while the British seemed to be having an easy time of it. The pressure was soon on for nazis over here to begin doing their bit in the war against the 'Jewish-Communist enemy'.

8

Inside the Terror Network

Looking back, it was clear that the signs in 1980 were ominous, although no one foresaw quite the deadly turn which events were to take.

Fascists in Italy, usually members of the Armed Revolutionary Nuclei, had for over ten years been pursuing what they called 'the strategy of tension'. It was very simple: they launched campaigns of terror bombings, random murder, or assassinations of police officials or magistrates investigating their activities, hoping to provoke a violent response from their left-wing opponents, who, in Italy at that time, were the only groups taking seriously the threat from the fascist movement.

The right believed that if they maintained this sort of activity for long enough, pressure would build up in the country for a 'return to law and order' and the path would be open for a military coup.

It very nearly succeeded in the early 1970s, when two attempted *coup d'états* failed – one led by the 'Black Prince' Valerio Borghese, a prominent supporter of the main fascist party, the MSI (Italian Socialist Movement).

In other European countries, however, the idea did not catch on until much later. The principal reason for this was simply that within the fascist movement the debate about the best road to power had to take into account the progress that the National Front had been making in Britain, where their clever exploitation of simple anti-immigrant propaganda was bringing considerable success in election contests and broad public campaigns. For a while at least, it persuaded important sections of the fascist movement in Europe that perhaps they too could build mass-based parties if only they got their policies into a similar sort of shape. So it wasn't any accident that in the mid- to late 1970s the MSI, the German NPD and others all seized upon anti-immigrant agitation and made it the centre of their activities.

But with one or two exceptions, the gamble failed. After its first flush of success, the NF was knocked back by the hugely successful campaigns of the Anti Nazi League which organized rallies of tens of thousands against the NF, and produced millions of highly effective leaflets which circulated in factories, offices and housing estates. And the Front received a mortal blow in 1978 when Prime Minister-to-be Margaret Thatcher appeared on television to shed crocodile tears for British people frightened of being 'swamped by people from an alien culture'. She stole their policies, thousands of their supporters, was brought to victory in the 1979 General Election and left the Front bleating from the sidelines that they had been robbed – which they certainly had.

At the same time, no one else in Europe was showing any real prospects of successfully exploiting this strategy: it wasn't until four years later that the Centrum Party in Holland and the Front National in France returned to it with spectacular success. For the time being, it was widely held in fascist circles that such a strategy would always fail. The road to power, they concluded, must lie in another direction.

There had always been opposition to the election strategy, of course, and now, in 1979 and 1980, those arguing that it was necessary to prepare for actual war against their opponents started to gain the upper hand. What was the point, they argued, of agreeing to fight the enemy on its own ground? While the left controlled the media and pulled the strings of political power, the far right would never be allowed to succeed in 'respectable' politics. It was all part of the same old 'conspiracy theory' that I encountered wherever I went in the movement.

In late 1979, *Notre Europe*, published by the French nazi group FANE (which changed its name to FNE in 1980) printed an article by 'Michel Leloup' arguing for 'a new strategy of tension'. The author's real name was Michel Faci, one of FANE's leaders whom I met in Diksmuide in July 1980. I don't know if his article simply reflected what was being discussed at the time, or whether it was a call to action, but soon events took a dramatic turn. In August 1980, a bomb exploded in the waiting room of Bologna railway station in Italy, killing eighty-five people. The city was the main stronghold of the Italian Communist Party, known as 'Red Bologna', so it was an obvious target for right-wing terrorists intent on waging open war against the left. Responsibility was quickly claimed by the NAR, whose members, as I recounted in the last chapter, flooded out of the country as police began hunting the perpetrators of this outrage.

Then just two months later, a German nazi organization, the Hoffman Group, planted a bomb at the world famous Oktoberfest beer festival in Munich. Here fourteen people died, including the young Hoffman group member, Gundolf Kohler, who planted the bomb.

Another attack followed in December, this time in Paris. A bomb was left in a motorcycle outside a Jewish synagogue in Rue Copernic. It was only because the service was running slightly late that the street was not crowded with worshippers leaving the building as the device exploded. But even so, four passers-by were killed.

I had been trying for several months to establish if there was any firm connection between these events and the

activities of British nazi groups, but not surprisingly
everyone who might know anything was being extremely
tight-lipped.

Then I got the break I was waiting for: I was invited to
Brighton to spend a weekend with the Hancock family.
The Hancocks were, in every sense, the godfathers of the
British nazi movement. Alan Hancock, the father, had
been a member of Mosley's blackshirts and, in the 1960s,
a central figure in the Racial Preservation Society. The
visit was not without a certain irony: it was the Racial
Preservation Society which had so deftly recruited me to
the nazi cause back in 1968. Now I was travelling to
Brighton ostensibly as one of the star graduates from their
academy of national socialism – in reality as the 'mole'
who was to cause them such acute embarrassment in the
coming months.

The son, Anthony Hancock, had belonged to the
National Front, joined the National Party split in 1975,
and been close to the League of St George – and
especially Steve Brady – since its birth. He had set up a
printing firm which churned out books, newspapers, magazines and leaflets for every conceivable group on the
extreme right. It wasn't confined to Britain: when NF
leader Richard Verrall, under the pseudonym 'Richard
Harwood', wrote his notorious pamphlet *Did Six Million
Really Die?*, denying the nazi mass murder of Jews, it was
published by the Hancocks in several languages and
distributed all over the world. Anthony Hancock was
always travelling to Europe and America meeting nazi
leaders to arrange publishing deals, and maintained extensive contacts with hard-line national socialists abroad.

I had been invited to Brighton to discuss a printing
deal: earlier I had told Anthony Hancock that I was
interested in buying a large quantity of copies of *Southern*

News, the old Racial Preservation Society paper published by the Hancocks, which had been prosecuted under the Race Relations Act in 1968. As far as he was concerned I wanted a supply of the paper updated and adapted for distribution in the Midlands. Not unnaturally, they found the prospect of a bit of business quite attractive. They owned a hotel (the Heidelburg!) but when I travelled down in February 1981 I was put up for the weekend at their house at 19A Madeira Place near the sea front.

I wasn't the only guest: staying there at the same time were the League of St George's international liaison officer Steve Brady, and a young Frenchman, Alex Oumow whom I had previously met at a League of St George meeting in London. His connection dawned on me when he asked me over a meal that evening if I knew his cousin, John Ormowe. As it happened, I didn't know him personally, but he was a well-known figure in nazi circles, having been a close associate of the Hancocks in the early 1970s when they were involved in an attempt to infiltrate and take over the Monday Club – the main right-wing pressure group inside the Conservative Party. They had all been expelled when their efforts were uncovered, and a number of Monday Club branches where they had seized control were closed down by the Club's leadership. I was told that Oumow was close to the FNE leader Mark Frederiksen and was held in high esteem throughout the European nazi movement.

The Saturday evening was spent in a local restaurant where a large crowd of us – myself, Oumow, Hancock, Steve Brady, an ex-National Socialist organizer called Denis Pirie (later exposed in the national press when it was discovered he held a senior civil service post in Whitehall), and the NF's local organizer Harold Jones – passed the time discussing some of the more obsessive points of far-right philosophy. I must admit, it was occasions like this that drove me to ask myself what on earth I was doing. There had to be better, more fulfilling ways of spending my middle age than sitting around with people like these discussing how Jews controlled the world. But later on, things got more interesting. Oumow told me that he had been sent from France by FNE leaders to help establish new and better links with the British far right. Up until now, this work had been done through the League of St George, but after a series of embarrassing stories about them had appeared in the press, they had been nicknamed the Leak of St George by other nazi hard-liners. So Oumow was by-passing them and making contact directly with other far-right activist groups 'in the field'. He had already visited British Movement leader Michael McLaughlin, he told me, but without much success. McLaughlin's ambition, he felt, was simply to build up a party which could provide him with a living through members' subscriptions. 'Such men', he said, 'have no place in history'. Much more promising, he thought, was the National Socialist Action Party, with whose leader Tony Malski he had already had a successful meeting.

I knew Malski through his former membership of British Movement. As a leading member in the South of England he had been rallying support for me in my battle against BM leader Michael McLaughlin, when he was trying to expel me. Malski was completely uncontrollable and extremely violent – but also extremely loose-lipped. Many a time he landed himself in trouble by shooting his mouth off about his activities when he had had a few drinks too many. Leaving BM, he set up his own National Socialist Action Party and boasted that he was building 'a paramilitary army'. He also bragged about having guns stockpiled in woods near his Watford home, a claim I had dismissed as empty boasting – until a nazi social evening which I attended in January 1981.

Once again the worse for drink, Malski was boasting that he and another leading BM activist had organized a raid on a Territorial Army barracks and stolen a quantity of guns and ammunition. The man he claimed had been with him was standing on the other side of the room drinking, but could hear Malski's every word. Known throughout the movement as a hard man, he visibly blanched, looked as if he was about to explode, and left the room quickly, obviously terrified that Malski's big mouth would get him into serious trouble. To this day, he has never again involved himself in right-wing activity, but that particular incident convinced me that there was after all some substance to Malski's boasting. On several subsequent occasions Malski told of raids on his home by Special Branch officers looking for the guns. 'What sort of prick do they take me for?' he would say, laughing, 'Do they really think I'm going to keep them under the sink?'

Malski claimed to have served with the regular army in Northern Ireland, but it later turned out that he had belonged only to a TA Regiment. Even then, he had been thrown out for 'not coming up to scratch'. But he had clearly learned something. One summer afternoon I sat in his kitchen in Watford while he expertly dismantled a wristwatch and showed me how to convert it into a timing device for a bomb. He trusted me so completely that at one stage he even asked me to become leader of his NSAP. When I refused he went off like a spoilt child. All in all, it was just a little amusing that having rejected the League of St George and British Movement, French nazis had decided to co-operate with this ludicrous – if danger-ous – figure.

At the time of my Brighton visit, however, I was widely regarded as the man who should replace McLaughlin as the BM's führer. When I told Oumow this he responded enthusiastically and indicated that such a development would change things as far as he was concerned. He went out of his way to encourage me to proceed with my battle against McLaughlin, saying he could work with BM if I could take it over.

But although he held the BM leaders in contempt, he obviously had a high regard for some of its members and told me of paramilitary training camps which had already been held in Dorset, where FNE members had trained very successfully alongside BM activists.

The real breakthrough came just before Oumow left Brighton to return to Paris. Having spent the weekend sizing me up, he concluded, fortunately for me, that I was sound and reliable. Before leaving he took me aside and asked if I would like to travel to Paris in the near future to meet 'some of the French comrades'. This was the opportunity we had been waiting for: a chance to move into exactly those top French nazi circles which we were convinced had been involved in far more than just publishing anti-semitic tracts. I accepted his offer eagerly.

In the meantime, Oumow told me, if I had difficulty in getting in touch with people in Paris, I could do it through a woman called Samantha Flynn, who was close to Tony Malski. He gave me her telephone number and an address in Camden Town, North London. Unfortunately, when I tried to contact her, she had moved, leaving no forwarding address, and I never did manage to get in touch. It was only months later that I learned that she had moved to Watford where she was sharing a house with one of Tony Malski's NSAP lieutenants on the same South Oxhey housing estate where Malski lived himself. It transpired that she had been chosen for this courier's role without ever having actually been consulted.

It wasn't until April that I had the opportunity of a free weekend, but as it happened that lent a little colour to subsequent events: the weekend which was eventually arranged coincided with the anniversary of Hitler's birth-day – always, without fail, celebrated by nazis all over the world.

I travelled to Paris by boat-train on the Friday evening to be met at the railway station by Alex Oumow and two of his FNE comrades. We travelled by car to Clichy, a Paris suburb, to an apartment occupied by a Vietnamese member of FNE, Yann Tran Long, and three or four other young nazis, including a young German.

Tran Long is one of the most sinister characters I met in my active time on the far right. He was only about twenty when I met him, but I quickly realized that when it came to paramilitary matters, he was at the heart of things. His flat was a veritable arsenal – as soon as I arrived he showed me rifles, grenades, handguns, and M16 carbines which had been specially modified to take easily available .22 ammunition. He had telescopic sights and silencers, which I was told had been smuggled in from Italy. His brother Minh shared the flat as well, but was away at that time. He had, Yann explained, joined the Foreign Legion the previous January. Yann had been arrested by French police on several occasions, but had never been charged.

On my first evening in Paris I had a dramatic taste of things to come. First my hosts produced guns from a cupboard and began taking pot shots from the window at pigeons on neighbouring roofs. They didn't even bother to use silencers, just blasting away with gay abandon. I fully expected the police to come banging on the door at any moment, but, to my amazement, none did.

Bored with this, someone suggested we go out 'for a little fun'. I wasn't quite sure what this meant but I confess I did begin to get a little worried when they started to pack guns and petrol bombs into two cars parked nearby. There were about eight of us – myself, Oumow, the German, about three male FNE members and two women – and we drove to a part of Paris I was totally unfamiliar with. It was, they said, inhabited by many Jewish people, and they had singled out for their 'bit of fun' a nearby Jewish restaurant. I sat mesmerized in the car as two of them climbed out and hurled petrol bombs at the outside of the café, screaming '*Sieg Heil*' as they did so. Then they stopped two passers-by, decided they were Jewish, and beat them viciously in the street, before running back to the cars. Minutes later we heard the sirens of police cars or fire-engines speeding to the scene of the attack, a sound which provoked whoops of merriment and glee from my fellow passengers.

I have to admit I didn't sleep easily that night. True, I was making the connections I had been working towards, but I hadn't expected to witness – let alone accompany – such activities quite as quickly as this. If this was just a boisterous night out, what else were these maniacs capable of?

The following evening FNE leaders had arranged the expected party to celebrate Hitler's birthday. After spending the afternoon doing a little shopping and sightseeing, I travelled with the others from the flat to a seedy-looking restaurant. From the outside it looked like a dingy corner shop, but inside, through an internal door, it opened up into a spacious, well-lit dining room, comfortably seating about forty nazis, almost all of them in full nazi uniform.

Taking pride of place on the top table was FNE's own

führer, Mark Frederiksen, and Alex Oumow and I sat near him. From the outset I was treated as an honoured guest. The meal, served by waitresses who were clearly aware of, and sympathetic to, what was going on and watched over by a proprietor who was equally friendly, was sumptuous, We struggled through about six courses accompanied by gallons of wine. I had to keep reminding myself to go easy, not to get carried away trying to keep up with the general level of wine consumption. It could have spoiled the purpose of the whole trip if I woke up the next morning remembering nothing of the night's proceedings and discussions.

On the top table I sat between one of the French nazis from the Clichy flat, and another Frenchman, to whom I was not introduced by name, but who was kitted out in complete paramilitary uniform and had a finger missing from his right hand. He was intensely curious about the state of the nazi movement in England.

For some time the conversation at our table revolved around the same old question of which strategy the movement should adopt. Everyone agreed that national socialism was not going to get anywhere through election campaigns. 'Things have changed since the führer's day,' one of them said; 'now the Jews control the ballot box.' Needless to say, I expressed my wholehearted agreement. Then the fingerless character beside me leaned over and asked, quite loud enough for those close to us to hear, 'Do you really want to make an impact in England?'

I asked him what he meant. For too long, he explained, the English comrades had been pussyfooting around. It was about time they did something. Comrades from Italy, Germany and France had begun to fight back – now it was the turn of the English. 'If you want to make a real impression,' he went on, 'we can arrange it – Bologna-style!' I knew right away what he was getting at, so I pretended in a guarded sort of way to be interested.

Warming to the idea, he told me he could provide everything necessary for a Bologna-type bomb – explosives, detonators and timing devices. He even gave me a price list for the various components – it was as matter of fact as if he were selling spare parts for a car. The whole device, made up and delivered would cost about £500, and would contain 15 kilograms of explosives. The whole discussion was quite bizarre. There we were discussing the possibility of exploding a bomb in Brixton, quite openly, as though there were no possible security worries. My hosts seemed totally confident that they were safe. The idea of bombing the best-known black area of South London was greeted with hoots of glee. One man even stood up to offer a toast: 'Bologna,' he barked, to cheers from the assembled national socialists. When I got the chance I had a quiet word with Alex Oumow and asked him bluntly, 'Is this guy giving me a load of bullshit?' 'No, he can deliver,' Oumow replied, explaining that the man, whose name I still do not know, had some connection with explosives in his job and could get his hands on them easily.

I returned to my place at the table to tell my neighbour that there might be interest in England in such a scheme, and I would be in touch with Alex about it. He nodded, but went on to explain that 'the job should be done like Munich', an obvious reference to the massacre at the previous year's Oktoberfest. I asked him what he meant. 'Make sure,' he replied, 'that whoever plants the device is dispensable. They should die with it. That way we can cover our tracks. If the bomb is set to explode at three o'clock, tell them it's set for three-thirty and they should put it in place at exactly three. That's the way we did it at

Munich.' At this point I began to feel sick in my stomach, as this grinning monster described how they had cheerfully blown to pieces one of their own comrades. It was only with some effort that I managed to grin back and nod agreement.

For the moment, it was left at that, and we returned to the flat, my colleagues considerably the worse for drink, and me wondering yet again what on earth I was doing here in Paris cheerfully hatching schemes to kill and maim dozens of people in London.

The following day, another 'bit of fun' was proposed, but this time it was to be rather better organized and executed. In the same car we travelled to a Jewish college in central Paris, accompanied by two young members of the Front National, who were told to hand out FN leaflets in the street outside the college entrance. The idea was, it transpired, to provoke Jewish students into rushing into the street to confront the leafleteers. At this point, two or three of the Clichy nazis, who had taken up positions on a nearby rooftop, would throw down petrol bombs and open up with the guns they had brought with them – replica M16 carbines modified to fire .22 ammunition.

I was left in the car with Oumow, desperately trying to work out what I could do to stop this madness. Thankfully the scheme didn't work out – the Jewish students ignored the leafleteers and the rooftop snipers were recalled down to the street. Before leaving their vantage point, however, they did loose off a few shots into the street in front of the school, causing panic among passers-by but fortunately not hitting anyone.

As everyone piled into the cars two petrol bombs were also hurled down into the street – again injuring no one, but causing considerable panic. Their adrenalin flowing, these young nazis to whom I was now a comrade-in-arms sang nazi marching songs at the tops of their voices as they drove back to Clichy.

It was with an enormous sense of relief that I left the flat the following day to be driven by Oumow to the railway station to begin my trip back to England – but even so, I still couldn't be absolutely sure that he wouldn't stop somewhere en route for another 'bit of fun'. Thankfully he didn't, but he did bring up again the question of a bombing in London. I told him that my present battle for control of British Movement, a legal political party, would not square easily with trying to carry out terror attacks, and that BM would be seriously damaged if I were caught. He was sympathetic but insisted nevertheless that something should be organized, and asked me to contact Tony Malski about the proposal when I got back to England.

This presented me with an extremely difficult dilemma. I knew that Oumow had himself been in touch with Malski at various times, so if I didn't pass on the message Oumow would quickly find out the next time he and Malski were in contact. Explaining such a lapse would be difficult and my standing on the right would be seriously compromised. On the other hand, I knew that Malski was quite wild enough to throw himself into such a scheme – and carry it out. The last thing I wanted to do was encourage him in a direction that might lead to tragic results.

In the end, after much discussion with my contacts at *Searchlight*, it was decided to pass on the message but in such a vague form that Malski might not understand its significance and might not bother to follow it up. I would tell him on the telephone so that later, if necessary, I could plead that the message had to be guarded, there being a strong possibility that his phone, or mine, or indeed both, were tapped by Special Branch. If the worst came to the worst and he did embark on this deadly escapade, we would try to sabotage the whole scheme by leaking it to the press. In the very last resort, if it were the only way to prevent a bloodbath, we would blow my cover and I would go public, exposing the plot that was being hatched.

I phoned Malski the day after I returned to England. After a very general chat about my trip, I casually dropped into the conversation: 'Oh, by the way, Alex wants you to get in touch sometime.'

But our first plan failed. Malski did get in touch with Oumow, and phoned me a few days later. I couldn't believe my ears as he told me – over the phone, despite the risks of interception – exactly what was being proposed. 'We're going to do Notting Hill,' he said. 'We've already got the geli, all we need now are the detonators. We'll give them a fucking carnival to remember.'

When we met several days later, he described the operation in almost exactly the same terms as had the fingerless madman in Paris: he was going to use someone dispensable 'to cover our tracks'. He already had someone in mind, he said, hinting that it would be a fellow NSAP member living nearby on the same housing estate. I couldn't help thinking that if using a neighbour was his idea of covering his tracks he wasn't going to last long, but I didn't say anything. It certainly wasn't for me to help him perfect his lunatic schemes. But the scale of his crazed designs became more alarming as he went on to describe how he planned to put two snipers in position on the roofs of buildings overlooking the Carnival. They were to open fire after the bomb exploded so that black people would believe the police were shooting at them and respond violently. 'We'll turn the niggers on the cops,' he said triumphantly. I tried to dampen his enthusiasm: 'Well, anyway, none of it's any good without detonators, is it?'

'No problem,' he replied. 'It's all fixed with Alex. I'm going to Paris to collect them.'

Not being the brightest, nor even the most security-conscious of Britain's small band of would-be führers, he even gave me the times that he was sailing from Dover on the approaching spring bank holiday weekend, thus presenting us with a heaven-sent opportunity to spike the whole operation with minimum risk to my cover, and at the same time have Malski taken out of circulation for a while. If he could be apprehended carrying detonators during an apparently random customs search at Dover we could kill several prize birds with one stone.

One of my *Searchlight* contacts duly made an approach to Special Branch, telling them that some sort of terrorist outrage was being planned, outlining Malski's involvement, and providing them with all the details of his trip to France. He was assured that the matter would be taken care of. Collectively, we breathed a considerable sigh of relief.

Then, the following Sunday night, Malski telephoned me. 'I'm back,' he said. I was incredulous, expecting him by now to be on remand facing serious charges. Trying to disguise my astonishment, I asked him guardedly if he had had a successful trip. He had. I concluded not unnaturally that he had brought the detonators into the country and was now planning to proceed with the outrage. What had happened to Special Branch's assurances that he would be dealt with, we were not to find out until nearly two years later when I managed to draw Malski out on the subject in a pub conversation that was being recorded for the Channel 4 television documentary. For the moment all we knew was that he was going ahead and we had to stop him.

After some thought we decided on a simple approach: we would give the story to a national newspaper and just hope against hope that I would not be uncovered as the source of the information. A few days before the carnival, the *Daily Mirror* carried 'Carnival Bomb Plot' all over its front page. Shadow Home Secretary Roy Hattersley piled in with demands for police action and a bewildered Tony Malski was left wondering what had hit him.

Not wanting to tempt fate too seriously, I didn't phone him, reasoning that I could always explain away my lack of interest as an elementary security precaution – something apparently lacking in certain quarters, I would add if necessary.

A few days after the story broke Malski telephoned me at home, obviously still fuming, and now swearing vengeance. He was going to 'fix *Searchlight*'. He didn't explain exactly what he had in mind but he asked me to travel to Birmingham to 'case' the *Searchlight* offices, which were then in Livery Street in the city centre. He particularly wanted to know about the movements of the editor, upon whom, I presumed, he planned to exact his revenge. I said I would.

I immediately phoned *Searchlight* and explained what was intended. Gerry didn't seem too put out. In fact, if anything he was rather amused, and told me to go ahead and do as Malski had asked. Well, I didn't think Malski should be taken so lightly, but I did as I was told. A couple of days later I travelled by train to Birmingham and duly took up position near the *Searchlight* office to watch and wait. It was only after several hours, with nobody arriving or leaving, that I ventured into the office building and asked the caretaker if anyone was expected in the *Searchlight* office that day. 'Oh no,' I was told, 'they moved out a week ago.'

I wasn't exactly overjoyed, having wasted a day standing around on a Birmingham street corner, but my friends at *Searchlight* thought it hilarious. By sheer coincidence they had decided to move office following the death a few months earlier of the magazine's editor Maurice Ludmer, who lived in Birmingham. Still, at least I could honestly report back to Malski that nothing could be done. He had picked just the wrong moment to try to get even.

Then he decided he was going to sue everybody in sight – *Searchlight*, the *Daily Mirror*, anyone for that matter who had repeated the Notting Hill story. I sniggered, pretending to be amused. 'Well, they can't fucking prove anything, can they?' he said.

In the end, he went only as far as the Press Council, complaining that he had been damaged by *Searchlight* calling him a psychopathic terrorist. Rejecting his complaint, the normally conservative Press Council concluded that, on the evidence, this seemed a perfectly reasonable description. In evidence the magazine had submitted a transcript of a telephone conversation which one of its reporters had with Malski just after the Notting Hill story broke. Posing as a journalist from a mercenary magazine, the reporter drew Malski into a very candid discussion about his paramilitary activities in Britain, and tape-recorded every word.

But if exposing the plot had been a setback for the people behind it, they obviously weren't completely discouraged from their endeavours. Only shortly afterwards Tony Malski phoned me again to tell me that the Vietnamese FNE member Yann Tran Long was in London and wanted to meet me. He gave me a telephone number where I could reach Yann in the evenings.

That same evening I contacted Yann and we arranged to meet a couple of days later at a Wimpy Bar in King's Cross, near the railway station where I would arrive from Leicester. Hurriedly, *Searchlight* journalists arranged for the meeting to be secretly photographed from the entrance to the neighbouring St Pancras Station which overlooked the café. Just to help the photographer, I met Yann in the street outside and gave him an especially flamboyant welcome, greeting him with my arms in the air like a long-lost brother. Yann responded in similar fashion and the photographer made no mistake – the meeting was recorded for posterity. Yann must have been more than a little surprised two years later to see us pictured together on television when the activities of his terror cell were exposed to the world.

But it wasn't just a social get-together – Yann had business to discuss, and had not been in the least discouraged by the failure of the Notting Hill plot. He was in the country studying English for about three months at a private language school and living in a bedsit in West London. He explained to me that he could supply weapons and explosives for British nazis if we needed them. Determined to nail him this time I tore a page from my address book and asked him for a price list. He duly put on paper, in his own handwriting, prices for detonators, sub-machine guns and ammunition, adding yet another piece of hard evidence to the dossier we were building up on his group's activities.

A week or so later I joined Yann, Malski and a couple of Malski's NSAP thugs at a meeting in London organized by WISE (Welsh Irish Scots and English), an anti-immigration group quite influential amongst certain Conservative Party MPs. The guest speaker was a West Indian who had been converted to the idea that blacks should be repatriated from Britain and who, as a result, was being patronized and touted round the country by people who inwardly loathed and hated him. Tony Malski, never well-known for his subtlety, responded to his appeal for repatriation with the immortal words, 'Well, lead the way then, you fucking nigger. Fuck off home yourself.'

After the meeting I had a chance to chat with Yann, who had been visited at his West London digs only a few days previously by Special Branch officers. He found the whole episode highly entertaining. They had searched his room, but failed to find a box of detonators which he had hidden under the bed. He joked that if this was the quality of Britain's 'political police' we would have no serious problems from them.

Yann was rather upset on this occasion, having only just heard of the recent death, of a close friend and comrade, Klaus Uhl, of the German nazi group VSBD. He had been killed in a gunfight with Munich police during an attempted night-time bank raid. A tax consultant in his mid-twenties, Uhl was in the forefront of German nazis who believed that they would only achieve their ends by force of arms. He had carried out a series of fund-raising armed robberies for nazi groups in both Germany and France, and was an important link-man between the FNE and the VSBD to which he belonged. When in France he would always stay at the flat of Yann Tran Long and the two men had become firm friends.

Yann told me he had been travelling around. As well as Malski, he had visited Major Ian Souter Clarence in Dorset (the man who had organized the joint training camps which, Alex Oumow had told me in Brighton, had been attended by FNE members) and Tony Hancock, the man whose invitation to me to spend a weekend at his

Brighton home had opened all these doors into Yann's terrorist world. Hancock had tried to persuade him to infiltrate an anti-nazi group in Brighton, taking advantage of his Asian appearance, but he had not been able to stay in the town long enough to carry out this particular little mission.

I asked him if he had had a good response to his offers of hardware for British nazis. He smiled and nodded, exchanging knowing winks with Malski. Malski, a man prepared to stop at nothing, had, it transpired, taken the detonators, which I could only conclude had now joined the gelignite and the weapons he had obtained from the armoury raid and were hidden, as he had boasted to me, in woodland somewhere near Watford.

It was at about this time that Malski asked me to become leader of the NSAP. After consultations with *Searchlight* it was decided that I should refuse: moves were already in hand to try to regroup the far right around John Tyndall's New National Front, which would later merge with a section of British Movement and the British Democratic Party into a new party. We felt it was important that I should try to involve myself in this at the earliest stages and at as high a level a possible. I was ideally placed, as McLaughlin's main opponent in British Movement, to lead any significant defection to Tyndall, giving the kiss of death to BM at the same time as placing myself in the leadership of the new outfit.

Malski was extremely put out when I turned down his offer. He became sulky and would not even speak to me for some time. Thankfully, all the adverse publicity which I had brought down upon him seemed to have cooled his terrorist ardour a little, and, to date, there have been no terrorist outrages in Britain such as those he was trying to organize. Even so, I still cannot understand why he remains at liberty. If left-wing terrorists had been planning what he intended they would be facing thirty-year sentences for conspiracy by now. He seems to have some sort of charmed life.

Yann Tran Long was not quite so fortunate. After I had paid him another visit while filming *The Other Face of Terror*, our information about the activities of his Paris flat was passed on, via anti-fascists in Paris, to the French government, and the building was raided by police. They arrested a Spanish nazi, Juan Lorenzo Martinez, wanted in Spain for a double murder and on the run. He was quickly extradited. That particular terror network would never be the same again.

One of my most successful achievements, but also one of the most disappointing, was in connection with another British paramilitary group, Column 88, run by private detective Les Vaughan. I had come to know him well during our mutual association with Tony Reed Herbert's British Democratic Party, and he had obviously developed a high regard both for my abilities and my ostensible commitment. Column 88 was a long-established underground group which boasted that it had recruited, and controlled, many of the leaders of overt nazi groups in Britain. A recruitment cassette tape, given to new members who had passed its rigorous selection and screening procedures, claimed that John Tyndall himself was a Column 88 man. As well as attempting to direct the efforts of public nazi groups by recruiting its leaders, and establishing its own 'intelligence gathering' facilities, it was heavily involved in paramilitary training.

One such enterprise, which had been exposed in *Searchlight*, was a joint training camp which had been held in conjunction with the League of St George in

November 1975. In charge of this were Birmingham British Movement leader Peter Marriner, Les Vaughan, a Manchester prison officer called Brian Baldwin, and Don Mudie, a fanatical Hitlerite with a handlebar moustache and monocle, who liked nothing better than parading around in full stormtrooper uniform and coal scuttle helmet.

Obtaining more information on 88 was always high on my list of priorities, but so secretive was the group that it was a major success when, in 1981, Les Vaughan invited me to join. I was issued with a membership card and told to await instructions.

Unfortunately this came only shortly before Reed Herbert and Vaughan were exposed so embarrassingly on *World in Action*. The former fled to Ireland, and Vaughan hurriedly dropped all of his dubious activities. Some months later, I made contact with Vaughan to tell him I was still awaiting instructions and was eager to be of assistance. 'Forget it for the time,' he replied, 'I'm keeping my nose clean. I don't want to end up living in Ireland like that other daft bugger.' And this was still the case when, two years later, my true story was told on Channel 4.

9

The Men who Rewrite History

Throughout the whole of the post-war period, the biggest obstacle which fascist and neo-nazi movements have had to face has been their own history. Quite rightly, the regimes of Hitler and Mussolini are held responsible for the conflict which led to death and destruction on an unprecedented scale, and which engulfed the whole world. But the blame goes deeper than mere responsibility for starting war. While allied and nazi armies were engaged to determine whether democracy in Europe should survive, behind the lines the Hitler regime was fighting another war: its race war against the Jews and other '*untermenschen*'.

It now seems clear that some news of what was taking place behind the barbed wire around death camps like Auschwitz and Treblinka did reach the allies before the war ended. For whatever reason, those camps were not destroyed, as they might have been, by allied bombing. It was only when the camps were liberated by British, Red Army and American troops that the full horror of Hitler's genocide programme was revealed to the world at large. An estimated six million Jews – along with socialists, communists, homosexuals, gypsies, the disabled, and others considered 'inferior' by the nazis – went to their deaths in those camps, and the images of emaciated, disease-ridden survivors, photographed and filmed by the liberating allied armies, are a permanent reminder of the genocidal logic of national socialism.

Or are they? There can be no doubt that for the thirty

years since the war closed, those images as much as anything else have led to such a deep and widespread hatred of national socialism that the re-emergence of such movements seemed a prospect only in the imaginations of the small bands of disciples who remained faithful to the creed. Many millions of people had also lost members of their families or risked their own lives in the defeat of Hitler, and were unlikely ever to be attracted by the ideology which had set the world at war.

All of this was well understood by extremist groups which have nevertheless survived on the fringes of political life ever since. But as a generation reached adulthood which had had no direct experience of the conflagration, which had been born and brought up in the post-war era, so latter-day nazis realized that there were new opportunities available to build themselves once again into significant political movements. The key lay in how successful they could be in challenging the historical record, which after all was the only concrete evidence available to new generations of nazism's culpability in the Second World War, and its attempt to commit genocide against the Jews. Out of this thinking was born 'historical revisionism', nothing less than an attempt to rewrite history in favour of the Third Reich.

For more than two decades, nascent nazi groups had plugged away at the notion that the Nuremberg Trials, where nazi leaders were accused of war crimes and crimes against humanity, were a travesty of justice. But memories were still too fresh for this to cut much ice. And anyway, the facts of the Holocaust were beyond dispute. In 1969, the first tentative effort to challenge the basis of the Nuremberg retribution, and the facts of the nazis' crimes, appeared in a booklet, written anonymously, called *The Myth of the Six Million*. It was published by

Noontide Press, an offshoot of Willis Carto's Liberty Lobby in America. Five years later it was followed by *Did Six Million Really Die?* written by 'Richard Harwood', and published by the Hancocks' Historical Review Press in Brighton. This was printed in runs of many thousands and in several languages, and was distributed widely throughout Europe, the United States, and the Middle East. It was the first major propaganda offensive to challenge the truth of the Holocaust, and was to spawn a whole far-right industry in the next few years.

Putting up the money for the Hancocks was a Warwickshire landowner and businessman called Robin Beauclaire. A stalwart right-wing extremist for more than thirty years, he was among those who set up the Racial Preservation Society in the 1960s and was a leading light in the NF when it was launched in 1967. When American Ku Klux Klan leader David Dukes visited Britain in 1978, Beauclaire generously provided a hillside on his Chapel Ascot farm for a Klan cross-burning ceremony attended by West Midlands NF and British Movement members. Beauclaire, apparently, was highly amused when one of Dukes's BM 'minders' produced a Kalashnikov rifle from beneath his German-style great-coat. When *Did Six Million Really Die?* appeared it was published from his farm, where the Historical Review Press printing press was at the time installed. Later it was moved to the Hancocks' premises in Brighton and, later again, to a small factory unit on an industrial estate in Uckfield, Sussex.

Beauclaire died in 1981, but by this time Anthony Hancock had firmly assumed the reins. It was he who travelled the world setting up new deals with the network of nazi 'revisionist' writers who all wanted to chip in with their contribution to demolishing the Holocaust 'myth'. When I got to know him in the early 1980s, he was making regular trips to Scandinavia, West Germany and the United States, and was a central figure in the burgeoning revisionist publishing empire.

But it is not just revisionist literature which tumbled from Hancock's presses: he also served as printer to virtually the entire British far right. With a degree of non-sectarianism rarely found in such quarters, he produced newspapers, magazines and booklets for the NF, British Movement and the League of St George, and for many years he has printed *Spearhead*, owned privately by John Tyndall and published 'in support of' whichever group he happens to be involved with at the time.

In addition to printing, HRP offered a comprehensive book sales service to the extreme right. In 1980, for instance, their cyclostyled wholesale lists included such nazi bibles as Hitler's *Mein Kampf*, *The Programme of the Nazi Party*, and William 'Lord Haw Haw' Joyce's *Twilight over England*. But it did not confine itself to national socialist nostalgia: also for sale were US army manuals on topics such as *Incendiaries*, *Booby Traps*, *Unconventional Warfare Devices*, and *Improvised Munitions*, which became widely distributed to young right-wing thugs through the various parties. They were supplied, for instance, to National Front and British Movement branches and to the League of St George, and were constantly available on bookstalls at events organized by these groups.

Did Six Million Really Die? was one of Hancock's all-time money-spinners, with thousands of copies sold all over the world. The scale of its distribution was finally revealed when the author – in fact, former NF deputy chairman Richard Verrall – sued Hancock for unpaid royalties in the High Court in 1982. His writ disclosed that the booklet had been sold in the UK, America, Eire,

Germany, France, Holland, Belgium, Italy, South Africa, South America, Norway, Sweden and Denmark.

Hancock himself is a hard-line nazi with an inclination towards populism which led him to line up with the doomed National Party splinter group in 1976. He has not made the same mistake since. In 1981 he was generally supportive of Tony Reed Herbert's 'populist' approach with the British Democratic Party, but stopped short of openly backing it. He and Reed Herbert did, however, become close friends, and spent weekends shooting together on the Leicester solicitor's Welsh farm. Even then, in the early days of John Tyndall's split from the NF, he correctly judged Tyndall to be a spent force, and while continuing to print *Spearhead* and Tyndall's New National Front paper at favourable rates, refrained from offering further support.

For Martin Webster, then leading what was left of the NF, he had nothing but contempt but, again, carried on publishing NF literature at preferred rates. In 1981 Hancock confided to me that Webster was believed to have 'defected to the Jews', and that 'somebody has been brought in from Europe to deal with him'. Whatever had been planned was foiled, however, by round-the-clock protection afforded to the NF leader by the Special Branch.

If anything, Hancock's sympathy was for British Movement. Michael McLaughlin he considered to be no more than a figure of ridicule, but he told me that BM's hardened young members would be the basis of a future Brownshirt Brigade modelled on the SA. BM, he said, 'contains the nucleus of youngsters who will be indispensable in the forthcoming battle to control the streets. The niggers must be as afraid of our youth as the Jews were of the Brownshirts.' He was anxious that McLaughlin should

be dumped, and offered to print literature for me at
heavily discounted rates if I would use it to mount a
serious challenge for the leadership of BM.

He was convinced, however, that the efforts being put
into historical revisionism should be kept quite separate
from the activities of any 'populist' right-wing group, and
was determined that the Historical Review Press would
remain totally under his own control. One project about
which he confided to me in advance was the publication
of a pamphlet called *Christianity: a religion for sheep*,
which, he claimed, would 'expose the Jewish conspiratorial nature of Christianity'. Sure enough, the pamphlet
began to be distributed only a few months later bearing
the fictitious author's name Ralph Perrier. But Hancock
had already told me that it was written by Revilo P.
Oliver, a notorious American right-winger who had been
expelled from the John Birch Society for the virulence of
his anti-semitic views. He had announced on radio that
the world's problems would be over if 'the Jews were
vaporized at dawn'. Needless to say he wrote often and
angrily that the Holocaust was but a Jewish hoax.

It was during my visit to Hancock's Brighton house in
1981 that I managed to discover who was behind the
publication of a nazi comic, *The Stormer*, which led to
prosecutions under the Race Relations Act later in the
year. Also staying at the house was Jimmy Styles, whose
activities I have recounted elsewhere. He had travelled
from London quite specifically to discuss with Hancock
the production of *The Stormer*, which was to be a cartoon-
style comic which would deliver a revisionist and pro-nazi
message to young schoolchildren. Also backing it was
Robert Relf, and the cartoons had been drawn by Robert
Edwards, who had done similar work for the League of
St George journal *League Review*. Edwards was eventu-

ally imprisoned for his part in what turned out to be one of the most pernicious pieces of anti-semitic propaganda to appear in many years. Bundles of copies were left at school gates in several towns and cities and it was this, as much as anything, which led to loud public demands for prosecutions. The paper on which it was printed had, it seemed, been stolen by a British Movement member in the East End of London. Although Styles discussed printing with Hancock, Relf later told me that while Hancock had done the layout and made the plates, the paper had in fact been run off on the presses of the Spanish nazi group CEDADE in Barcelona.

Another attempt to get revisionism into schools was made in 1980, when British Movement launched a series of broadsheets called *Fact Finder*. The first issue featured a major article denying that the massacre of Jews by Germany had occurred. Like *The Stormer*, it was aimed specifically at the impressionable minds of young school-children. Like almost all of BM's literature, it was produced on Anthony Hancock's presses.

Hancock's network of revisionist colleagues spanned the globe, and in the course of our many conversations I was able to identify who his main collaborators were.

In Sweden he works closely with Dietlieb Felderer, a crazed former Jehovah's Witness who publishes *Bible Researcher* from Taby near Stockholm. Austrian-born, he somehow manages to produce a veritable torrent of anti-semitic leaflets and booklets which he mails free to thousands of horrified recipients all over the world. The Holocaust is his favourite obsession; he calls it 'The 6 million race hate swindle'. Perhaps his most grotesque operation was to run guided tours to concentration camp sites in Germany and Poland where he would 'show you the fakes'. His leaflets, distributed outside Swedish schools, told children, 'Don't believe your teachers: they are lying about Hitler.' It was this sort of propaganda directed at young minds that finally moved the Swedish authorities to prosecute and imprison him in 1984.

In Germany, Hancock dealt especially with three neo-nazi writers: Udo Walendy, Thies Christopherson and Manfred Roeder. Christopherson wrote a seminal 'revisionist' work called *The Auschwitz Lie*, which was distributed widely in Britain through Hancock's Historical Review Press.

Roeder, leader of the Citizen's Initiative and Teutonic Unity groups in Germany, received even more direct assistance. When he wanted to sue a Jewish newspaper in England for accusing him of having been a guard at a concentration camp, it was Hancock who arranged a British solicitor – Anthony Reed Herbert, inevitably – to prepare his case. Roeder visited Hancock during his several trips to the UK, and through his travels to meet expatriate nazis and war criminals in South America, was an important link between the old nazis and the new. In 1982 he was gaoled for thirteen years for terrorist offences after being found guilty of participating in bomb attacks on Vietnamese immigrant hostels in West Germany. Two people died when Roeder's underground squad, the 'German Action Group', blew up eight buildings in 1981. Udo Walendy, himself a major German proponent of revisionism, was responsible for importing and distribution *Did Six Million Really Die?* in West Germany. He was also involved in German editions of several other works published by the Historical Review Press.

A former executive committee member of the neo-nazi NPD, he specializes in trying to prove that photographs of concentration camps and their victims were faked, and he runs his own 'Revisionist Historian' publishing company through which much of his business with Hancock is conducted.

But far and away the most lucrative market for revisionist enterprises is the United States and when, during the production of *The Other Face of Terror*, I was asked which was the most important operator, beside the Hancocks, to investigate, I unhesitatingly answered, 'the Institute for Historical Review'.

Based in Torrence, California, IHR was the joint creation of two men: Dave McCalden from Northern Ireland and an American called Willis Carto, who had written the unsigned introduction to *The Myth of the Six Million*. In the early 1970s, McCalden had made something of a name for himself as a bright young thing in the National Front. Very quickly, while still a university student, he had become editor of the party newspaper, then called *Britain First*, upon which he stamped his own 'radical' Strasserite mark. When party chairman John Kingsley Read led a breakaway in 1976 to form the National Party, McCalden joined him – as did Anthony Hancock and Steve Brady. But the NP came to nothing and when it collapsed less than two years later McCalden emigrated to America to team up with Willis Carto, leader of the long-standing anti-semitic organization Liberty Lobby. At McCalden's suggestion, Carto agreed to launch IHR as a major exercise in trying to establish the academic credentials of theories which disputed widely-held truths about the Hitler period. It was not just the truth or falsity about the Holocaust itself which IHR was to insist was open to challenge, but other questions like the war guilt attaching to the allied bombing of German cities; whether the entire war was the fault, not of Hitler, but of Jews determined to destroy him; whether Churchill was in the pay of the Jews; and whether Britain and America should not have made an alliance with Hitler and struck east to destroy the Soviet Union. Of course, the Holocaust and the death camps are still a major target (and even *Anne Frank's Diary* has been denounced as a forgery), but the whole history of the inter-war period was also to be reappraised from a pro-Hitler point of view.

Central to the success of this ambitious project, however, was the involvement of respectable academics in the disputes which IHR wanted to open up. A number of revisionists who had been ploughing individual furrows were assembled together at Northrop University for the first IHR Annual Conference in 1979.

Present were:

Arthur Butz, a Professor of Electrical Engineering at North-Western University, Illinois, who had written *The Hoax of the 20th Century*, disputing that the Holocaust took place;

Robert Faurisson, Professor of History at the University of Lyons, who also disputes the truth about the Holocaust;

John Bennett, Secretary of the Victoria Council for Civil Liberties in Australia, who has publicly supported the views of Faurisson.

All of these participants were highly prized by the conference organizers because of the academic or respectable credentials which they might be seen to confer upon the Institute. Alongside them were people like Udo Walendy and Austin J. App, the subtlety of whose thought is perhaps expressed in the titles of some of his books: *Can Christianity Survive when the Jews control the media and the money?*, *Ravishing the women of conquered Europe*, and *Kosher food racket exposed*!

Only months later, to keep up the momentum of

establishing itself as an academic force to be reckoned with, IHR launched its own magazine, the *Journal of Historical Review*, in which the papers delivered at the inaugural conference were reproduced. It has since become a regular publication.

Arthur Butz presents us with a particularly strong link back to the Hancocks' operation in Brighton. When his book, *The Hoax of the 20th Century*, appeared in Britain, it was published by the Hancocks' Historical Review Press. And, interviewed on *The Other Face of Terror*, former National Front chairman John Kingsley Read revealed how, sitting down to dinner with Hancock, he had personally designed the motif (a swastika intertwined with a Star of David) which appeared on the cover.

The Institute's conference has now become an annual event, and has succeeded in drawing ever-bigger audiences to its proceedings. Its central preoccupations can be summarized as follows:

– that the Jews and not Germany started the Second World War;
– that Hitler was really only an anti-communist defending civilization from communism;
– that the Holocaust did not happen, and evidence that it did has been fabricated to justify reparation payments from Germany to Israel;
– that the real atrocities were committed by the Allies, for instance in the bombing of Hamburg and Dresden;
– that the USA was forced into the war by the Jews, and collaborated with communism in enslaving half of Europe.

But it is not so confident of its case that it is prepared to allow its proceedings to be public. When Ludi Boeken's film crew arrived at a Los Angeles hotel to film its 1983 conference, the IHR's organizers went into a blind panic and called security guards to throw them out. Robert Faurisson refused to answer questions at all and began legal proceedings in France when he was shown at the conference in the finished programme. Film of scenes shot secretly over the shoulder of one of the conference security guards was the first time that the IHR had been thrown open to public gaze, and their furious reaction is perhaps a measure of how much their claim to academic standards and respectability is just a ploy to peddle a message with a quite sinister political intent.

The 1983 conference allowed the IHR to parade their biggest catch to date: the star attraction was none other than the well-known British historian of the Hitler period, David Irving.

Now, while Irving states unequivocally that he does not share their view that the Holocaust never happened, he did provoke an enormous public controversy in 1977 with the publication of his book *Hitler's War*. In it he argues that although the murder of Jews in Hitler's Germany did take place, Hitler himself knew nothing about it. The mass killings were the responsibility of his subordinates who concealed from him that they were being carried out. Irving has even gone so far as to offer a reward for anyone who can prove that the Führer either ordered or knew of the extermination programme.

The IHR made much of Irving's appearance at their 1983 Anaheim proceedings, where his audience included Ku Klux Klan leaders and a bevy of far more uncompromising 'revisionists' than Irving himself. One contributor, H. Keith Thompson, earned a rapturous ovation when he exhorted the audience to 'Stand by the Third Reich. Stand by the Holocaust – whether imaginary or real. And if it was real, so much the better.' He expressed the eternal dilemma of Hitler's latter-day admirers. They are never really sure whether to deny the Holocaust or defend it.

At the time, Irving was deeply involved in trying to establish his own 'new right' political movement in the UK which, in its embryonic form, took the name of the Focus Policy Study Group. His ambitions were well known. Over many years he had made it quite clear in press and television interviews that he nursed political aspirations. From the start he had been more than a historian, and when, in 1958, as a student at Imperial College, he had edited the student magazine *Phoenix* and a rag magazine called *Carnival Times*, it was pretty clear that his views were well to the right. He said, for instance, the Notting Hill riots of 1958 had been started by 'coloured wide boys with knives'. He announced his belief that Britain had fought on the wrong side in the Second World War ('against the first great unifying force Europe has known in 600 years'), and there was a hint of the future when he said that 'we need a leader in this land; we need a leader in Europe. A leader who can rise above the pettiness of party politics, a leader who has the courage to do what he thinks will serve the future of Europe and the Nation best.'

These views, of course, would have remained buried in the past had not Irving himself sprung to international prominence in the mid-1970s with *Hitler's War*. Earlier works like *The Destruction of Dresden* and *The Destruction of Convoy PQ 17* had earned him a certain reputation for his anti-Churchill sentiments (and the latter volume cost him £40,000 in damages after a successful libel action by the convoy's commander) but it was *Hitler's War*, with its controversial claim that Hitler knew nothing of the

Jewish extermination programme, that firmly established him as a public figure.

It was with this reputation fixed, and with his earnings from sales of *Hitler's War* and subsequent books, that the Focus Policy Study Group was launched in 1980 as the precursor to a fully-fledged party of 'the new right' to be led by David Irving himself.

The preparatory moves were made through a small, informal dining group called the Clarendon Club. If Irving's intention was to draw in figures from the respectable right, it was in no way apparent from the guest list at the first dinners in 1979 and 1980.

On 30 March 1979, the Clarendon Club met at the Portman Hotel in London to hear Irving speak, according to one report, 'of the perfidy of Churchill and how the allies had lied about the Holocaust'. His audience consisted mainly of League of St George activists including Lucy Roberts (whose home is used by the League for its annual Hitler birthday parties), Robin Rushton, Tony Creese, and Mike Griffin. Also present was the far right's paramilitary 'godfather' Ian Souter Clarence and a couple of extremist former Monday Club members, part of the crowd expelled for infiltration in 1972, who had clearly been invited by John Ormowe who was at the time acting as Irving's *aide de camp*. Ormowe, himself expelled from the Monday Club, was, of course, the cousin of my terrorist acquaintance, the French nazi Alex Oumow. The high point of the meeting was Irving's announcement that he was starting a small study group to look at the possibilities of launching a new political party. And he appealed to those present for their support.

John Ormowe was in the chair when the second meeting took place at the Ecclestone Hotel in early 1980. This time a premium was put on security arrangements, and

Ian Souter Clarence turned up with a team of heavies which he called 'The Unit'. One of them, then a British Movement member, was Tony Malski. Again, Irving's audience contained many League of St George members, who this time included Steve Brady, the League's international liaison officer.

It was almost a year later, before a right-wing audience at the Europa Hotel, that Irving finally announced the establishment of his new group. With Ormowe in the chair beside him, he told his admirers that it would be known as the Focus Policy Study Group.

Irving threw himself energetically into promoting this vehicle for his own 'destiny'. A couple of months later there appeared the first edition of his journal *Focal Point*, and he himself embarked upon a speaking tour of British university campuses where he intended to recruit 'brains' who could later be expected to hold positions of importance in their chosen careers.

Focal Point declared itself to be 'a new beginning for the New Right', and subscribers were told that they would 'not only be buying the magazine but helping to launch an unusual venture on a broad front'. It began to appear more or less regularly, reached a print run, Irving claimed, of 2,000 in 1981, and at its peak was being published twice a month. Much interest was raised, not unnaturally, by a series of exclusive articles by Irving himself, based upon his researches, which claimed to throw new light on various curious episodes in history. For instance, he revealed for the first time that Mosley's British Union of Fascists had been directly funded by Mussolini. Other articles, on the entry of the United States into the Second World War, and on Churchill, reflected long-standing favourite themes in revisionist circles.

Irving was not shy of acknowledging his affinity with that tradition, which has usually been associated with neonazism. In *Focal Point* he proudly proclaimed his 'crusade of historical revisionism' and told readers of his visit to the Liberty Lobby headquarters of IHR leader Willis Carto. Carto he criticized for allowing Liberty Lobby's link with the IHR to 'call down unnecessary fire . . .' and Irving was particularly critical of McCalden's preoccupation with the Holocaust, which he said was 'of purely academic interest to historians, and of no relevance whatever to modern European, let alone British, problems'. But for Carto's newspaper, *Spotlight*, with its reputation for blunt anti-semitism, Irving had nothing but praise, describing it as 'excellent'.

At least occasional contacts were also admitted with Britain's own revisionist publishers, Anthony Hancock's Historical Review Press. After their print shop was destroyed in an arson attack in 1980, Irving reported the subsequent court case in *Focal Point*. Without revealing that the pro-nazi Hancock was 'the print shop proprietor, he quoted him as having 'told *Focal Point*' that 'we are politically libertarian ourselves, we are prepared to print commercially for any lawful organization that pays us to do so'.

But none of this revealed just how deep the relationship went. Many of Irving's more respectable supporters would have been shocked to learn that *Focal Point* was actually being printed by the Historical Review Press, a fact which was never disclosed in the magazine itself. Its imprimatur only ever declared that it was 'published by Focal Point, Suite 411, 70 Shoe Lane, London EC4'. Whether Hancock was offering favourable rates to subsidize Irving's political efforts is not known, but clearly something was attractive enough to tempt the historian into a commercial relationship which, had it become known at the time, would surely have damaged him in the eyes of some of his Conservative admirers. And the fact that he did not, as is normal practice, disclose in the magazine who the printers were suggests that he too was alive to the potentially embarrassing consquences of such a link.

At the time Irving was advertising for 'lists of right-wing names' which he was willing to purchase from 'patriotic' officials and secretaries of right-wing groups. Curiously, in December 1981 he sent out complimentary copies of *Focal Point* to individuals on the Historical Review Press mailing list – a fact established by *Searchlight*, who had entered a fictitious name on HRP's lists in order to receive its literature. This particular name and address was used only to subscribe to HRP, but it became a recipient also of 'mailshots' from David Irving. Other groups whose membership lists found their way into Irving's hands included WISE and the Federation of Conservative Students.

Focal Point became very much a sort of bulletin board for the extreme right, and carried advertisements for a wide range of racist and nazi-controlled groups. WISE and Tory Action, for instance, were often publicized in its pages, as were journals like *Excalibur* (published by the National Front Constitutional Movement), *Sussex Vanguard* (by Brighton National Front) and *National Democrat* (another 'new right' venture published by a London member of the NF). The letters columns were dominated by items sent in by known members of nazi groups and, indeed, two letters which I wrote to Irving while I was a leading activist in the British National Party were printed without a murmur.

As well as his speaking engagements in British universities (which were frequently disrupted or cancelled following protests) Irving busied himself with lecture tours abroad, most notably in West Germany, where he associated himself closely with the German People's Union run by Dr Gerhard Frey. This group organized entire tours for the 'Britische Historiker' and plugged him heavily in their journals. The DVU, however, has rather more hardline views on the Holocaust than Irving; their newspaper *National-Zeitung* serialized Arthur Butz's book *The Hoax of the 20th Century* under the headline 'The truth about Hitler's concentration camps'. Another DVU group, the *Gesellschaft für Freie Publizistik*, which arranged a series of lectures featuring Irving in 1979, reviewed Butz's book in the same year and concluded that any reader 'will find it difficult to believe in mass murders at Auschwitz'.

But Irving's slowly growing venture in Britain was beginning to concern some of his far-right competitors. They were obviously attracted by the audience he had established for revisionist ideas, even if he would not go so far in denouncing the Holocaust 'myth' as many of them would have liked, and they were clearly impressed by the potential which he was displaying in successfullly involving a small group of Conservative MPs in informal Focus activities.

They were worried, however, that he might undermine their own efforts to build new organizations after the débâcle of the NF split, especially when his views on race and immigration were considered to fall considerably short of what was required. He had refused to back, for instance, the notion of compulsory repatriation, although he conceded the need to reduce the size of Britain's black communities and proposed to do it through schemes of voluntary or 'benevolent' repatriation. After many letters on this matter had been received by *Focal Point*, Irving did move some way towards meeting the desires of the constituency he was aiming at: he wrote that benevolent repatriation was only the first step in dealing with the problem and 'does not preclude the introduction of a compulsory repatriation programme' in the future.

Column 88 boss Les Vaughan, trying in 1981 to sew up control of Tony Reed Herbert's British Democratic Party by making Reed Herbert financially dependent upon him, was particularly concerned that Irving's progress was undermining the BDP's 'respectability' strategy by providing an even more attractive and influential alternative. This was behind his growing antagonism towards Anthony Hancock, whom he believed was supporting Irving's efforts. John Tyndall, with whom I was in almost daily touch in 1982, was equally concerned that his only recently launched British National Party would suffer from Irving's efforts when he put out informal feelers to Irving in May 1982. Tyndall told me that he was anxious not to sit back and let Irving make the running, as they were both trying to address essentially the same audience. However, simply to launch into an attack on the historian, using his 'soft' views on repatriation to lever racist support away from him, might easily have been seen in some quarters as infantile, given the strides that Irving was making. He proposed, therefore, to engage in ostensibly friendly debate with Irving, where he could mark out the differences between them without antagonizing grassroots right-wingers who felt there might be potential in Focus.

Irving had already agreed, Tyndall told me, to carry a letter from Tyndall in a later edition of *Focal Point*, where the BNP leader would take issue with Irving's Europeanism. And sure enough, the following month, a letter along those very lines appeared in *Focal Point*. Tyndall quickly dropped this idea, however, when he realized that his followers might see such an approach as conferring a seal of approval on Irving and Focus and be more ready to drift away from the BNP. Instead, he decided to ignore Irving's efforts and hope for an early demise of his group. At that stage it was quite clear that the historian was still having to underwrite *Focus* from his literary earnings and was struggling to reach break-even point. Tyndall concluded, and was eventually proved right, that Irving's ability to subsidize his political work would collapse before Focus could fund itself and he would be forced to abandon the whole project.

This stage was effectively reached by mid-1983 when the last issue of *Focal Point* appeared. Irving's standing on the right, however, was still considerable and, as we have seen, the Institute for Historical Review considered it a major coup when he agreed to address their conference that September in Los Angeles. They believed, not without justification, that his attendance would help bring them in from the academic cold.

Revisionism, it had been decided, was to be a major theme of *The Other Face of Terror* and both the Historical Review Press and the Institute had been identified as well-springs in this area. It seemed logical therefore that some attention should be paid to David Irving.

I made contact with Irving in the summer of 1983 through the man then acting as his secretary, Robin Davies. Davies had a colourful political background himself, and when some of his associations (he was sharing a flat with a wanted Italian terrorist) were disclosed in *Searchlight* a few months later, Irving was a little put out. They parted company soon afterwards. It was clear that my simply attending Irving's Focus Policy Study Group meetings – even those private ones held in his Mayfair flat – would not add significantly to our knowledge of him.

Searchlight had already succeeded in penetrating those events and were monitoring activity at that level. For any contact to be useful, I had to meet him on a one-to-one basis.

I had already had letters published in *Focal Point* in February and May of that year, one taking to task those who criticized 'extremists' on the right, and the other admitting my attendance at the neo-nazi rally in Diksmuide, Belgium. Even before my approach, therefore, he could have been under no illusions as to where I stood, and in any event he followed the right-wing scene quite closely enough to be aware of my leading position in the British National Party. I invited him to Leicester in the summer of 1983 to address a meeting of BNP activists and he readily agreed.

By arrangement, we dined together at the Central Hotel in Leicester prior to the meeting, which was to be held in the hotel's conference room. It turned out that Irving was familiar with my role in the BNP, and indeed he congratulated me upon my performance as BNP candidate in the recently-held General Election. After the usual introductory small talk about his journey and his health I plunged into the the question of 'the six million'. Surprisingly perhaps, he showed no reluctance at all in discussing the issue, and told me bluntly, 'The figure is ridiculous.' Pushing my luck a little, I pressed him further.

Why, if that were the case, and if he could substantiate it, did he not publish the facts as he saw them? After all, I said, the story of six million murdered Jews was the single main obstacle to the progress of national socialist ideas ever since the war. A refutation from someone of his scholarly reputation could have a tremendous impact. He listened with what appeared to be amused tolerance. 'The time still isn't right,' he said. Why not, I wanted to

know, and if six million were not killed, how many, if
any, actually were?

'There may have been a million or so,' he replied.

I looked at him quizzically. 'But surely a million deaths
would be enough to cause public revulsion?' Why should
Jews risk being caught out inflating the figures if Irving's
'true' figure would itself be enough to have the desired
effect? Why tell a lie when the truth would do just as
well?

Irving sat back in his chair and smiled. Did I know
anything about the attempted genocide of the Armenian
people by the Turks, he asked me. I said I had never
heard of it. 'Exactly,' he replied, a little triumphantly,
and went on to explain that the reason I knew nothing
about it was because the total number of people killed
had 'only' been about a million. 'History,' he declared, 'is
littered with such incidents.' If it had been admitted that
only about one million Jews had died in the Holocaust,
then the whole affair would have begun to fade from the
memory of the world just as the massacre of the Armeni-
ans had done. The Holocaust issue had to be kept alive as
it was still the main source of income for the state of
Israel, and provided political and diplomatic *carte blanche*
for Israel to behave however it pleased in the Middle
East.

He reiterated strongly the pet far-right theme that
communism is essentially Jewish, and drew my attention
to the main thesis of his book, *Rising!*, about the Hungar-
ian uprising of 1956, that the anti-communist revolution
was also firmly anti-Jewish in nature, thus demonstrating
the predominance of Jews in communist governments and
movements.

We had about an hour and a half together before the
meeting was scheduled to start and our conversation

ranged over the whole spectrum of far-right politics. A couple of months earlier I had entertained Keith Thomson of the League of St George at the same hotel, and he had claimed to be secretly helping Irving in the production of *Focal Point*. I asked Irving if he knew him, but I was not really surprised at his somewhat guarded response. 'I believe I may have met him,' he told me. Clearly I still had a way to go before I was taken completely into his confidence but, even so, to someone he was meeting for the first time he had already been remarkably candid. If I could strike up a long-standing relationship with him, I reasoned, it could be very profitable indeed. This, unfortunately, was not to be.

The meeting itself was attended by about forty people, most of them BNP members, with a few refugees from Reed Herbert's British Democratic Party who had yet to find a new political home. Irving's chosen subject was 'The New Right', and echoed his views in *Focal Point* about the need for a new departure on the right and for new leadership. It struck me, however, that for someone as clear about his 'destiny' as Irving, he was still remarkably unsure about the track his new group should be taking. In particular he seemed torn between, on the one hand, using a bridging organization to secure a foothold in the Conservative Party and, on the other, giving up the Tories as a lost cause and seeking support among the established extremist groups outside the Tory Party, whose members might quite easily be prised away from their tin-pot leaders by an appeal from someone of rather more stature. I am convinced that it was his inability to make up his mind about exactly what he was trying to do in the short term to establish the basis of his new movement that led to its demise in 1983. That its collapse coincided with his own financial problems is clear, but had he struck out in one direction or the other at a much earlier stage, he just may have laid organizational foundations sound enough that his own problems would not have made the difference between carrying on and becoming extinct. As it was, the whole enterprise ground to a halt and was abandoned.

I was convinced when we met that the reason he refused to be drawn on his political plans (as opposed to his literary ones) was simply that he was not in a position to answer. His perspectives were still too blurred to be exposed to scrutiny. It was quite abundantly clear, however, that he had a deep and abiding faith in his own destiny, and a conviction that if he pressed on cultivating like-minded people within and outside the political establishment, the day would surely arrive when he would be recognized as the leader of vision which the nation so desperately needed. So he was to carry on continually broadening his contacts in order that, come that day, he would have a fund of helpers and admirers upon which to call.

Irving is, however, a very charming man, and it is easy to see the impression he can create upon right-wing activists who come into contact with him and who would, in the normal course of things, have a certain contempt for the right-wing intellectual who keeps his hands clean. Irving seems to be able to rise above this and command a respect that is not enjoyed by others.

But later, when he was interviewed by Ludi Boeken's co-producer for *The Other Face of Terror*, Irving betrayed one grave weakness. When asked whether he had had any dealings with extreme right groups he flatly denied it. And when pressed specifically about the British National Party, he claimed never to have heard of it. This was only a few short months after he had so readily attended the

BNP meeting I had arranged in Leicester, where he had congratulated me upon my election performance and taken me to task over certain areas of BNP policy. It is quite possible, of course, that it was all a simple lapse of memory, but, if so, it would have been utterly out of character.

When he visited Leicester it was a warm summer evening and I accompanied him through the city centre as he walked back to the railway station. On the way he talked at length of the Conservative Party, describing Harvey Proctor MP as 'a sound chap' and expressing near unprintable views on Mrs Thatcher and Edward Heath. And, passing members of Leicester's Asian community on our way, he could not hide his distaste for coloured immigration and talked bitterly of the politicians who had 'imposed' this state of affairs upon the people of 'our country'.

As I took my leave of him at the station I could not help reflecting upon the future as David Irving would have it. Although I felt his somewhat arrogant faith in his own 'destiny' was a little misplaced, it seemed to me that with his charm, his confidence and his undoubted intellectual ability, he was the sort of man who would be easy prey for others more powerful to use and manipulate. In other words, he might be an ideal 'front man'. Given the sort of political company he seemed happy to keep at the time, I rather hoped that his 'day of destiny' would never arrive.

10

Funds from Abroad

Despite his dabblings with the far right, David Irving remained very much his own man. Apart from tokens of help, like extremists voluntarily distributing copies of *Focal Point* or giving a little help with its preparation, the whole effort was sustained by himself. He paid the printing bills, financed his own full-time help, and generally oversaw the magazine's production. He funded the whole operation privately from the income generated by his literary efforts. When those funds ran out, the operation ground to a halt. He did admit, quite publicly, that he had approached one or two Middle Eastern embassies for financial support, but was politely turned away.

But it's easy to see why Irving felt that such sources might be forthcoming, because there had been a regular pattern of Arab financial backing for the extreme right, and especially for revisionist causes. Two examples spring readily to mind. In 1981, for instance, a thousand prominent figures – including hundreds of members of both Houses of Parliament in Britain – received free through the post copies of a book called *The Six Million Reconsidered*. As its title suggests, it was yet another hard-core revisionist tome, purporting to cast doubt on whether the nazi Holocaust had ever actually taken place. Behind this expensive mail-out were, not surprisingly, the Hancocks in Brighton, who organized it under the auspices of the Historical Review Press.

When he was interviewed on *The Other Face of Terror*, former NF chairman John Kingsley Read reported that copies of Arthur Butz's book, *The Hoax of the 20th Century* (published by the Hancocks), and of an anti-semitic pamphlet written under a pseudonym by another NF leader, had been mailed out in a similar fashion. The mail-out had been organized by National Party members, after the split of 1976 which he led. He had been told, he said, that funding for this had come from Arab sources, although he was unable to specify which sources. He did know, however, that 'the intermediary' involved in obtaining the money was Richard Lawson, formerly a young rising star in the Front and a very close associate of Dave McCalden, who had also left the NF to launch the NP and later co-founded the Institute for Historical Review. The sum involved was said to be in the region of six thousand pounds.

In the case of the 1981 mail-out, organized directly by the Hancocks, it is possible to be even more specific about where the money came from. It was supplied by a Pakistani called Inamullah Khan, who is also an adviser to the royal court of Saudi Arabia. In this case, he had arranged for the funds to come from the World Muslim League, which is funded by the Saudis and operates from Karachi, and of which he is Director-General.

Khan has now publicly admitted his role in bank-rolling this particular operation, and I know for a fact that Anthony Hancock was beside himself with rage when his link to the World Muslim League was uncovered. In funding the Hancocks thus, Khan said, his aim was 'to correct many wrong notions held by Jews'.

But Saudi backing for revisionism has been shown to go even further. *The Six Million Reconsidered* was written by an American called William Grimstad. A former Ku Klux Klan employee and editor of the nazi paper *White Power*, he also wrote another anti-semitic volume called *Anti-Zion*. Both books were included in yet another

mailing, direct from the World Muslim League's headquarters in Karachi, which in 1983 was despatched to
every member of the United States Senate and to members of the Houses of Parliament in Britain.

In America, it is more difficult than in other parts of
the world to conceal links with foreign powers, especially
where this involves the receipt of funds, and Grimstad
was forced eventually to declare his Saudi backing. He
registered as a 'foreign agent' with the US Department of
Justice, and his registration document disclosed that from
1977 he had been in the pay of the Saudi government.
After an initial payment of five thousand dollars, they
paid him twenty thousand dollars to 'research' and write
Anti-Zion, which the documents described as 'a humanitarian and educational project'. The money, authorized
in the Saudi capital Riyadh, was paid out through the
embassy in Washington.

The Saudis have not, however, been the sole Middle
Eastern source of finance for the extreme right. As long
ago as 1962, John Tyndall, then national secretary of
Colin Jordan's National Socialist Movement, was involved
in secret negotiations with the Egyptians for more than
£16,000 to fund a whole series of anti-semitic publications
and a pirate radio station. The negotiations, which
involved military attaché Colonel Saad Eddin el-Shazli,
collapsed when Tyndall, Jordan and others were gaoled
for organizing the 'Spearhead' paramilitary group. The
affair became public some years later when el-Shazli was
sent back to the UK as Ambassador. When Egyptian
President Anwar Sadat was assassinated in 1981, el-Shazli
claimed to have been behind the plot.

Much more recently, the National Front has found two
or three Arab embassies sympathetic to its requests for
financial assistance. Until its closure in 1984 in the wake

of the murder of policewoman Yvonne Fletcher, the Libyan People's Bureau was becoming increasingly helpful. In 1984, for instance, it put up the money for a special supplement to the Front's magazine *Nationalism Today* which, whilst calling for 'Victory for Palestine', was little more than an anti-semitic tract. Intermediary in this particular case was a young Front leader, Derek Holland, whom I knew well from his days as a young nazi activist at Leicester Polytechnic. We had fallen out when, at a meeting in the town, he was wildly declaiming that we should have been out fomenting 'chaos in the streets', and declaring that only 'violent struggle' held any future for the right. Not unnaturally, I was concerned at the effect that wild talk like this might have on my admittedly excitable followers in Leicester, so I publicly accused him of being an '*agent provocateur*' and belted him under the chin. 'If you want a bit of "violent struggle",' I told him, 'I'm happy to oblige.' To the amusement of those gathered around, he stormed from the room. In 1983, however, he was a key member of the clique that toppled Martin Webster from the NF leadership. He was a founder of the Italian-Strasserite venture, *Rising*, which I describe later, through which the internal coup was organized.

But others may have been getting Libyan backing as well. As far back as October 1980, Column 88 boss Les Vaughan was boasting to me that he had arranged Libyan money for his political operations. True or not, it was quite clear at the time that his expenditure, both political and personal, was far in excess of anything he might have been earning from his activities as a private investigator.

When the Libyans were packed off home after the siege of their 'People's Bureau' in 1984, the Front began to look elsewhere. Through Joe Pearce, the party's education and training officer and another *Rising* stalwart, tentative approaches were made to the Iranian Embassy in London. Soon, large quantities of glossy, well-produced, but extremely anti-semitic literature were being delivered to Front headquarters from the embassy and distributed through NF branches all over the country.

A meeting planned to discuss financial assistance was called off at the last moment when police raided Pearce's home (and the homes of other NF leaders) and brought charges against them under the Race Relations Act. Ironically, it was only four years earlier that the NF had demonstrated in London demanding 'Iranian and Libyan killers out of London'. Understandably perhaps, it is not a theme which has been taken up on their more recent marches.

I know, however, that one place in London where the Front received no joy at all was at the office of the Palestinian Liberation Organization. The NF's anti-semitism not unexpectedly leads them to be vociferous on the question of the Middle East and, although they privately loathe Arabs as an inferior racial type the principle that 'my enemy's enemy is my friend' leads them to line up on the side of the Palestinians in their struggle with Israel. On each occasion, however, that they have tried to exploit this by touching the PLO's London representatives for money, they have been shown the door in pretty short order.

In 1982, still reeling from the barrage of publicity which followed exposure of their links with European terrorists, the League of St George also began touring London's Arab embassies, cap in hand. Making the rounds this time was a long-standing League activist from North London who later tried to organize a *putsch* of the men who had controlled the group since its birth in the early 1970s. He too was making the most of the far right's 'anti-Zionist' record, but received little for his troubles. He confided in me that only the Kuwait Embassy had shown any interest at all, and I gather that even this fizzled out shortly afterwards.

It would seem, from everything I managed to pick up from far-right sources that such finance, while available from time to time for one-off projects, has never been so regularly available as to fund the day-to-day work of nazi groups in this country. Still the main sources of regular income are membership fees and receipts from the sale of literature and regalia that form an important part of groups' activities. There are also, of course, relatively wealthy supporters in all these organizations who can be prevailed upon to find regular contributions, often of thousands of pounds, which they believe are being invested in the salvation of their race and nation. When the Front expelled Martin Webster, for instance, they soon found themselves faced with a battery of legal actions from Front backers who left with him, who had loaned the party many thousands of pounds and decided that they now wanted it back.

But, having said this, I did uncover one definite source of financial support from abroad. From my contacts with the far right in South Africa, where I spent almost ten years, I learned that wealthy right-wingers were raising funds there for both the National Front and the League of St George.

The League, in 1980, was receiving money raised on its behalf by Roger Enskatt, a close friend of one of the League's leaders, Keith Thomson. This man, touring South Africa, stayed for a while at the home of Herstigte National Party leader Jaap Marais, and was using the access which this gave him to prominent and wealthy HNP backers to organize fund-raising for the League. At a series of HNP meetings he was introduced by Gert Beetge, the leader of the White Building Workers' Union and a staunch HNP supporter. Enskatt had impressed him by writing to him from England in Afrikaans, and HNP members were urged to dig deep for this representative of an openly nazi organization. Given HNP's election successes in recent years, this fondness for Hitler supporters abroad must give cause for concern. Enskstt returned to the UK with a large sum in HNP donations. This may help partly to explain how the League, only ever a few hundred members strong, was able to publish a relatively expensive monthly journal, *League Review*, and finance all of the international contacts, visits and exchanges that made it such an important part of the European nazi network.

Also receiving funds raised in South Africa was the British National Front. Expatriate nazis like Brendan Wilmer, who had emigrated to South Africa, took responsibility for exploiting wealthy contacts for donations and sending the money back to the mother party in the UK. Wilmer told me that in the three years or so that he had been fund-raising for the Front he had sent several thousand pounds 'back home'. Like Enskatt, he was enthusiastically helped in this work by White Building Workers' Union President Gert Beetge. Even more sinister, however, was the evidence I obtained of very large sums being smuggled illegally from South Africa to the National Front. I have it on first-hand authority that, in 1979, a South African NF member who was returning to England was visited by members of the South African police shortly before his departure. Ostensibly, they wanted to interview him about some public disorder involving SANF members which had taken place only shortly before. One officer, taking him aside, pressed a small package into his hand and told him it was to be delivered to a National Front leader in Britain. He did as he was told. When he got back to England, he went to a National Front demonstration, took to one side a member of the 'honour guard' which protects NF leaders on such occasions, and passed him the package with instructions to hand it over to a particular NF officer. He saw it handed over. He discovered later that the package, which he had dutifully refrained from opening, had contained diamonds.

What happened to them after that is not known. But it is perhaps worth reflecting that in May 1979, to field more than 300 candidates in the General Election, the Front had to find in excess of £45,000 in election deposits alone, all of which it could expect to forfeit. All the costs of conducting election campaigns in 300 constituencies were extra again and amounted, according to the NF's official returns published by the Home Office, to over £63,000. To have raised such funds internally would have been a remarkable achievement for a party whose membership at the time was only about 12,000 and who, in any event, already had to find the regular month-to-month finance simply to keep the party apparatus functioning and its team of full-time national officers employed.

One major mystery concerning far-right funds still remains to be cleared up. In 1983, the Italian terrorist Luciano Petrone was arrested by armed police in London. He was wanted for murdering two policemen in Rome, and for a massive bank raid in Marbella, Spain the previous Christmas where more that $10 million was stolen. Only about a third of it was ever recovered, and there were persistent rumours on the extreme right that much of it had found its way into the hands of other Italian terrorists who had also taken refuge in Britain. Certainly, as I have described elsewhere, Petrone is known to have made contact with other wanted right-wingers as soon as he arrived in England.

On the British far right, the informed view was that large amounts of money had been used by NAR members here to buy properties in rural areas. True to the spirit of their fascist mentor, Julius Evola, they intended to 'return to the soil' and establish fascist communes in the country where they could raise a second generation of 'front-line fighters' away from the decadent and corrupting influences of the cities. Where they were, or how many people were involved, I was not able to establish before my enforced departure from the right-wing scene. But I was confidently told, by members of the League of St George, that this was what had happened. Despite the close co-operation between fugitive Italians and the NF which developed over the same period there does not seem to be any clear evidence that the money, in any substantial amounts at least, has found its way to the NF.

11

The Other Face of Terror

The old, run-down, typically Parisian street where the terrorist Yann Tran Long lived with his brother seemed almost claustrophobic. As I pushed open the entrance door I glanced nervously down the street. Parked up on the corner was a large Renault van which I knew concealed a film crew and recording equipment. Further up, nearer the entrance, but out of direct line of sight, was a Lancia car in which sat two *Searchlight* journalists. I was uncomfortably aware that snuggled into the small of my back, lashed on with sticking plaster, was a battery-driven sound transmitter attached to a microphone concealed under the collar of my jacket. It was being picked up by a tape recorder in the van. All being well, every word of my conversation with Yann would be recorded. If anything went amiss they would know immediately, and my two *Searchlight* colleagues would be hammering on the front door to create as much fuss as possible and, if necessary, drag me out. When Yann saw me his eyes lit up in genuine surprise as he recognized me immediately. 'Ray,' he exclaimed, throwing his arms around me. For a moment I was terrified that his hand might chance upon the transmitter. It didn't. He ushered me in. 'No problem', I thought.

Ludi Beoken's Channel 4 documentary had become a painstaking project and it was over a year after I had agreed to participate that I returned to Paris to pick up again on the contacts I had made during my 1981 visit. This time, however, it was to be different. Every word of conversation was now being recorded and, wherever possible, my meetings were being filmed. If our talks were half as unguarded as they had been on the last occasion, all this expensive effort would be well worth it.

A major theme was to be an attempt to expose the web of right-wing terror groups who had plagued the continent for the previous three years with a succession of outrages in which many innocent people had been slaughtered. The bombing of Bologna railway station in 1980, where more than eighty people died, was the most horrific of these attacks and had been quickly followed by explosions in Munich, Paris and elsewhere in Europe. I have already described how my earlier trip to Paris, in April 1981, had helped *Searchlight* expose in part the co-ordinated, international character of these attacks. Now, in Paris for only the second time in my life, my task was to gather hard evidence on film and recorded sound that would prove beyond doubt the allegations I had already made.

An important breakthrough was accomplished in the space of a single weekend at the end of May. From England I had telephoned FNE leader Mark Frederiksen to arrange a Friday afternoon meeting at my hotel. From there we would play it by ear. Ludi's film crew were waiting when I arrived at Charles de Gaulle Airport and from a nearby car filmed me taking a taxi into the centre of Paris. This was to be the dramatic opening sequence of the film. Checking in at a rather seedy hotel near the Hôtel de Ville, I made contact with Gerry Gable who had travelled separately and booked into a room immediately above mine. I stripped to the waist and a French sound technician strapped a concealed transmitter to my back. Two film crews were stationed nearby; one on a facing rooftop and one in a large van in the street. In the second hotel room was a sound monitor through which my conversation with Frederiksen could be heard. In the van was a tape recorder to log every word.

Frederiksen and his group had adopted a relatively lower profile since the bombing of the Rue Copernic synagogue in 1980. It had been widely assumed that their members were responsible and, indeed, an anonymous telephone call had 'claimed responsibility' on their behalf. As a result, FANE had been banned by the French authorities but had quickly reorganized under a new name, the Faisceaux Nationalistes Européens (FNE), and were still printing their pro-Hitler magazine *Notre Europe*. They had become much more cagey now about contacts with outsiders but Frederiksen still remembered me well from the 1981 meeting, and welcomed my suggestion that we should meet when I phoned him from England.

Because I had no 'political' pretext for travelling to Paris I told him that my wife and I were taking a few days holiday while I recovered from the hectic campaign I had conducted as a British National Party candidate during the May General Election. It was more of a social visit, I told him, but I did not want to miss the opportunity for us to get together again. This meeting, unfortunately, was to produce little hard evidence of FNE's terrorist activities. Frederiksen refused to be drawn whenever I tried to open up the subject by declaring that the ballot box approach to national salvation was doomed, and when I announced that 'Bologna' was the way forward. He merely grunted vague assent and stared at the floor, giving the impression of a man who now regarded such talk as highly dangerous, even in the most select of right-wing company. It was all in very marked contrast to his behaviour during my previous visit. The evidence we needed on FNE was to come from another quarter, but Frederiksen did reveal some startling information about developments on the far right in France and Germany.

When he arrived at my hotel he was clutching a large case of beer, and it was pretty apparent that he expected us to consume the lot during the afternoon. It was a mixed blessing. Undoubtedly, the ready supply of alcohol loosened his tongue a little and encouraged him to speak more frankly than he might otherwise have done. On the other hand, I had to remain fairly sober myself if I was to steer the conversation in the directions we wanted and elicit new information.

A number of fascinating things transpired from our discussion, but none more astonishing than the news that a former German general, Otto Ernst Remer, was in Europe trying to set up a new political party in Germany. Not only that, Frederiksen revealed, but Remer, who commanded Hitler's security entourage, had travelled secretly to France only the previous week to meet Frederiksen and other FNE leaders and discuss his new organization. Even more intriguing was Frederiksen's claim that Remer would be financing the new party with money which had come from Arab sources in the Middle East.

In Remer's case, this was not at all surprising. A senior and highly regarded nazi officer during the war, he had emerged from the process of de-nazification absolutely unshaken in his national socialist beliefs. When tried by a de-nazification court in 1949, however, he was inexplicably acquitted. For three years afterwards he tried to establish a new nazi party called the Socialist Reichs Party, but just before this was banned by the authorities in 1952, and after getting a short prison sentence for slandering the German officers who tried to assassinate

Hitler in the famous July Plot, he dropped out of sight. For the next eighteen months he travelled in Egypt, Syria and the Lebanon, before returning to West Germany in 1954 to serve his sentence.

In the 1960s it became clear that he was working with an organization of former nazis who were smuggling weapons to Arab countries, motivated largely by their desire to see the state of Israel wiped out. Through a Damascus-based company called Orient Trading, secret arms deliveries were organized to several Arab countries. Remer ran the Cairo end of the operation. At its head-quarters in Damascus, Syria, operating under the false name 'George Fischer', was an equally interesting figure – Alois Brunner, Adolf Eichmann's assistant and, after Klaus Barbie and the 'angel of death' Dr Joseph Mengele, probably the most wanted war criminal in the world.

Brunner had been an enthusiastic exterminator of Jews whilst serving with the SS in Eastern Europe. Later, posted to the concentration camp at Drancy near Paris, he pulled out the stops to ensure that Jews were deported to death camps before the allies reached Paris. From there he was moved to Hungary where, again, he speeded up the process of deporting Jews so that they should not survive to be liberated. As the war ended, he fled to the Middle East, where he worked for the Syrian intelligence services. In 1962 he was implicated in a plot to assassinate the head of the World Jewish Congress. The Syrian authorities have persistently refused to expel him, even though he has already been sentenced to death *in absentia* in France.

Together, Remer and Brunner had considered how best to prosecute their deep enmity for the Jewish people following the collapse of the Third Reich and, as they saw it, the steady rise once again of 'Jewish power'.

They were joined in the Middle East by numerous nazi scientists and military figures who travelled to Egypt after the war to offer their services in the struggle against Israel. Remer himself rose to the position of political adviser to Egypt's President Nasser; one can only wonder at the nature of the advice he offered.

One thing was clear: Remer had not changed his views. Why else should he meet secretly with the leader of an openly nazi outfit like FNE? Why else should he disclose to a leader of FNE his plans for a new party and his sources of funds?

From Frederiksen I also found out where Remer could be found, and when, a few weeks later, Ludi travelled to Munich to interview him, it became clear that his ideas had not changed: criticizing what he called 'the Zionist influence in Wall Street', he declared that, 'I see all evil coming from there – because Israel is continually following policies of war and Israel is the long arm of Wall Street.'

Just how deep runs Remer's animosity towards Jews may be gauged from the radical new departure which his new party in Germany was to announce. Against America, which they see as hopelessly under the thumb of Zionists, they advocate an alliance between a re-united Germany and the Soviet Union. Clearly, the old nazi's antipathy to the forces of godless Bolshevism takes second place to the struggle to end the influence of 'world Zionism'. In part, possibly, he has been attracted by the Soviet Union's own less-than-tolerant treatment of its Jewish citizens. In fact, he had begun expressing a similar view as far back as 1951 when, as leader of the Socialist Reichs Party, he declared that, 'Rather than have our women and children overrun by the Russians . . . it would be better to post ourselves as traffic policemen, spreading our arms so that the Russians can find their way through Germany as quickly as possible . . .' en route to destroying the British and Americans.

'I would very much like to meet the man,' I told Frederiksen.

'Perhaps,' he grinned, 'but he hates the British . . .'

At the time of our meeting, France was being rocked by the dramatic advance of the Front National led by Jean Marie Le Pen. In by-elections it had achieved astonishing local success, polling as high as 18 per cent, by playing much the same anti-immigration card as the British National Front had deployed so successfully for a period in the mid- to late 70s. At a time when nazi groups all over Europe were abandoning election work in favour of more violent 'direct action' it was threatening to confound the argument of those who maintained that electoral tactics were doomed. When I raised this, Frederiksen surprised me by revealing that he had met with Le Pen on a number of occasions. 'He is nationalist,' he said, 'not national socialist', but nevertheless, the progress that the Front was making was an encouraging development. Even so, Frederiksen added, someone had to keep alive the spirit of true national socialism. Among those who had deserted the fold, he said suddenly, was the perfume heiress Françoise Dior, a bitter anti-semite whom I knew personally from her days as a National Socialist Movement member in Britain. It was her marriage to Colin Jordan in 1963 that led a scorned John Tyndall to break away and form his own organization. Even today, Tyndall remembers being jilted by his fiancée with incredible anger. Later she was gaoled for her part in arson attacks on synagogues in and around London.

So I was taken completely aback by the news, from Frederiksen, that she had joined up with Jacques Chirac's conservative RPR opposition. (We discovered later that she was also a member of the Paris branch of the British Conservative Party.) This was a leopard, I felt sure, who would never trade in her spots, an assessment which was borne out a couple of years later when she was found to be financing Our Nation, Martin Webster's ill-fated group set up after he was expelled from the National Front.

Frederiksen could not understand her attraction to the RPR. 'Chirac is no good. He says he dislikes fascists and national socialists. He's not even a nationalist, he's an internationalist, a liberal. And there are many Jews in the RPR . . . I don't understand it . . .'

Frederiksen's FNE had always prided itself on its links with other European groups, and indeed, in reconstituting itself after the French Government's 1980 ban, had taken a new name with a distinctly European, rather than French, flavour.

Frederiksen, it became clear, was preoccupied with the problem of bringing Europe's nazi groups closer together and desperately wanted to organize some sort of nazi summit meeting where the respective leaders from each country could sit down together to plan common approaches and co-ordinated activities. One problem would be the location; he had ruled out France, Britain and Germany because of the close police attention that such a gathering would attract. Sweden, similarly, would present problems. The options, he felt, boiled down to either Norway or the Channel Islands, where there was not much supervision.

Apart from confirming that the terrorist Yann Tran Long was still in Paris, the only light which Frederiksen seemed prepared to throw on the activities of the FNE terror cell was the news that Alex Oumow, their link-man with British nazis, would no longer be able to perform this particular function. He had made one attempt, it seemed, to return to England after his exposure during the Notting Hill affair, but he had been stopped at his port of arrival by Special Branch officers and refused entry. 'The government said "go away, you are not British",' Frederiksen said. He also rather spoiled any plans we might have had of secretly filming a meeting with Oumow by revealing that he had left France and was now living in Germany, where he was establishing contacts with other hard-line nazi groups. But Yann Tran Long, with whom Oumow had been living in the suburb of Clichy two years earlier, was still there and would, no doubt, be glad to see me. I said I would contact him, and Frederiksen staggered from my hotel room considerably the worse for wear.

There was a certain despondency over the proceedings later that evening as we ate cous-cous in a fashionable Algerian restaurant.

Despite all the care taken in the advance preparations, we did not have a single foot of film of Frederiksen entering or leaving the hotel. Everything which had taken place in my room had been recorded on the sound recorder, but inexplicably, neither film crew had spotted him in the street before or after our meeting. It was as if, on leaving my hotel room, he had evaporated into thin air. We had all the evidence we needed on sound tapes, but moving pictures are, after all, what television programmes are made of. After almost a whole day's effort, we had nothing visual to show for it. The gloom was understandable.

The next day, Saturday, would be crucial. On the schedule was a visit to Yann Tran Long and his brother. It was at their flat that I had stayed during my 1981 visit, and where I had been so readily initiated into the terrorist activities of his group. The flat was a meeting point for fascists from all over the Continent and, as I had discovered, the base from which terrorist acts were planned and carried out. We knew, for instance, from my previous visit that it was used to store weapons for their night-time attacks on Jewish targets. Tomorrow, hopefully, we would have the evidence. It would be difficult to film the proceedings, of course, but at least we should obtain pictures of me arriving at and leaving the apartment. And, if things at the flat had not changed, the evidence recorded on sound should be totally damning.

And so it was that I found myself in Rue Morice, Clichy the following day, somewhat nervously pushing open the main entrance of number 19, the apartment block where Yann Tran Long lived. He was without doubt one of the most dangerous men I had encountered in all my years on the far right, willing to use guns and explosives against the enemies of national socialism without a second thought.

It would be dishonest to pretend that I wasn't a little frightened as I struggled up several flights of stairs to his flat at the top of the block. Acutely aware of the transmitter strapped to my back, I also noticed a slight tremor in my hand as I pressed the doorbell. It was answered by a hard-looking young man who filled the doorway and scowled at me. '*Oui?*' he demanded.

I was a little thrown, but managed to stammer, '*Parlez-vous anglais?*' '*Non!*' he replied firmly. Only when I mentioned Yann's name did his attitude change and the Vietnamese was summoned to the door. He recognized me instantly and threw his arms around me. He did not notice the transmitter. Laughing, he ushered me in.

The place was busy and noisy. Yann thought I had come to stay, as I had on the previous occasion, and began to apologize that the flat was full and it would be difficult to put me up. I explained that it was only a flying visit and he introduced me to his brother, Minh, and two others, all members of the French Foreign Legion and all members of FNE. One of them spent the entire duration of my visit doing press-ups and shadow boxing in the bedroom which led from the main living room. They made me feel distinctly uncomfortable. Yann introduced me as 'Ray Hill – British Movement'. He was clearly out of touch with what had been happening on the British far right but I saw no advantage in correcting him.

The last time we met had been in London, where he wrote out for me his price list of weapons and ammunition for sale, and told me of his visit by Special Branch officers who failed to find a box of detonators hidden under the bed at his bedsit in West London. Ostensibly there to study English, he had packed his bags and left without finishing his course. I asked him why he had gone back to France so soon. 'Troubles, troubles,' he replied, 'with the police.'

We wanted the business with the detonators on the record. 'You were lucky,' I told him. 'The last time I saw you, you told me of the search . . . how they missed the detonators.'

'Oh, yeah,' he replied, laughing, 'Someone very near was with the police. I don't know who. The police got some photos.' If only he had known how near. The photos, he said, were of him together with Tony Malski, the nazi who had later obtained detonators from Yann for use in the planned Notting Hill attack.

He had lost touch with Malski, he complained, because the phone numbers Malski had given him had been changed. Now he wanted to get in touch with Malski urgently. Could I give him a new number? Happily, as it happened, I couldn't, as I was not carrying my address book, but I promised to tell Malski to get in touch with him when I got back to England. 'Tell him it's better to send me a letter,' said Yann. He was convinced his telephone was tapped.

At this point, and for the first time, I became really frightened. As Yann disappeared into the kitchen to fetch me a drink, one of the Legionnaires put a Wagner record on the record player and turned the volume up very loud. For an instant I thought I had been tumbled and that the music was intended to drown out anything the transmitter might hear. I was much relieved when Yann re-appeared and insisted that I should stay a couple of days with them. I explained that I was on a short holiday with my wife to rest up after the election campaign.

'Was the election good for you?' he asked.

'So so. I got 500 votes. But votes are no good. Elections are no good. Boom . . .' I did a passable impression of an explosion in an effort to draw him out.

'Yeah,' he laughed, 'fucking democracy . . .'

I seized the opening. 'Have you still got the M16?' On my last visit he had told me that it was his favourite weapon.

'Oh, yeah. It is always good to buy guns. Look – this is a .44 Magnum.' With that, he pulled a gun from beneath an armchair. It was followed by a Luger and another Magnum.

'Beautiful,' I said. 'How much?'

'2,000 francs.'

'Not much, can you get them into England?'

'Yes, but it would be difficult.'

'What about a machine pistol?'

'More difficult – but better too.'

Opening a cupboard he proceeded to show me two semi-automatic weapons which, if my memory of my army days serves me well, were sten guns. At the bottom of the cupboard were boxes of ammunition. All of them were for sale, he told me.

'So if I want to buy one of them, you can fix it for me?'

'Sure,' he replied.

'Next time I come, I'll bring some money. For one of those.' I pointed at the sten gun.

'OK,' he laughed.

Making the excuse that I had to collect my wife from the airport, I got up to leave. 'Don't forget to tell Tony to get in touch,' he reminded me as he showed me to the door.

'Don't worry, I'll tell Tony . . .'

It seemed like an age had passed in that flat as he showed off his collection of hardware. In fact, I had been in there no more than twenty minutes. Trying not to hurry, I walked to the end of the street and turned the corner. The Lancia pulled up alongside and I jumped in. At this point, I began to shake with what can only have been delayed fright. My companions were ecstatic. 'We got it. Every single word. As clear as a bell. You were terrific.' Just then, I found it difficult to share in their enthusiasm. 'For God's sake, just get me a drink.'

The starting point in our investigation of far-right terrorism had always been the planned bomb attack on the Notting Hill carnival in London in 1981. The Munich attack on the 1980 Oktoberfest had been alluded to by nazis I had met in Paris in 1981, but Notting Hill was still, by far, the operation about which we knew most, and where there was the clearest possible evidence of an international conspiracy behind right-wing terror. My previous evidence of the link between Paris, where the idea originated, and Tony Malski, the would-be perpetrator of the outrage, had been gathered in piecemeal fashion: first from my conversations at the Hitler birthday party in Paris; then by telephone conversations with Malski himself. It had been confirmed by his trip to collect detonators from Yann. What was essential was to be able to bring forward hard televised evidence of the plot. Yann Tran Long was now on record agreeing that he had been lucky to escape arrest when he arrived in London with a consignment of detonators. Malski's involvement now had to be established beyond doubt and a secretly recorded meeting with him was the obvious next stage.

The problem with Malski had always been to separate what was plainly fantasy from what was deadly reality. He was just as capable of actually plotting and organizing a bomb attack in Notting Hill as he was of constructing an elaborate fantasy which existed only in his own head. As we were to discover, his claims about the size and success of his National Socialist Action Party were ludicrously inflated. But we knew, with certainty, of his involvement in the dreadful plan to create havoc at the carnival. We now needed him to admit travelling to France for the detonators, and to admit his connection with the Paris terror cell.

Despite the closeness of our relationship a year or so earlier, it was not easy to tempt him to a meeting in 1983. The reason was simple. After his break from British Movement, which he regarded as irredeemably soft, he had launched his own National Socialist Action Party in mid-1982. True to style, he had imposed upon it a complicated, almost comic, military structure. There were no less than fifteen ranks in its pseudo-military hierarchy. And, parallel to that, there were four other sections of the party ('Black Wolves', youth, women and 'workforce') each with its own ranks. The leader of 'Black Wolves', for instance, was accorded the rank of

'Lieutenant-General'. Beneath him were 'Brigadiers' and 'Colonels', all the way down to 'privates'. Little wonder that in far-right circles he quickly became mockingly known as 'the Field Marshal'. All of this was, of course, grotesquely out of step with the true size and strength of his organization, which only ever numbered a few dozen. But he had influential friends: his glossy (but only barely literate) magazine, *The European*, was being produced by leaders of the League of St George.

Comic though his organizational efforts might have been, there was no mistaking the sinister intent behind them. A circular letter to sympathizers openly declared that, 'We are a political party which will support any action of paramilitary groups which come to the rescue of our so much corrupt and infested country.'

I have already described how he boasted of having caches of guns and ammunition stockpiled in countryside near his Watford council home, and how he demonstrated to me how to turn a harmless wristwatch into a timing device for a bomb. In fact, his ambitions ranged much wider than the leadership of a small suburban terror cell.

The European openly declared that the NSAP was building 'an effective paramilitary army' and 'stockpiling all types of guns and ammunition'. It laid out a blueprint for establishing a right-wing terror force.

'For many years now, parties, movements and individuals have tried to set up a paramilitary force capable of defeating the reds completely on the streets, and when the time comes, in the field . . . there are small paramilitary groups up and down the country but they are small and not organized in such a way that people of the right can get the protection they need.'

What was needed, he argued, was 'all paramilitary groups to unite into a new organization . . . a strongly organized military command'. It would be important, he went on, that the political party, the NSAP, should remain distinct from this 'revolutionary army' otherwise 'our military activists will get the party banned'. Having recognized the need for this sort of separation, however, he seemed quite incapable of carrying it out in practice, and openly pushed his paramilitary ideas in the magazine of his self-styled 'political party'.

Although he has only one criminal conviction – for an assault on a disabled Labour Party supporter – he has had many close shaves. In March 1981, police raided the homes of several of his supporters on the South Oxhey estate where he lives. This was prior to the formation of the NSAP, but even then he was organizing local British Movement members into cells which infiltrated a local territorial army unit. In one house, belonging to John Deighton, police found a gun, and Deighton was subsequently convicted. In fact, the gun had been left with him by Malski, to whom it belonged, and Deighton was bitter at having, as he saw it, to take the rap for Malski. But Malski made no secret of what he was up to. To a *Searchlight* reporter purporting to be involved with mercenaries he boasted that his group would send trained men into riot-torn inner city areas to exacerbate conflict between police and black people. He admitted his involvement in the Edelweiss Group, a highly secret international paramilitary training operation run from Dorset by former major Ian Souter Clarence. And, to a *News of the World* reporter, of all people, he bragged of the secret arms dumps where he had hidden caches of guns and ammunition.

Up until the early days of the NSAP, Malski had a high regard for me as a political leader, and was particularly impressed by the welcome I received from the violently-inclined nazi hard-liners in Europe whom he admired so much. Such was his regard for me, however, that not long after the NSAP was formed in late 1982 he approached me to become NSAP party leader. It did not take much in the way of consultations with friends at *Searchlight* to decide that this would not be a good idea at all. Infiltration is one thing, even seeking senior positions in the far right may be justified, but to assume the leadership of a group bent on violence and terror would be quite unjustifiable, and would, in any event, carry the real possibility of my becoming seriously implicated in major criminal offences for which I would risk imprisonment. The course of action decided upon was that I should politely decline, but try to remain personally close to Malski in order to keep abreast of what he was up to. There was no reason why he should not continue to trust me.

We counted without one thing: Malski's childish petulance. He took my refusal as a personal affront, and sulked. As far as he was concerned, the NSAP was a major political and paramilitary initiative. Any national socialist worth his salt would be proud to stand at its head, yet here was I, rejecting his offer on the grounds that I felt, for the time being, that it was more important to address the slightly wider audience of experienced nazi cadres who seemed then to be rallying around John Tyndall's New National Front. I was, of course, heavily involved with Tyndall at the time in mopping up the remains of British Movement and some of the NF splinter groups with a view to launching a new party in 1983.

But Malski, piqued, would have none of it and told me, more or less, that he never wanted to speak to me again. If we were going to coax him into admitting his part in the bomb plot, he would have to.

It took a couple of placatory telephone calls over the

next few days before he finally agreed to meet me in London. The pretext I used, of course, was that I had been to France and had a message for him from Yann. Unfortunatly, he was at work during the day and would only meet me in the evening, so filming the event was made difficult.

When he insisted that we meet in a particular pub in West London, there was no option but, somehow, to conceal the camera in the bar. When Ludi and others went to scout the location it was clear that it would be a difficult operation. At the time we were due to meet, the bar usually had only a sprinkling of customers and a camera crew would stick out like so many sore thumbs. Nevertheless, with a camera cleverly concealed in a bag to be placed on a stool at the bar, and with a transmitter hidden in my briefcase, we decided to go ahead.

It was October, and although we had arranged to meet as the pub opened at 5.30 P.M. the light was already failing. Even so, to ensure against the failure of our concealed camera, we had agreed to try an outdoor shot with whatever light was available. I spun him a transparently thin tale about meeting a 'French comrade', a friend of Tony Reed Herbert, outside the pub at 6 o'clock, and persuaded him to join me outside while we waited for him. After a few minutes in the cold Malski was getting impatient and insisted on going inside. 'Surely he'll have the sense to come in,' he said, and I could not really argue with him. I just had to hope the cameraman had done the trick. In fact, it had been too dark.

He had arrived with his NSAP 'second-in-commmand', Phil Kersey. I didn't have the nerve to ask what rank Kersey held in the party's military hierarchy, but we must assume that it was at least major-general. With a French cameraman sitting nonchalantly at the bar nursing a holdall containing a camera, and with two *Searchlight* journalists playing pool nearby 'just in case', I settled into a corner table with Malski and Kersey. Quite brazenly, I placed the bugged briefcase smack in the middle of the table around which we were seated. Technical breakdowns aside, there was no way it could fail to record every word.

Before we had even had a chance to order drinks he was boasting that members of his NSAP who lived locally were 'going shooting three times a week at a gun club just round the corner. The "old bill" (the police) are going mad about it but there's nothing they can do.' The party, he claimed, now had almost a thousand members (a claim which I could not take seriously) and they were planning the first national meeting in London in the near future. 'All in uniform,' he assured me, 'everyone's issued with a uniform.'

He was not at all worried, he said, by earlier publicity surrounding demands by Joan Lester MP that the DPP should investigate the activities of his organization. As it turned out, he had nothing to worry about anyway: the DPP concluded that an investigation would only feed his ego. Nor was he too upset that Special Branch had raided his home on number of occasions looking for hidden weapons, although he conceded that such attentions meant he had to be careful about what was kept in the house. As far as he was concerned, any publicity was good publicity. I wondered if he would hold the same view after the programme we were making had been shown.

Servicing the party, he said, was more than £90,000 of printing equipment, another claim which I felt was just a shade on the outrageous side, but he was very specific about the make and model of computerized type-setting equipment which was attested to by Kersey sitting next to him. All of it, he said, was paid for out of the earnings of his own business, which had also financed sending his wife on a week-long user's training course costing £150 a day. How his small painting and decorating firm was generating this sort of income, if indeed it was, mystified me. Jokingly, I suggested that he obtained it by other means, at which point he became noticeably agitated and denied it vehemently. I could not help feeling he was protesting just a little too much.

Quickly, I got him on to the subject of Yann. 'He wants you to get in touch, but not on the phone. You should write to him.'

Malski knew why Yann was nervous about the telephone. 'He's worried about the Special Branch . . . but if you get involved in this sort of thing you've got to expect it.'

He had, he admitted, been surprised when Special Branch officers stopped him as he left for France on the Spring Bank Holiday in 1981, to collect the detonators for Notting Hill.

'They said, "we know where you're going." They said, "we know you're going to pick up some things in Paris." They said, "we were tipped off . . . we've got your description, your name" . . . he says, "we were tipped off, we know you're going to bring in some gear." They said, "don't bring it back in."

'And the only three that knew I was going over to see him was Alex Oumow, Yann and me. And Alex was the one who introduced me to Yann in the first place.'

And he confirmed that while in Paris, he had visited Yann Tran Long's flat where the guns and detonators were stored.

Somehow or other, he had completely forgotten that he had also told me of his plans in detail – down to his port of departure and the time of his sailing. As it was, with only two foreigners knowing about the trip, the leak to British Special Branch, he concluded, could only have been through Oumow's British contact – and that meant the circle around the Hancocks in Brighton. 'It's definitely someone on the south coast. That's a fact.'

'It couldn't be anyone else,' I agreed.

So within ten minutes of sitting down with me, Malski had confirmed for the record his involvement in attempting to bring explosive devices into the country from the continent. For the next hour he regaled me with further grandiose tales of the progress his NSAP was making: how the leadership included nine Oxbridge graduates and ex-public schoolboys; how he had built up an intelligence network which had successfully found the 'secret' *Searchlight* office and the address of a particular *News of the World* reporter who had run a series of uncomplimentary stories about the NSAP; how he and fifteen NSAP members had joined a BNP march recently and 'done the communists' before the march ever began.

Much of this I knew to be fantasy. The *Searchlight* 'address' he had published in *The European* was about nine miles from where the office was actually located, and had led to some puzzling moments for London Transport officestaff who occupied the office he had identified. And I knew from my own experience that neither *Searchlight*'s editor nor the *News of the World* reporter had 'shit themselves' and 'gone into hiding' as he claimed.

But he did provide other useful information, confirming that he was still in regular contact with Major Ian Souter Clarence in Dorset, and that he had recently been in touch with Oumow who was now in Spain working with the nazi group CEDADE. This was one of the wealthiest European nazi outfits, which frequently made printing

and other facilities available to their less well-off comrades in other countries. It was almost certainly through
this connection, I discovered later, that Lorenzo Martinez, the wanted killer, had fled from Spain to be found at
Yann Tran Long's flat in Clichy when French police
raided it later that year.

As far as he was concerned, only the NSAP stood any
chance of building a national socialist party in the UK.
The NF, he proclaimed, was 'run by poofs and Jews – it's
hardly right-wing, is it?' The British National Party would
fail because Tyndall, while himself a sound national
socialist, was surrounded by Monday Club types to whom
he was beholden for support and finance. The newly
launched, and extremely violent, National Action Party
was saddled with a leader, Eddie Morrison, who 'can't
handle it' and who was, anyway, seeking a merger with
the NSAP.

He was saddened, however, by the demise of the NF
which was, after all, a household name. The problem, as
he saw it, was Martin Webster, who had saddled the party
with a reputation for homosexuality and intrigue.

'Tell you what,' he said bluntly, 'if Martin Webster was
a headache to me, he wouldn't be here, after the next
four or five hours, on this planet.'

A 'final solution' to the continued embarrassing presence of Webster in the leadership of British nationalism
was one I had heard canvassed more than once. On
several occasions, when such proposals were being discussed seriously, the 'Fat Man' had been known to
disappear from public view for weeks on end, surfacing
only to meet major commitments and then surrounded by
teams of heavies.

When Malski and I parted company in the pub car park
later in the evening, we arranged that I should visit him

in Watford after Christmas for a further meeting where we might discuss the contribution I could make to the NSAP. In particular, I promised him a series of articles about 'The Jewish Problem through the Ages'. He was enthusiastic and plainly flattered that a prominent figure on the right was prepared to publicly associate with him. I knew the meeting would never take place.

The programme went out at the end of March 1984. It included much of the secret filming that we had carried out both in the UK and in France and a lengthy interview in which I described how I had become involved with the nazi movement almost two decades earlier, and the process of disenchantment which had led me secretly to change sides. It was the first time that the movement's sinister underground activities had been exposed from the inside, and the damage it inflicted on some groups, like NSAP and the League of St George, was lasting. Their fury, impotent though it was, was not long in revealing itself. Only days later I got my first piece of hate mail.

I knew the handwriting on the envelope immediately. Robert Relf, one-time race martyr, had obviously found it impossible to contain himself. Having known him, and witnessed his speechless, spluttering, apoplectic temper, I could more or less imagine what he would have to say.

My 'coming out' on Channel 4, and a few days earlier in the *News of the World*, had sent shock waves through the nazi movement in the UK. I imagined it had achieved a similar result among my former 'comrades' abroad, but about that I was in the dark. What I did know was that among British nazis stunned disbelief had given way to the sort of rage you only find among guilty men who have finally been found out by subterfuge.

On the Sunday prior to transmission, many a far-right activist woke up to find the *News of the World* announcing

'Top fascist quits to uncover the threat to Britain'. And there, spread across two pages in the old, larger, broad-sheet-style *News of the World*, were many of the dirty little secrets that they had been convinced would never see the light of day. It was a mouth-watering sample of what was to come in the television programme – the Notting Hill episode, the weapons dumps, the football violence, the trips to Diksmuide – but we knew from the start that my erstwhile comrades would not wait until the television show had been aired before the reprisals began. I could not make a permanent move from Leicester at that stage because my daughter was just about to sit her mock 'A' levels and it would have been a serious interference with her education, but a move, temporary at least, was essential. We spent the next couple of weeks in the country well away from Leicester.

Having been part of the movement for so long I knew exactly what we could expect, and it was not long after we moved back to our Leicester home that the trouble began. Twice in less than a fortnight I left my house to find my car seriously vandalized with paint stripper. My front door was daubed with nazi slogans and windows were broken. It was typical of the sort of people involved that they did not have the courage to meet me face to face to say what they thought of what I had done. On the one occasion that two young nazis did accost me in the street they turned and fled when I simply threatened to turn my dog loose on them. The most serious incident came a couple of weeks after the programme when a team of them waylaid a friend and neighbour of mine and beat him savagely on the doorstep of his own home. They told him, 'We can't get that bastard Hill because of his dog. So we'll have you instead.' Fortunately we were able to identify the individuals involved and two of them were subsequently arrested and charged by the police.

When my daughter's examinations were over we finalized plans to move away from Leicester, something which I would rather we could have done earlier. The whole family felt utterly vulnerable in our Leicester council house, an address only too well known to too many nazis. It was not so much the random threats from BM members or NF hangers-on that concerned me. What frightened me more was the possibility that some of the more professional, armed men of violence in Europe would feel angry enough to arrange the kind of reprisal against which there is no real protection other than their not knowing where you are. In Leicester I was a sitting duck, and it was with enormous relief that we finally left the town to begin a new life in a different part of the country.

But apart from the incidents I have mentioned, a sort of blind, helpless rage seemed to be the best response that the British far right could manage. If the style of the letter from Robert Relf was inimitably his, the sentiments were pretty close to those expressed to me in a pile of letters (often anonymous) and a stream of telephone calls (usually anonymous) that followed in the wake of my 'betrayal'. Relf did not hang on letter-writing etiquette: 'Hill: You obnoxious traitorous cowardly bastard', his missive opened. And the pace did not slacken: 'I have always thought that there was nothing lower on the face of the earth than the evil stinking Jew. However, you have proved me wrong, you have achieved what I thought was impossible, you have sunk even lower than those hooked nose deformed bastards.' It finished with a threat: 'It's said that you are about to write your memoirs, I would hurry up if I were you, you stinking bastard,

because somehow I think that it's your obituary that will
soon be written.'

Quite apart from being a revealing insight into the
darker thoughts of the fascist mind, Relf's letter seemed
to provide him with an almost sexual relief. Similar efforts
had got him into trouble in the past; a letter not unlike
the one I received, published in the *Sunday Times*, had
seriously undermined nazi efforts to present him as a
wholesome martyred Englishman when he was in gaol in
1976 for contempt. And no less than eight manic tirades
(including two addressed to the Prince of Wales and Lord
Whitelaw) had already earned him convictions in Leamington magistrates' court. His little epistle to me was quite
true to form.

As it contained an obvious threat to my life, I passed
the letters to the local police. Two weeks later, Relf wrote
to *Searchlight*, repeating most of the insults he had already
addressed to me directly, but complaining that he had
been visited by police who had told him that the letter to
me was considered offensive. (I was told later that they
did not intend to prosecute him as the threat was apparently not to be taken seriously.) 'For the life of me, I
can't see how it is possible to offend scum like that,' he
wrote. For good measure, he had taken a thick felt-tip
pen to add a postscript – a carefully drawn swastika, and
the words 'Hitler was right'.

Much more interesting than all of this was what was yet
to come. There was no way that my 'defection' could be
ignored by people like Tyndall and McLaughlin, nazi
leaders who had taken me into their confidence and
trusted me with high office in their organizations. Tyndall,
particularly, had gone overboard in defending me against
detractors in the BNP, publishing spirited little pieces in
his BNP journals affirming his trust in me and the views

we held in common. The rival führers were now left with not inconsiderable quantities of egg on their faces, and they would be hard put to explain to their supporters how they had been so completely taken in. But they would have to try. I awaited their published reactions with keen anticipation.

McLaughlin's was the first to appear. He had long since given up publishing regular periodicals. With the demise of British Movement there was nothing to sustain them. But, funded presumably by his increasingly lucrative nazi literature, militaria and survivalist business in Chester, he did produce an occasional broadsheet called *Comment*, which accompanied book lists and catalogues mailed out by his Phoenix Publications. Needless to say, the percipient former milkman had not been taken in for one moment by the wiles of this particular infiltrator:

'It is said that everyone is shocked by the Ray Hill fiasco, and this feeling of "shock" more than anything else symbolizes the sheer lunacy of Britain's nationalists. From the moment he stepped from the 'plane bringing him from South Africa, that man didn't even need to hide his true intent. He joined every right-wing group; ingratiated himself with the leadership of each. He agitated the membership, subverted the comradeship and conspired against the leadership. He was a wolf among the lambs.'

But McLaughlin, naturally, had spotted my 'true intent' from the first:

'Exposed as an agitator, he was hurled out of the British Movement while still a probationary member. He took out a writ claiming wrongful expulsion and must have been happily bemused when "stalwarts of the British right" egged him on, encouraged and assisted him. Of these, Colin Jordan provided the most assistance preparing and providing his legal papers . . . Ray Hill a mole? No. Hill was never a mole. Hill was revealed

and exposed for what he was publicly five years ago to the
month. It was the British right wing that had its head in the
sand.'

How he expected any of this to be believed by activists
who knew quite well that he had assigned me an important
position in BM, asked me to stand in for him at the head
of BM marches, and even, at one stage, asked me to run
BM's internal security arrangements, is quite beyond
understanding. Why all this, if my 'true intent' was clear
from the moment I stepped off the plane from South
Africa?

But he did pay a handsome tribute to the impact my
mischief had had in bringing the squalid life of BM to a
premature close. To meet my legal challenge

'the Movement had to borrow over £1,000 to defend itself, and
coinciding with this crisis the leadership had to divert its energies
and finances to holding a membership together because, rumour
was rife, loyalties were torn and disillusionment was everywhere.
Collapse was postponed but the pre-Hill era when the Movement had at last emerged as the true voice of British nationalism
was gone forever . . .'

Could I possibly have asked for a better testimonial?

John Tyndall's response, to be found in the subsequent
issue of his own journal, *Spearhead*, was altogether more
considered, representing an unusual excursion, for Tyndall at least, into the realms of amateur psychology. My
revelations posed Tyndall with a twofold problem: not
only did he have to explain how he had been taken in,
he also had to face up to the fact that someone exposed
to him at close range had not arrived inexorably at the
view that here, truly, was a man born to be 'leader'. In
other words, he felt compelled to explain his own

rejection. This, inevitably, could only be the consequence of some maladjustment of the mind on my part;
some character defect which explained both my plausibil-
ity and my failure to recognize him as the führer he so
clearly saw himself destined to be. And this was exactly
the tack taken by Tyndall in a wordy two-page piece
entitled 'Impressions of a turncoat'. Rigorously laying
out different categories of treachery, he concluded that I
fell into the group of 'traitors' whose actions are 'the
product solely of a weak, unstable, corruptible and
opportunistic character, liable to collapse and surrender
itself to another's will under stress of circumstances . . .'
Having in all likelihood joined the movement with a
genuine ideological commitment to it, I had 'turned'
because of 'some innate character deficiency'. And, of
course,

'in some respects this type of betrayer can be more dangerous,
precisely because the actions and words he employed to build
confidence among his associates were perfectly genuinely motivated at the time they occurred, thus conveying the sincerity of
a stage or film actor who so absorbs himself in his allotted role
that he actually starts to think and believe in the same manner
as the one whose part he is playing.'

So there we have it. John Tyndall was only taken in
because I suffered from 'some innate character defect'.
And who could possibly blame him?
His explanation, however, skated over the (by then
well-known) fact that I had been collaborating with
Searchlight for five years, ever since my return from South
Africa. Given that my first meeting with him did not take
place until 1981, two years later, it is hard to see how he
could have been taken in by views 'perfectly genuinely
motivated at the time . . .' But then, rewriting history is

almost second nature to a right-winger as long in the tooth as John Tyndall.

To soften the blow, however, he felt compelled to claim that I had been a little suspect, in some quarters, from the start, and as a consequence had been given no position of influence or trust in the BNP. In particular, he alleged, I was never his deputy. His earlier announcements in the BNP newspaper stood in marked contrast to these rather weak, *post hoc* claims.

The lesson of it all, he concluded, was that nationalist groups should look to even more rigidly hierarchical leadership structures than had hitherto been the case if 'the probability and effect' of treachery such as mine was to be reduced. So, the man who had been so completely duped was to be, in the future, the sole bulwark against any repetition of such episodes.

There was one curious comment in his article. The harm I did BNP, he argued, was small:

'all the truly damaging information . . . involved people and groups not connected with the BNP. I am tempted to feel sorry for those people and groups but, if they think themselves aggrieved, they ought to ponder on their wisdom in allowing a character like Ray Hill to get so close to their operations – we never let him get too close to ours.'

Up to a point this is true. *The Other Face of Terror* focused primarily on the paramilitary operations of nazis to which I had successfully 'got close'. So what might these 'operations' of the BNP from which I was kept away be? It might usefully be recalled that two years later, one of Tyndall's principal BNP lieutenants, Tony Lecomber (alias Wells, alias East) was arrested in his car near the offices of the left-wing Workers' Revolutionary Party in South London. He had just been seriously injured when a home-made bomb went off in his hands. At his home, police found other explosive material including home-made hand grenades.

It was, perhaps, a little ironic that for several months following disclosure of my treachery, Tyndall's *Spearhead* continued advertising for sale cassettes of BNP meetings featuring speeches by Tyndall, Charles Parker . . . and Ray Hill. Only when this was pointed out somewhat tongue-in-cheek in *Searchlight* did it occur to him to amend the advertisements.

By then, my family and I had moved to another part of the country to begin a new life. Through *Searchlight*, a series of meetings was organized around the country where I spoke to trades unions branches, Labour Party groups, anti-racists and other interested audiences about my time in the far right and what I felt had to be done now to deal with the threat of increasingly violent racist organizations. Everywhere I spoke, I was received with remarkable warmth and affection. People who must have hated my guts up to a few months previously went out of their way to commend the work that *Searchlight* and I had been carrying out 'behind the lines', and there was not a single instance that I encountered of anyone doubting that whatever I had been compelled to do to establish my credentials as a top nazi had paid a handsome dividend in the long term. I was genuinely touched by the generous tributes that were so often offered, and which confirmed for me that all the anguish and pressure – and, if truth be told, the fear – which had characterized my five years of undercover work had indeed been worthwhile. But more important to me, on a personal level at least, was that at last I could be among those whose commitment to democracy and freedom and tolerance I had come to share, no longer having to conceal my own commitment to these things. Whether the debt I acknowledged in South Africa has been fully repaid I will leave others to judge; at least I know I have tried.

Postscript: an Ever-Present Danger

It is, perhaps, only with the passing of time that a true balance sheet of the achievements of my five years of undercover work can be drawn up. We were never foolish enough to presume that my activities, nor those of any other single individual, would eradicate the threat from extremism of the right, but looking back, it is clear that major successes were chalked up. The British Democratic Party and British Movement, both of which were showing considerable potential for growth at the time when I became involved with them, are dead and buried as political forces. A major terrorist outrage planned for London was sabotaged and the secret safe housing network for European terrorists has collapsed after being exposed. Attempts to stockpile weapons for a 'race war' were foiled through our co-operation with Granada Television's *World in Action*, and the chief culprit, Tony Reed Herbert, is still in self-imposed exile in Ireland as a result. Exposure of the role of the League of St George in safe housing and in maintaining British links with terror groups all over the world brought such a blaze of publicity to its activities that to all intents and purposes it is now a spent force, publishing its magazine only rarely and holding meetings more rarely still. Tony Malski's National Socialist Action Party, an embryonic self-styled paramilitary group, has not dared raise its head in public – or private, for that matter – since my intimate conversations with him were broadcast to the world on *The Other Face of*

Terror. BNP leader, John Tyndall, with difficulty maintaining his claim to be a divinely inspired leader after
being taken in so thoroughly, came to face exactly the
problems that we had anticipated when the decision was
made that my secret work was over. He has lost the
financial backing of his father-in-law, and has failed to
build support beyond the couple of thousand who
responded to the unity appeal out of which BNP was
born.

But none of this should give any cause for complacency.
True, the far right is still divided, now largely between
the BNP and the National Front, but the NF has taken a
modest new lease of life over the last two years, and, if
anything, poses a more sinister threat than at any time in
its earlier history.

Even as I left the nazi movement amid considerable
publicity in early 1984, events were taking place which
were fundamentally to alter the picture of the threat that
the forces of the far right pose to our democratic way of
life. Most significant of these, as it turned out, was a
further split in the National Front which paved the way
for something of a rebirth of the party, but at the same
time relaunched it on a completely new and threatening
political path.

Ever since John Tyndall quit the Front in 1980, it has
been in the grip of a particular variety of nazism associated with the Strasser brothers during the pre-war Hitler
regime. They placed considerable emphasis on the 'socialist' component of national socialism but, when it was
necessary to secure the support of the industrial barons,
Hitler had their Brownshirt followers butchered in what
became infamous as 'the Night of the Long Knives'.

It was a brand of national socialism which always
enjoyed a certain minority support on the British right,
and featured in the earlier split in the Front in 1975, out

of which the short-lived National Party was formed. At that time, Martin Webster had railed in *Spearhead* against young dissidents, dubbing them 'spotty Strasserites'. By 1981, however, he had apparently become thoroughly committed to their ideas and wrote enthusiastically that the British middle class was soft, indecisive and corrupted. Only in the white working class could the NF build the sort of committed, dependable support upon which a serious political movement might grow, he argued.

Given the growing influence of such ideas within the party, it could be said that Martin Webster had little option but to go along with them. But there were other problems looming: a younger breed of up and coming leaders was anxious to thrust him aside and break with the older generation of fascists that he represented. And, with his utterly intolerable manners and behaviour towards other members, his fits of violent temper, his possessive attitude towards control of all areas of party work and, not least of all, the spicy tales which constantly circulated about his private life, they had any number of pretexts upon which to move against him.

They made their play at the end of 1983. After some clever moves involving the apparent resignations of Nick Griffin and Joe Pearce – the latter popular among younger members and crucial to holding on to the support of the NF's many skinhead members – Webster was relieved of his post as National Activities Organizer and his seat on the ruling National Directorate. Soon afterwards he was expelled from the party, leaving it wholly under the control of the Strasserites.

Working alongside them in orchestrating this takeover were members of the Italian terrorist cell which had only narrowly avoided extradition back to Italy in 1983.

Together they had published a magazine, *Rising*, and organized training seminars to educate up and coming young activists in the politics of Strasserism, to which they now added the ruralist fascist policies of Julius Evola upon which the Italians drew heavily. All of this was leavened with some of the most virulent anti-semitism that the Front has ever given voice to. In Italy, the fugitives had all belonged to the Third Position, which proclaimed Evola's belief in a return to rural societies, but which was, in 1985, judged by a Rome court to be the public face of a terrorist group, the Armed Revolutionary Nuclei (NAR). Among other things, NAR had claimed responsibility for the 1981 bombing of Bologna railway station. Several of those in England, including their leader, Roberto Fiore, have received heavy gaol sentences *in absentia* as a result. That has not stopped the NF from working closely with them, much to the publicly expressed disgust of Martin Webster. Labour MPs have pressed persistently for their deportation, and it is their presence in Britain that has led directly to a new extradition treaty being agreed with the Italian government.

But at the same time as proclaiming a new affinity with the white working class and a concern for the environment and British folk culture, the Front have managed to address themselves to a younger generation of nazi recruits and have succeeded in reversing the decline which had set in up until Webster's departure. From an all-time low in paid-up membership in 1984, they have begun to recruit steadily and are once again growing.

But it is not just a change of political direction which gives cause for concern. Equally worrying is evidence that NF members have been involved in paramilitary training under the direction of two former SAS officers, and that firm links have now been established with loyalist paramilitary and murder squads in Northern Ireland. The province has witnessed a major drive by the Front, whose leaders now travel regularly to Belfast for meetings with paramilitary commanders. One of the key figures behind this has been Steve Brady, although he has shared the work with Joe Pearce and others. It seems that Northern Ireland has become one of the most important areas of recruitment for the Front in its new phase.

Running in parallel with their adoption of the Italian Third Position ('between capitalism and communism') is an acknowledgement that these politics range you against the democratic state. As a result, the Front has now openly adopted a revolutionary pose, declaring the need to destroy existing society before a nationalist 'folk state' can be built. Taking this to its logical conclusion, they now educate Front members in the need to become 'political soldiers', and to prepare for the overthrow of the state. It is a theme constantly reiterated in their publications and, no doubt, explains the paramilitary preparations which take place at discreet locations in the countryside, and a new internal party structure where much stricter procedures are now used to screen and recruit members, and where the most promising are quietly creamed off into élite cells for various forms of training. They appear to be basing their organization increasingly upon models previously adopted by underground terrorist groups.

A more recent split in 1986 divided the Front into two factions each claiming the organization's name. One is led by Nick Griffin and Derek Holland, and managed to hold on to the party's infrastructure; the other is led by Andrew Brons, Joe Pearce and Ian Anderson. This split, however, appears to be more to do with form and personality clashes than with the substance of politics, for both groups remain wholly committed to the Strasserite, Third Position policies which are so worrying, and both are pledged to build organizations of street-hardened young 'political soldiers'.

They draw particular inspiration from a novel published in the United States, written by nazi National Alliance leader William Pierce. *The Turner Diaries* is a fictitious account of a race war launched in the US by a small group of underground nazi fanatics which culminates in genocide and nuclear war. This type of scenario is presented in the book as the only feasible means of re-establishing white domination across the globe. Fantastic as it appears, the book has already been adopted as a blueprint for action by American nazis, many of whom were gaoled in 1985 after carrying out robberies and murders exactly as ordained in the *Diaries*. They even called themselves The Order, after Turner's fictitious terror group. Now the same book is being peddled eagerly among the NF's young, impressionable and violently-inclined new intake of recruits.

The consequence of all this has been a dramatic rise in the incidence of racial and political violence. One of the most notable features about the NF in recent years has been the sickening regularity with which its members face the courts charged with violent assaults on black people, Jews, or political opponents. Others have been convicted for arson, or attempted arson attacks, and a number have even been sentenced for murder or manslaughter.

What was widely predicted when the Front's efforts to make an electoral breakthrough collapsed in ruins in 1979 has come to pass. Increasingly, they and their supporters are turning to other, more direct methods of achieving their goals. The awful upsurge of racist violence, especially in inner city areas where Asians in particular are facing an undeclared war from racist thugs, is one feature of this. But it would be an error to regard this violence as simply the spontaneous expression of some irrational hatred. One theme which I heard time and again on the far right was the need to 'drive them out'. Given the tiny support that exists for a policy of repatriation, nazis have resolved to make life so intolerable for racial minorities that they begin to flee from this country. It is precisely with this in mind that younger, easily-aroused nazi supporters are wound up and turned loose on the streets by other more calculating figures who remain in the background. In these circumstances, and given the apparent inability of police forces around the country to get a grip on this problem, it is perfectly understandable that many minority communities now feel that the only protection they can depend upon is that which they organize themselves. And that is a tragic indictment of a democratic society's ability to guarantee the rights and liberties of its citizens.

The Front, of course, will deny all of this, claiming that members convicted of violent offences are quickly expelled. But this is a lie. Its ranks are full of fascists who sport with pride their convictions for racial or political violence. In 1983 and 1984, more than twenty known NF members were convicted of crimes of violence, ranging from threatening behaviour to possessing offensive weapons, to grievous bodily harm and murder. And these are only the ones who were actually caught and whose NF membership was known or was revealed in court. The NF, on the other hand, has announced not one single expulsion for such activities.

Increasingly, the real bedrock views of the NF are revealed, not through the pronouncements of its leaders, but through the statements and activities of its members.

Front publications, for instance, have become increasingly open about the party's anti-semitism in recent years, but it was left to a local branch, in Bedfordshire, to produce a newsletter which announced, in the wake of the hijack of the liner *Achille Lauro* by Palestinians, and the murder of a Jewish passenger: 'The Bedfordshire National Front would like to congratulate the PLF (Palestine Liberation Front) who successfully proved that Jews cannot float in the Mediterranean Sea (Leon Klinghoffer). The Bedfordshire National Front will try to test this theory in lakes, streams, ponds etc. . . . until the supply of Jews have run out.'

And it was left to the NF's Leeds branch to proclaim on the cover of their local newsletter that: 'The future belongs to the few of us still willing to get our hands dirty. Political Terror: it's the only thing they understand.'

We cannot say we have not been warned.

Glossary of Right-Wing Organizations

Afrikaaner Resistance Movement (Afrikaaner Weerstandsbeweging – AWB)

Hard-line South African nazi party formed in 1973. Led by Eugene Terre'blanche, its symbol is similar to the swastika. Its aim is racial partition in South Africa; it is opposed to 'The Zionist Money Power'.

Anti-Immigration Movement (AIMS)

A Leicester-based anti-immigration pressure group active in the late 1960s. Its strenuous campaigns against black immigration laid the foundations for the exceptional successes of the National Front in the city in the 1970s.

Armed Revolutionary Nuclei

See Nucleii Armati Rivoluzionari

British Democratic Party

Leicester-based NF splinter launched by Anthony Reed Herbert in 1979. It collapsed after its members were exposed as part of a gun-ring in 1981.

British Movement (BM)

Founded in 1968 by Colin Jordan, and until its demise in 1983 one of the most hard-line pro-Hitler groups in the

UK. Jordan was succeeded as leader in 1970 by Michael McLaughlin.

British National Party (BNP)

Born in 1960 out of a merger between Colin Jordan's White Defence League and John Bean's National Labour Party, the original BNP was led by Jordan and Andrew Fountaine. Pro-nazi and anti-semitic, it split in 1962 when Jordan left to form the National Socialist Movement. It was one of the groups which merged to form the National Front in 1967.

When former NF leader John Tyndall launched a new party in 1982, the BNP name was resurrected. It is now a few hundred strong, and publishes *British Nationalist* and *Spearhead*.

British Union of Fascists (BUF)

Sir Oswald Mosley's pre-war Blackshirt Movement. Its full title was actually the British Union of Fascists and National Socialists. It collapsed when its leader was detained during the war.

Column 88

Taking its name from the eighth letter of the alphabet (HH: Heil Hitler), Column 88 is a British paramilitary nazi group run by private detective Les Vaughan. It is very secretive and highly organized and its small élite membership is recruited only from the most capable and fanatical members of public nazi organizations.

Committee for Nationalist Unity (CNU)

Set up in 1981 as a front for John Tyndall's efforts to poach members from other groups to launch his own British National Party.

Faisceaux Nationalistes Européens (FNE)

The name under which the French nazi group FANE (see below) was re-formed after being banned in 1980.

Fédération d'Action Nationale Européene (FANE)

French nazi group led by Mark Frederiksen. It was behind a number of terrorist incidents and was banned by the French authorities in 1980, to be re-launched as the Faisceaux Nationalistes Européenes.

Fronte Universitario di Azione Nazionale (FUAN)

The student organization of the Italian fascist party MSI. Many of its members have been implicated in political violence and terrorism.

Focus Policy Study Group

Right-wing historian David Irving's group launched in 1980 as the precursor to a 'new right' party under Irving's leadership. It tried to attract support from both fascists and conservatives but collapsed only three years later.

Greater Britain Movement (GBM)

Formed by John Tyndall in 1964 when he split from Colin Jordan's National Socialist Movement. It dissolved in

1967 when Tyndall instructed his members to join the National Front.

Herstigte National Party (HNP)

Hard-line break-away from South Africa's ruling National Party. Led by Jaap Marais, it campaigns against any liberalization of the apartheid system.

Historical Review Press

A nazi printing and publishing operation run from Brighton by Alan and Anthony Hancock. Operating under the name Wilson Laminates, it produces periodicals for British nazi groups and 'revisionist' literature for far-right groups all over the world.

Hoffman Group

The Wehrsportegruppe Hoffman Truppe (WSG) was an openly paramilitary German nazi group in the late 1970s and early 1980s. Many of its members, including leader Karl-Heinz Hoffman, received military training from the PLO in the Lebanon.

Imperial Fascist League

A pre-war British nazi organization led by Arnold Leese.

Institute for Historical Review

California-based pseudo-academic body behind campaigns to make theories which whitewash nazism respect able. Founded by Liberty Lobby leader Willis Carto and former British NF activist Dave McCalden.

League of Empire Loyalists

A group of British extreme right-wingers and conservatives pledged to oppose Macmillan's dismantling of the British Empire. Headed by A. K. Chesterton, it joined the merger which gave birth to the National Front in 1967.

League of St George

Avowedly nazi umbrella organization formed in the early 1970s by former Mosley supporters in Britain. It maintained contacts with nazi groups all over the world, and was central in safe housing foreign right-wing terrorists in the UK.

Movimento Sociale Italiano (MSI)

Italy's established fascist party, set up in 1946. It has deputies in the Italian Parliament and the European Parliament. Led by Giorgio Almirante, its members have frequently been involved in terrorist activities and plots to overthrow the Italian government.

National Front (NF)

For twenty years the most important British far-right party. Born in 1967, when several small outfits combined forces, it achieved temporary election successes in the mid-1970s. When these evaporated in 1979, it split into four warring factions. Since then it has lurched in an increasingly violent 'Strasserite' direction.

National Front Constitutional Movement (NFCM)

Led by Andrew Fountaine, NFCM was one of the factions
which split from the NF in 1979. After a change of name
much of its dwindling membership joined the Conservative Party.

National Party

A coalition of 'populists' and Strasserites who split from
the NF in 1976 under the leadership of John Kingsley
Read. It collapsed two years later.

National Socialist Action Party (NSAP)

A fanatical paramilitary outfit set up by former British
Movement member Tony Malski in 1982. Its members
have been implicated in serious terrorist activity and
attempts to provoke violent racial clashes.

National Socialist Movement (NSM)

Led by Colin Jordan, NSM was set up in 1962 to propa-
gate a pure form of undiluted Hitlerism. Prominent
members included later NF leaders John Tyndall and
Martin Webster. After a group of activists were gaoled
for paramilitary offences in its first year, Tyndall led a
walk-out to form the Greater Britain Movement. NSM
was wound up in 1968 to be replaced by British
Movement.

National States Rights Party (NSRP)

American nazi organization linked to the Ku Klux Klan,
with extensive contacts in Europe. Led by Dr Edward

Fields and Attorney J. B. Stoner, it is virulently anti-semitic and has frequently been implicated in violent attacks on American blacks.

New European Order (NEO)

International hard-line neo-nazi network set up in 1951 by European nazis and former SS members. Based in Lausanne, Switzerland, it is led by George Amaudruz and still operates as a co-ordinating centre for underground activity by European nazi groups.

Nucleii Armati Rivoluzionari (NAR)

The 'Armed Revolutionary Nuclei', an Italian terrorist group linked to the Third Position (see below), which was behind a wave of terror attacks in the late 1970s. Some members, later convicted of terrorism *in absentia*, fled to England in 1980 where they were safe housed by British nazis.

Racial Preservation Society (RPS)

Well-funded racist propaganda outfit in Britain in the 1960s. The RPS achieved a notorious victory in 1968 when it successfully defended itself against the first prosecution under the Race Relations Act. Its membership transferred to the NF when the latter was founded in 1967.

South African National Front (SANF)

South African version of the British NF launched by Jack Noble and other British expatriates in 1977. It collapsed in 1980 after some leading members were discovered to have set up a terror group, the White Commando, in league with Italian fascists.

Spearhead

A paramilitary nazi unit set up by Colin Jordan, John Tyndall and other members of the British National Party in 1961. Control passed to the National Socialist Movement when these individuals split from BNP in 1962. Spearhead members were arrested, charged with paramilitary offences and gaoled later in the same year.

Third Position (Terza Posizione)

A fanatical Italian fascist group which grew up in the 1970s and leaned heavily on the teachings of anti-semitic philosopher Julius Evola. It spawned the terrorist Armed Revolutionary Nuclei and many of its members were gaoled in 1985. Some found refuge with British fascists in London in 1980.

UNIDO (International Union for the Defence of the West)

An organization of far-right expatriate Italians set up in South Africa in 1976, UNIDO joined forces with the South African National Front in 1978. With SANF leaders, some of its members were later convicted of belonging to the White Commando terrorist group.

Vlamese Militanten Orden (VMO)

Belgian nazi group, one of the strongest and most highly regarded in Europe. It was prosecuted by the Belgian authorities for its involvement in terrorist activities. Each year it organizes the international nazi gathering at Diksmuide.

Volksocialistiche Bewegung Deutschland (VSBD)

The German People's Socialist Movement, despite its name, was a hard-line pro-Hitler organization led by Friedhelm Busse. It had strong links with the Hoffman Group until its collapse following the arrest of Busse and other members on serious criminal charges including armed robbery.

Wehrsportegruppe Hoffman Truppe

See Hoffman Group

White Commando

Although adopting an Afrikaans name (Wit Kommando) this white South African terror group was made up entirely of fascist immigrants from Britain and Italy. Its members, including leaders of the South African National Front and UNIDO, received heavy gaol sentences for terrorist bombings in 1981.

WISE (Welsh Irish Scots and English Association)

A pro-repatriation pressure group based in London since 1976 and organized by veteran race-campaigner Joan Mason. It attracted support from all sections of the right-wing spectrum; from hard-line nazis to Tory MPs. After a spate of bad publicity in 1984, many 'respectable' supporters drifted away and it fell into decline.

Index

Modern society – now available in Grafton Books

Dougal Dixon
After Man (illustrated) £4.95 ☐

Germaine Greer
The Female Eunuch £3.95 ☐

John Howard Griffin
Black Like Me £1.95 ☐

Peter Laurie
Beneath the City Streets £2.50 ☐

Desmond Morris
The Pocket Guide to Manwatching (illustrated) £5.95 ☐
Manwatching (illustrated) £8.95 ☐
The Naked Ape £2.95 ☐
Intimate Behaviour £2.95 ☐
The Human Zoo £2.50 ☐
Animal Days (autobiography) £1.95 ☐
Gestures (illustrated) £3.95 ☐

José Silva and Michael Miele
The Silva Mind Control Method £2.95 ☐

Ivan Tyrell
The Survival Option (illustrated) £2.50 ☐

Michael Binyon
Life in Russia £2.95 ☐

To order direct from the publisher just tick the titles you want
and fill in the order form.   GM881

The best in biography from Grafton Books

Dirk Bogarde
A Postillion Struck by Lightning (illustrated)	£2.50 ☐
Snakes and Ladders (illustrated)	£2.95 ☐
An Orderly Man (illustrated)	£2.95 ☐

Elizabeth Longford
Wellington: Piller of State	£3.95 ☐
The Queen Mother (illustrated)	£3.95 ☐
A Pilgrimage of Passion (illustrated)	£3.95 ☐

Ted Morgan
Churchill: The Rise to Failure 1874–1915 (illustrated)	£4.95 ☐

Kim Philby
My Silent War	£1.95 ☐

Michael Bentine
The Door Marked Summer	£1.95 ☐
The Long Banana Skin	£1.95 ☐

Doris Collins
A Woman of Spirit (illustrated)	£2.50 ☐

Claude Duval
Lester (illustrated)	£1.95 ☐

Steve Ovett with John Rodda
Ovett: An Autobiography (illustrated)	£2.50 ☐

Martina Navratilova
Being Myself (illustrated)	£2.95 ☐

Ian Rush
Rush: Ian Rush's Autobiography (illustrated)	£2.50 ☐

To order direct from the publisher just tick the titles you want
and fill in the order form.

History – now available in Grafton Books

Douglas Botting
In the Ruins of the Reich (illustrated)   £3.50   ☐

Sir Arthur Bryant
Set in a Silver Sea (illustrated)   £3.95   ☐

'The Alanbrooke Diaries'
The Turn of the Tide 1939–1943   £5.95   ☐
Triumph in the West 1943–1946   £5.95   ☐

Stephen Knight
The Killing of Justice Godfrey (illustrated)   £2.95   ☐

Joyce Marlow
The Tolpuddle Martyrs (illustrated)   £2.95   ☐

Angus Calder
The People's War (illustrated)   £3.95   ☐

To order direct from the publisher just tick the titles you want
and fill in the order form.   **GM782**

All these books are available at your local bookshop or newsagent, or can be ordered direct from the publisher.

To order direct from the publishers just tick the titles you want and fill in the form below.

Name _____

Address _____

_____

Send to:
Grafton Cash Sales
PO Box 11, Falmouth, Cornwall TR10 9EN.

Please enclose remittance to the value of the cover price plus:

UK 60p for the first book, 25p for the second book plus 15p per copy for each additional book ordered to a maximum charge of £1.90.

BFPO 60p for the first book, 25p for the second book plus 15p per copy for the next 7 books, thereafter 9p per book.

Overseas including Eire £1.25 for the first book, 75p for second book and 28p for each additional book.

_____

Grafton Books reserve the right to show new retail prices on covers, which may differ from those previously advertised in the text or elsewhere.